Y0-BCV-499

J. M. HODGES LEARNING CENTER
WHARTON COUNTY JUNIOR COLLEGE
WHARTON, TEXAS 77488

Generations

Generations

A Collage on Youthcult

Clifford Adelman

PRAEGER PUBLISHERS
New York · Washington · London

43790

J. M. HODGES LEARNING CENTER
WHARTON COUNTY JUNIOR COLLEGE
WHARTON, TEXAS 77488

The author wishes to express his thanks for permission to quote material from the following sources:

The Last Whole Earth Catalog, edited by Stewart Brand, © 1971 by the Portola Institute.

"Open Land: Getting Back to the Communal Garden," by Sara Davidson, reprinted by permission of Curtis Brown, Ltd. Copyright © 1970 by Harper's Magazine, Inc.

Domebook 2, by permission of Pacific Domes.

"Honest Bob's 42nd Street," by permission of *East Village Other*.

The Movement Toward a New America, edited by Mitchell Goodman, © 1970 by Mitchell Goodman, by permission of Alfred A. Knopf, Inc.

"Growl to Me Softly and I'll Understand," by William Hedgepeth, by permission of Cowles Communications, Inc.

How to Survive in Your Native Land, by James Herndon, Copyright © 1971 by James Herndon, reprinted by permission of Simon and Schuster.

Young Radicals, by Kenneth Keniston, by permission of Harcourt Brace Jovanovich, Inc.

Shelter and Society, edited by Paul Oliver, Copyright © 1969, by permission of Praeger Publishers.

One Dimensional Man, by Herbert Marcuse, by permission of Beacon Press.

"A Conversation with Charles Reich," by Alan Rinzler. From ROLLING STONE, © 1971 by Straight Arrow Publishers Inc. All Rights Reserved. Reprinted by permission.

The Making of a Counter Culture, by Theodore Roszak, Copyright © 1968, 1969 by Theodore Roszak. Reprinted by permission of Doubleday & Company, Inc.

"Death in New Mexico," by Michael Blake, and "How to Fuck the Networks," copyrighted articles by permission of the *Los Angeles Free Press*.

PRAEGER PUBLISHERS
111 Fourth Avenue, New York, N.Y. 10003, U.S.A.
5, Cromwell Place, London SW7 2JL, England

Published in the United States of America in 1972
by Praeger Publishers, Inc.

© 1972 by Praeger Publishers, Inc.

All rights reserved

Library of Congress Catalog Card Number: 72–168334

Printed in the United States of America

301.4315
Ad 33g

43790

To
My Parents
and to
Jonathan:
The Generations Roll

Contents

THE CONTRADICTIONS OF COUNTER CULTURE

THE COMPLICITIES OF THE ACADEMY

Preface and Acknowledgments

The subtitle of this book—A *Collage on Youthcult*—weighs heavily with its author. My notion of what constitutes a specifically literary collage should be manifest not merely in the yoking of pieces of polemic, analysis, criticism, reportage, and speculation, but also in the shifting tones and styles, the arrangement, implicit assumptions, process metaphors, etc., of the whole. No collage, however varied its materials, surfaces, techniques of composition, really coheres without those unseen but inferable strands. As method, such strands are novelistic; but I hope they are strong enough so that the tentative landing places of this book will not strike the reader as the constructions of a fantast.

In the vernacular, the purpose of this book is to clear the air of a lot of bullshit. It seeks an analysis which I do not think has been formulated by too many of us old, tired radiclibs. It seeks a prophecy it hopes will never be realized, and tries to head it off by a broadside in the narrows. For that reason it is addressed to youthcult and its sympathizers.

If, indeed, the prophecy is never realized, and if, in its small way, this potpourri has some staying influence, there will be many to thank. There are many to thank anyway.

There are, for openers, the hundreds of college students, acquaintances, friends, friends of friends, passers-by who took the considerable time and energy to fill out a lengthy questionnaire, which provided critical data for a portion of the book and/or who were dearly obliging in formal interviews and less structured raps. There were many whose mere presence generated illustrative anecdotes. There were the nameless others whose fragments of conversation were simply overheard and shamelessly employed. The presence of some was continuing. Others were birds of passage. They all spanned some years. More years, when one adds those old acquaintances whose names were recognized on mastheads, bylines, and jacket covers. Add to these last the critics, journalists, educators who have provided masses of fact for us to work with and opinion from which we can rebound. The author of every document cited, whether honorifically or pejoratively, holds a slice of a mortgage on my soul.

Closer to the direct production of the book are, first, friends, former colleagues and students, at CCNY: Chris Mulvey, Jerry Kauvar, Ed Tomarkin, Ed Quinn, Lenny Kriegel, Jim Greene, Bill Herman, Ed Volpe, Alan Rosenwasser, Ira Kaufman, Marc Alper, Karen Winter, Marge Marash, Mike Rusinak, Stu Glass, Larry McGowan, Leo Hamalian, and I'm sure more. And secondly, those elsewhere: Horace Newcomb, Scott Colley, Lou Goodman, Dick Hendrix, Elaine Kauvar, Steve Weiland, Chris Herbert, Mike Salkin, Rubin Rabinowitz, Anne Kelley, father-in-law Gil Taverner, and, I know, more.

I save out Bob Hamburger because he falls in a separate category as an Eternal.

Indirectly, there is a world. I recall with particular gratitude neighbors Frank and Hope Mell, Bob and Carol Ballard, Chris Johnson and Ellen Foscue, and relatives Joe Adelman, Bette Taverner, and mostly Nan Barker.

Lastly, Nancy, who has been so forbearing and instructive, who, with intuitive understanding and greater love, was encouraging at moments when she knew not, and for whom a New World should arise.

CLIFFORD ADELMAN

T-House
Thanksgiving, 1971

The Generations
of Youthcult

1

Either/Or and Other
Elitist Distortions

I suppose this thing accumulated like the materials of a collage—
many midnights' thoughts spoken to walls, angry marginalia, curious research, whispered speculations, conversations real and imaginary—all revealing their hidden metaphors only by accretion.

Many of us walked too sedentary through this ongoing era of
youthcult, lulled to joy by the accessible fictions we were told sur-
rounded us, and then entered the Academy and the streets around
it too often. Too often because it took little time to discover that
the fictions were too convenient. To find, as James Herndon
found in a junior high school situation, a mass of our hopes for
whom there was nothing to do in here, and nothing to do out
there, and to suspect, against oneself, that all the excuses, high
culture and low, literati and illiterati, were unfathomably just that.

Reality has a fortuitous way of inducing frustration. Sometime
in the middle of the past decade the obliging *cognoscenti* began to
explain it all for us, lending a host of assuaging theories, coupled
with the weight of their imprimaturs on a half-dozen respected
academic books, to words about universal angst, mythic quest patterns, and what we ultimately had to perceive as a tissue full of
runny nonsense.

The frustration doubled not merely because we feared to sound

3

like reactionaries, but also because we were not, in fact, reactionaries. Within the Academy, one dreaded being identified with the line of Sidney Hook, Sam Hayakawa, and the Rational Boys. But the dialectics of the hyperbolic '60's demanded that one either accept the whole youthcult package (no matter how confused it was with elite counter politics) or risk the ranch brand of "fascist" or "chauvinist" or whatever the hate term in vogue that month.

So this double frustration was fortunate, because it had the historical inevitability of pushing us beyond that stale dialectic. If the apologetics have become clichéd required readings in the new book of common prayer—those between-the-cheesecake-ads articles in the Sunday *Times Mag* that rehash arguments on the politicization of the university or the viability of acid rock as "poetry"—so have all the comforting horror stories of mainstream America: the big stories, the little ones. Somehow we always fervently wished to be transported into a realm beyond petty arguments over hair, beyond elementary facts of repression, beyond what is unquestionably an anal-retentive society, beyond the hypocrisies of the real elders. We talked about the clothes in the closet so much that we came to live in the closet. We reinforced our disgust and anger so often with those stories, we became so inured to them, that we did not realize we were burying our own reality, not confronting it. We had been bombed into insensitivity by escalating confrontations with one dragon after another until they all seemed to emanate from the same dark Manichean source.

The solution went two ways: Blow it up (counter politics), or abandon it (counter culture). A Thomistic set of either/ors. Of course, all along there has been another and prior set—mainstream sensibility or alternative—one which really projects a single answer, for that "or" is the sign of the only chance we've got. That much is a given. Now we have been fortuitously forced into a position in which, while acknowledging the excruciations of the society writ large, we turn critically to the Alternatives we are being offered, and to that generation most involved with, and affected by, those oblations. We are forced to do so in the analytical spirit on which any deep reformation attends. We must look for extents and drifts, for contradictions and myths. Having crossed the divide of that first either/or, we have no other choice. One must delve for that which will enable an Alternative to survive, and for that task one must understand fully those factors actually in operation which have the paradoxical potential to give birth to a stillborn babe. As Sidney Zion noted in that last suppressed issue of *Scanlan's*: "To diagnose the disease is not to prescribe the poison. The fact that we do not like the way people are treated does not justify advocating their suicides. The nation's Radical Sheikdom ought to be a little careful about whose song it sings, while the wine it pours is laced with hemlock."

When we discover one set of poisons replacing another, forces only partially beyond the control of individuals which will vitiate even a great and loving spirit, and a new wilderness of either/ors, we have no choice but to call the tune. Besides, one cannot trust either the reactionaries or the "liberal" Rational Boys with that task.

It is more than appropriate that the seminal work on what we popularly conceive of as Youthcult, Theodore Roszak's *The Making of a Counter Culture* (1968), takes as a portion of its epigraph these lines from the Preface to Blake's *Milton*:

> Rouse up, O Young Men of the New Age! set your foreheads against the ignorant Hirelings! For we have Hirelings in the Camp, the Court & the University, who would, if they could, for ever depress Mental & prolong Corporeal War.

Roszak's choice of these words, and its accompanying misunderstandings, is prophetic of the new wilderness of either/ors. For there are a number of curios in the dialectic of that mythic cycle which informs all of Blake's "Prophetic Books," which the spirit of Roszak's choice overlooks, and by which the perceptual apparatus of this collage is very much informed. Thus, the myth must be set out early, and, by concentrating on three of its principal characters, in highly reduced form. As authentic prophecy, Blake's vision reflects a set of eternal and dynamic options, the recycling of which we are very much witness to in our time. The occasional reappearance of the characters then becomes more than appropriate as one of our major metaphorical strands.

Roszak has conveniently plunged into that stage of the cycle which best serves the call to revolution. So it is, whether in Blake's days or our own, that the "Hirelings in the Camp, the Court & the

University," sons of the Jehovic God, Urizen, have prolonged "Corporeal War." That is, Urizen's sons have protracted a vision of this world based wholly on the prison of the five senses and their corresponding abstract moral injunctions—in our time, technology and its accompanying subtle repressions.

How fraught with Blakean irony is the fact that the major revolt against Urizen is carried out through the agency of Orc, the revolutionary child who, like Urizen before him, binds others to the religion of himself. One oppressive and limited vision replaces another, and Orc, like Urizen, is metaphorically trapped in the Tree of Mystery that "grows in the human brain." In viewing each other as enemies, as negations (read "fascist pigs" v. "commie fags" in our contemporary corporeal dialogue of violence and limitation), both are guilty of the blindness of Blake's Man of Experience confronting the Tyger in the forested night of his mind, the Tyger who, he reasons, must issue *either* from Heaven *or* from Hell, with no stops or combinations in between. Neither Urizen nor Orc is capable of realizing that they, in their very contrariety, can be independently productive, as the war of (mental) Contraries is "necessary to Human existence." Thus Urizen as rigid reason and Orc as anarchic energy must be perceived in the dialectic of a third mythic figure, Los, the eternal artificer.

Los can and does build the City of the Imagination, the real Jerusalem, brick by brick, with the Hand and the Eye, with *words* and *shapes*, on the anvil of time, the forge of space—recognizing that these tools of time are all we have in a world of Generation. By his logic, both Urizens and Orcs will have to continue to exist as they did in Eternity. What his prophetic vision would urge is that *we* perceive them as Eternal and dynamic contraries, and not as they perceive themselves in the iron either/or logic of negations.

That the new Orcs of our Alternatives turn out to be as bound, elitist, and jealous—as "fascistic," if you wish—as the Urizens should descend with no mythic surprise. That they, too, clothe themselves in delusive self-righteousness and self-serving moral purity is a fact that should occasion confrontation, not muddy excuses. The greater problem from the perspective of these pages is that they pretend to play at Los without the insight of Los. They pretend to be artificers of Eternity while denying themselves the tools of time.

Since the counter culture commands the attention of both mainstream media and academic analysts like Roszak, it possesses a power far outweighing its ontological status. As long as that power exists, and as long as we've got Teddy Roszaks and Charlie Reichs joining the Abbie Hoffmans in hyping the counter culture as the only alternative to the coming technological anti-Utopia, the lesson of such a seemingly minor battle of footnotes as Roszak's misunderstood use of Blake should persuade us to take a less apocalyptic look at where we're going. Shaking out the illusions is a primary task.

Let's get some jargon out of the way early on. We've been too indulgent with the either/orists, their reductionistic tendencies, and the corresponding confusions—both qualitative and quantitative—of their labels.

That basic *qualitative* confusion first equates counter culture with counter politics and, on a more fundamental level, interchanges these two directions of what has been lumpingly headlined as The Movement with the idea of Youth Culture. Our primer of terms, however, should really require no extensive elaboration. The principal thrust of counter *culture* is behavioral, and oriented toward the self. The ground of counter *politics* is power and is theoretically oriented toward the community, the idea of *polis*. It may be a surface irrelevancy to subject the counter *culture* to ideological analysis since, as Roszak accurately indicated, its revolt is against organization, not against any particular ideology. A significant fraction of counter politics, on the other hand, requires at least the rudiments of organization, and thus opens itself to ideological judgment. Although, in the pages following, I am bent on avoiding the rhetoric of alienation, principally because I think it has explained itself out, it might be enlightening here to note that, under the rubrics of the either/orists, the counter *culturist* is relatively "alienated," whereas the counter politics man, to paraphrase Kenneth Keniston, is relatively committed to precisely the values that the "alienated" reject.

If one further confuses the "ideology" of The Movement with the *thought* of its many gurus and explicators, the belief that counter culture and counter politics overlap more frequently than not is a logical *sequitur*. In practice, however, the two divisions of The Movement overlap only sporadically. That is, once one breaks through the rhetoric of many counter politics poseurs, one finds counter culturists who are in no conceivable way directed toward the idea of *polis* or the realities of power. It is the persistent judgment of these pages that *some* overlappings of alternative culture and politics *may* offer hope for America. Such conditionals, though, point to the most critical factor of all—the identity of the practitioners. We have to look to the generations of the broader youth culture coming along, the directions in which they are being drawn, and what the combinations bode. There are a far greater number of contingencies than the pied pipers would have us believe.

With these conditionals, the *quantitative* distinctions begin to emerge in solution with the qualitative. The operative jargon of these pages is founded on the terms "core," "hard core," and "gravitational field." These quantitative distinctions are frequently ignored but are of immeasurable aid in discriminating both the qualitative subdivisions of counter culture and counter politics, and degrees of individual commitment. I would illustrate them *in vitro* primarily by example.

Core counter *culture* envelops decidely apolitical "alternative life-styles." To borrow from Charles Reich, its "Con I Division" involves the New Agrarians, Hip Craftsmen, "alternate media" people, the organic food table, geodesic domers, et cetera. The "Otherworldly Division" embraces the cults of drugs, assorted mysticisms, Jesus freakisms—in effect, just about all the tent placards at The Whole Earth Fair and Festival of Peace held at Boulder, Colorado, in July of 1970: Krishna Consciousness, Yoga exercises (big draw), Zen, Astrology, Bucky Fuller's World Game, Christ-consciousness, Chasidism, various Yoga theorists, combinations of the above. Even the small cult of Mao Tse-tung as an enigmatic great Buddha, a secular Eastern saint whose thoughts are so intense in their simplicity that they must hold the answers to all earthly dilemmas, falls into this category.

Adjacent to these two divisions of counter culture are more eclectic core groups, including sensitivity-trainees, ecologists who keep Kosher homes with a vengeance, architectural visionaries other than the domers, free schoolers, most phases of the world of rock, and, despite their political rhetoric, most communards.

In the broadest possible application of the word, I suppose the counter culture expresses a dominant "politic." But it is another major thesis of these pages that that "politic" is hardly the one shrilled by counter culture pitchmen.

Core counter *politics* runs a genetic chain from anarchist revolutionary trashers and street theater people to a division that recognizes a social order, a division that thus includes New Left ideologues and heavy black revolutionaries. But mere recognition of the social order does not imply any concessions to it; so, for example, law communes, the cooperative "food conspiracy" movement, black community organizations that usually don't make the papers, et cetera, are specifically excluded.

Immediately around the core moil the tent cities of the Movement divisions: the women's lib guerrillas, the gay activists, the lesser black militants, the political classroom radicals—and the anthill proletariat of Movement functionaries: the print collectives, "free store" operators, Liberation News Service people, and the ever ready marchers and sloganeers (that is, those one can always count on to turn out, no matter what the issue).

The *gravitational fields* of both counter culture and counter politics encompass involvements ranging from sympathizing to outright dabbling. With each chapter and verse of the above, too, there are obviously varying degrees of commitment and motivation. Here, *hard core* is used to signify a high degree of both. The stable, long-term hard core in any of the regiments can probably be indexed in no more than four figures. The *cores* can probably be expressed in six figures, the sometimes overlapping gravitational fields in seven.

What this brief catalogue *excludes* from the *cores* is as important as what it embraces. I have excluded activists in law, medicine, consumer affairs, and those ecological projects that confront the monster in his lair. I exclude community service people and community organizers. Nader's Raiders, Saul Alinsky's community organizers, Jesse Jackson's Breadbasketeers are out. Politically I exclude the New Populists, those who believe that the constituency defined by "the people" to whom "all power" is to be given must and can include far more than the young, the poor, and the black. I exclude, too, and for reasons we'll examine in the second block of this collage, the implications of *The Whole Earth Catalog*, that is, the potential cultural force of Stewart Brand–Portola Institute-type projects.

I exclude not because my own sensibilities (coincidentally, really) identify passionately with the excludables, but because, in the terms we have inherited, they are not "counter." That is, harking back to the Blakean distinction Roszak overlooked, they are not negations of either culture or *polis*. Not that agrarianism *per se*, or the *ideology* of women's liberation, or the *concept* of a print collective is a negation; but if one is more intrigued by practice than by abstract form, if one is more interested in the history of culture than in cultural history, one swiftly discovers that the practice has been effectively a negation, not a dynamic constructive contrary.

Let us call the excludables, then, the Sons of Los. They are eminently an elite, and tragically likely to become more so. That is, their core—the social activists, the serious long-term organizers, the alternative community builders—is small, and getting on now. For reasons hypothesized later, their potential gravitational field is being drawn off by the counter *culture* these days and, outside of the black community, the possibilities for a significantly numerous succession appear dim.

A full appreciation of this last judgment demands a detailed examination of the totality of a generation currently and recently of college age. When in the context of daily mainstream atrocities, one gazes beyond the too soothing exaltation of potential to the realities of that generation and to the shaping forces of those realities, he feels like a man locked into an oppressive job, unable to find another, and simultaneously ineligible for unemployment benefits. Combine the dominant characteristics of that generation with the fact that mass fragments of it are being drawn into the gravitational fields of counter *culture*, and we've got a very existential limit situation coming up. The first two sections of this book are devoted to an itemized expansion of that demoralizing recognition.

Briefly, now, why is it specifically counter *culture* of which one despairs? Our lives are shrouded with a manifest nightmare: a complex post-technological culture in which poverty, hunger, racism, mindless bureaucracy, and closet power-brokers remain, impenetrable as a great swamp of deceiving sunken roots and thick water-grass. The counter culture provides the most convenient and irrelevant rituals for an out, for an excuse not merely not to do, but not to perceive, feel, think, or express as well. All one has to say is that he is practicing "a revolutionary and alternative life-style," and presumably that will cover the abdication. The night-mare endures; and no communard, no dome-builder, no New Agrarian, no Hare Krishna chanter, no guru freak is going to con-front that swamp to which the wretched of this earth have been consigned. The elastic sensibility sweeps into counter politics, too. No bombardier or street-theater guerrilla will realistically put an end to the lingering nonsense in America. No "busload of slogans" (the phrase is Norman Mailer's) stopped the Vietnam war. But it's oh so much easier to play counter.

Yet it is precisely because the buried root of the counter culture is creative in impulse, it is because the Alternate Ways seek to re-establish a lost culture of small units of control and the spiritual values those units contain, that the humanist in particular is at-tracted to it. His disillusion is all the more severe when the imagi-nation is betrayed, and that tangled vine of mystery grows its stunted, self-consuming way. The line between the truly imagina-tive and the baldly delusive is not that thin, after all; but if one fails to sense a border-crossing, he is lost.

So were I a reactionary, a clever one, and wanted the spirit of counter culture to expire, I would keep my mouth sealed because the incarnations of that spirit are so loaded with contradictions now, so blinded by their own non-reality dilations, that the spirit is on a direct course to self-destruct. Since we're off on a critical jag in a few pages, let us again allow the assertion to stand large here: I genuinely wish for viable Alternatives (that's plural—op-tions, not either/ors), Alternatives that will not simultaneously violate the idea of *polis*, that will not vitiate their own professed ideals by abrogating reconstructive relationships to the Other. The erection of such permanent options requires more than gossamer commitment from more than four figures' worth of polyfoam dome-builders. Eddying around out there in youthcult is a frag-mented assemblage of Christmas tree ornament people who have been deluded by a parliament of pitchmen into believing that they are, in fact, providing resilient Alternatives. With them, applaud-ing or not, are a mass of elders who have been likewise deluded by that same parliament. Together, the collective swindle will pre-clude the vision. The critique, then, has got to run deeper than it has in order to discover what we have to do to alter the course.

This collage in particular has to run deeper in its critique because our primary subjects are not the elites that have been subject to previous explications but those who compose the vast gravitational fields. That shift in perspective, I hope, will wash some phantasms away.

A critical, archetypal case: The explicators of youthcult have tended to confuse its "ideology" with the *thought* of academic resources and gurus. To read the media pitchmen, one could believe that any streetcorner phreak, sloganeering days-of-rage radical, or just the ordinary college cafeteria-hanger could discourse at length on the likes of politipsychologist R. D. Laing, primal-scream therapist Arthur Janov, French theater-of-the-streets theoretician Antonin Artaud, Norman O. Brown, McLuhan, Marcuse, and on. I don't believe I exaggerate in claiming that even among the core counter culture life-stylists (particularly those existing beyond the elite academic meccas on the Cambridge-Berkeley circuit), few have even heard of most of those named. In the survey discussed in the following chapter and presented in full in the Appendix, less than 10 per cent of those who *claimed* involvement in group therapy or other forms of sensitivity training could even identify Arthur Janov, and only slightly more than 20 per cent could indicate an attitude response to R. D. Laing (and, in the case of those under twenty-five, the attitude response was decidedly tepid). And to college teachers outside the Big Twenty or so: Ever try McLuhan with a class of sophomores? Think, then, of Artaud or Marcuse with a seventeen-year-old St. Marks Place panhandler who can chant "free all political prisoners" with effortless guile.

To claim that blanket counter culture or blanket counter politics embodies the theories and then to concentrate on the theories without examining the minute particularities of those whose behavior supposedly expresses the theories is an exercise that can never come to terms with popular culture. A class of upperclass university students who have never heard of Antonin Artaud—and do not understand his theoretical justification for theater in the streets when it is presented—is a far more significant index of where youthcult is at than the word of some Artaud huckster who perceives the man's theories reflected in contemporary cultural politics.

In one very important sense, I am raising an ancient question in historiography: Does one emphasize cultural history or history of culture, does one look to the theorists for the trends, or to the cultural artifacts, dominant forms of activity, dominant habits of mind? In attempting to stick to the artifacts, one must recognize that the importance of the gurus and academic resources, the "relevance" of Marcuse, Paul Goodman, Bucky Fuller, Laing, *et al.*, lies in the ways they are being used and responded to—if at all—by various segments of youthcult. Equally relevant, if of slightly lesser importance, is the process by which the academic resources filter down to the college cafeterias, let alone the street. Even here one is required to hone to the modes and *effects* of the interpretations, not to the thought of the gurus *an Sich*. Thus the primary source material for this study and polemic lies in the artifacts, behavioral patterns, solicited opinion, and expressions of its subjects.

But the accessible written records of youthcult, the monuments of expression, present a very distinct problem; in fact, they offer the first major collection of illusions we are enjoined to explode. For when one fronts the reality of *exactly who it is* among the young who is writing about youthcult or speaking as its representative, one looks squarely at a member of an elite vanguard. The distortion that emerges from an elitist point of view may be compactly illustrated in a moment of deadpan seriousness in *The Strawberry Statement*, in which James Simon Kunen (not merely Columbia, but Andover as well) informs us that "Columbia is New York," a statement that, only by virtue of its forthrightness, distances Kunen from his elder, Charles Reich, who only *assumed* that Yale was America.

Since the mass democratization of higher education in America, we have developed a curiously blinding mentality (Reich claims it is constitutive to Consciousness III) which does not ask of the details of one's background or education. We pretend, in our romance for the wholly laudatory, that the difference between students at Harvard and students at the subsidiary branch of the State U. campus is negligible. Still, consider: Those who have been proffering ecstatic pronouncements on youthcult have usually, in effect, been talking about Harvard students, and, metaphorically speaking only in part, Harvard kids are the ones who write the books on which the popular image of what's goin' down is based.

Doubt it? Ponder, in the abstract, what personal experience youthcult commentators and Yale faculty members Charlie Reich, John Hersey, and Kenneth Keniston can possibly speak from? Keniston, whose work one must approach far more seriously than that of the other two, is hyperconscious of the distortion. In both *The Uncommitted* and *Young Radicals* he not only acknowledges but consistently underscores the fact that his subjects are drawn from the upper atmospheric regions of elites. Thus, for example, when he asserts that the life-style of the "alienated" possesses, as one of its "crucial features," "intellectual passion," we must recognize that he is decidedly not describing the great number of "alienated" college students whose literacy is simultaneously threshold. Or, when he claims that his small group of alienated and highly verbal Harvard undergraduates are reacting, in part, "out of historical losses that affect their entire generation," we cannot cloud the doors of our perception by applying such grandiloquent statements to others whose behavioral patterns *seem* to be similar, but who read little, possess less of a sense of history, and therefore are generally incapable of reacting out of a sense of historical loss.

We have also inherited the distinct and evidently indelible impression that current youthcult is "the media generation," in particular, the film generation. The survey that follows and a significantly large number of these pages are devoted to that illusion. But let's see where it comes from:

> Today's student generation has grown up with television, getting information and entertainment from some kind of rectangular screen all their lives. It's no surprise that the audio-visual experience is what it's all about for them.

Thus spake filmmaker Maurice Rapf after four years of teaching film at Dartmouth and Brown.

Run swiftly, too, through the bookshelf produced by those who are simultaneously "representatives" *and* explicators: Kunen and Dotson Rader (*I Ain't Marchin' Anymore*) of Columbia, Mark Gerzon (*The Whole World Is Watching*) and Paul Cowan (*The Making of an Un-American*) of Harvard, Jacob Brackman (*Esquire* film editor and prolific free-lancer on youthcult matters) of Chicago, and, in the category of the raree show, Abbie Hoffman of Brandeis. In clawing at the bookcases to disinter a whole book that will break that pattern, the best I can manage is a diary of counter-culturists in New Mexico, *Chamisa Road* "with . . . Paul & Meredith," Paul and Meredeith being a couple of dropouts from the prestigious Bronx High School of Science.

I think, too, of a young author, not mentioned above, whom I have not seen since days of heavy gabardine high school band parades, his trumpet solo-raised, from a high-powered family of kids striving in the world of the mind, and making it. President of his high school class, he flows naturally 'cross the river to Harvard, then the inevitable Berkeley, and back. From Cambridge burnished-room reflection, the book on Berkeley youth days is here now, of course, and the very effort of the book speaks as a paradigm for an elite perpetuating itself, however much it may profess the Mao-istically leveling values of the New Consciousness. There are too many fine moments in his book to disparage it; but consider that we have been paying a heavy purchase for a youthcult image produced by people on the Cambridge-Berkeley-Cambridge run.

The gravamen will be borne by Mark Gerzon, Harvard '70, artificer of *The Whole World Is Watching*. I single Gerzon out because he, too, employed a survey as the ground of his flights into youthcult phil, as the gessoed surface on which he washed bold statements of the essence of his generation. Gerzon's survey, needless to say, was confined to Harvard undergraduates. In what I hope the following chapter will convince, the patterns Gerzon recorded—not merely the spirit but the facts of the case—for students between the ages of eighteen and twenty-two in 1969 approximate those I found in a broader reach of young people who were between the ages of twenty-six and thirty-two in 1971. The coincidence, as will become manifest, has little to do with age *per se*.

With some apologies to Gerzon, one must note that, buried in the "Foreword" prior to the acknowledgments prior to the table of contents, i.e., in those paragraphs in any book that few will read, is a kind of fuzzy notation of the group he is describing. He honestly does not want to claim that his "youth" is wholly representative of a generation, but, like so many other commentators on youthcult, he commands us to a trackless task of figuring out just whom he is talking about, and how we should evaluate their ambassadorial credentials: "The type of young man I describe is one who comes from a middle- or upper-class background; who is white; who attends college or is capable of doing so," and who, in addition, "perceive[s] . . . new social circumstances and who rec-ognize[s] the new challenges." Whether Gerzon recognizes the fact or not, he is describing nearly *a third* of his generation.

To begin with, America has simultaneously democratized and enshrined higher education to the extent to which at least 50 per cent of those between the ages of eighteen and twenty-four have attended college for at least one year. If my 1971 survey has the slightest credibility, approximately 75 per cent of that group fits Gerzon's socio-economic description. When one adds a judicial index of political and social sympathies such as those Gerzon indi-cates (however vaguely), he is speaking, in turn, of 80 per cent of the 75 per cent of the 50 per cent, i.e., 30 per cent of a generation. In other words, if we took all the white middle-class and up kids in college and asked them (as I did in what, for convenience sake, we'll call the "Generations survey") to mark their sympathies and degrees of sympathy for a whole range of groups, individuals, issues, cultural artifacts—and these regardless of their stated politics—we find a vast majority with positive attitudes toward *most* of those groups, individuals, issues, etc., which Gerzon would no doubt col-lect under his honorific rubric (for an indication of the validity of this proposition, see Appendix, section C).

So Gerzon is actually talking about a lot of people, a gravita-tional field in seven figures. Yet, although they do *not* form an elite, Gerzon (and he is not alone) represents them, figures them forth for public inspection, with the behavioral patterns of a stratospheric elite. The behavioral patterns of his immediate sub-jects, those from which he generalizes, bear only a smidgen of an analogy to those of the group which is purportedly being pried open to a watching world.

Gerzon's treatment of the required youthcult reading list, and of the importance and influence of the Mentors, should be suffi-cient to demonstrate the elitist distortion that results and to pro-pel us toward some less turgid and fuzzy modes of defining the generations of the young.

Gerzon's first three required heavies are Marcuse's *Eros and Civilization*, Norman O. Brown's *Life Against Death*, and Camus's *The Myth of Sisyphus*, the last being "the most popular book of philosophy in youth culture." In a later excursion, "The Youthcult Bookshelf," I present a little list, culled from interviews, of the cultbooks of three successive generations of college students. *The Myth of Sisyphus* appears indeed—on the list of what I call the "elder juniors" (b. 1939–45). It was not even mentioned by anyone *under* twenty-six. Brown's *Life Against Death* was sporadically indicated by those in the "mid-generation" (b.1946–50) but did not receive enough backing to make the cultbook list. Those who did mention Brown were or had been students at Ivy League–genre colleges or Big Ten–quality universities. Marcuse, needless to say, appeared nowhere. As one of my more politically conscious former students who tried *One-Dimensional Man* asked, "What the hell is that guy talking about? I couldn't get through ten pages of that bullshit."

In other words, and on the grounds of simple surface behavioral patterns, Gerzon and other elitist preceptors lead us all to believe not merely that kids are actually reading, but that they are reading fairly demanding works and generating spontaneous passion and involvement with the ideas of their philosophical Mentors. In so doing, he confuses the media habits and conceptual abilities of elites and non-elites of at least two—and more probably three— "generations." In a slick media production with its own satirical distortions, "Staying Hip" (*Harper's*, September, 1971), Sherman Chickering compares the behavior of "the Relevant Teen-ager" of 1966 (the people Gerzon thinks he is talking about) with that of his 1971 counterpart. Chickering's hyperboles do not mitigate the accuracy of the thrust. *Cf.* Gerzon while perusing the reading list for the "relevant" eighteen-year-old:

> 1966: Has library of some 200 volumes. Leading off the fiction list are: *Catch-22* (Heller), *The Green Berets* (Moore), *Thunderball* (Fleming), *Candy* (Southern), and *Lord of the Rings* (Tolkien), followed by a whole series of existentialist and sci-fi titles. . . . The nonfiction list features: *The Art of Loving* (Fromm), *The Prophet* (Gibran), *The Secular City* (Cox), *Growing Up Absurd* (Goodman), *The Gospel According to Peanuts* (Short), *New Radicals* (Jacobs/Landau), and *Understanding Media* (McLuhan), plus the usual overweight assigned in the social sciences. . . .

> 1971: Does not own any books. Has five paperbacks temporarily in his possession: *Hot Cherry* (stolen from a bus station newsstand); *Pre-Columbian Burial Rites* (found in a campus parking

lot); *The Aesthetics of Rock* (borrowed from the pocket of a sleeping musician); *The Boy Scout Handbook* (picked up hitchhiking from well-meaning driver); and Abbie Hoffman's *Steal This Book* (stolen from a friend who bought it).

Granted, Chickering's 1966 model is in college and in 1971 is on the street. Still, the list for seventeen-to-twenty-year-old college students that the Generations survey presents is far closer in *spirit* to Chickering's 1971 street kid than it is to Gerzon's mirror-image of Roszak's roster of "leading influences"—Marcuse, Brown, Paul Goodman, Allen Ginsberg, Alan Watts—to whom Gerzon adds Camus, C. Wright Mills, Swedish sociologist Gunnar Myrdal (!!), and, implicitly through heavy citation, that shopworn under-every-arm guide to 1960, Reisman's *The Lonely Crowd*. By comparison, our list:

Single works: *Demian* (Hesse), *One Flew over the Cuckoo's Nest* (Kesey), *Soul On Ice* (Cleaver), *Do It!* (Rubin), *The I-Ching*.

Authors: Richard Brautigan, Kurt Vonnegut, Jr.

As we'll note later, and in considerable reviewer's detail, that list, with the exception, perhaps, of Kesey and Cleaver, is a cartoon. It has none of that grim, high-powered seriousness of Gerzon's heavies. Its demands on the conceptual abilities are minimal; on the range of the emotive life, only moderate. For large segments of the young who are no longer touched by the print-visual media complex (and *therefore*, as it turns out, *not* subject to elitist projections), the tone and demands of our list (let alone the lengths of the individual books) are most fitting.

There is an ideological argument, too, which helps to explain the confusion of elites and generations which we have been too willing to accept in "insider's" analyses such as *The Whole World Is Watching*. One retraces a time when, for example, it was possible to accept Camus's notion that masochistic Sisyphus was happy and, wholly conscious, to revel in that and attendant absurdities. One walks a thin line of transgression if he suggests the viability of those values to the mass of those who, stridently or less so, "want the whole world and want it NOW," who cannot imagine anal-retentive Sisyphus happy at all. I, too, have wandered, assuming the values of a college generation of the early 1960's would hold through, attempting to introduce Camus to college classes, rolling that stone until I was shriven. Since few could follow the rage of Camus's moral logic when it was described for them (fewer actually read it), we shifted to some of the less demanding and sustained essays in *Resistance, Rebellion and Death* ("Why Spain?", the four "Letters to a German Friend") as a way in, and even there, trying to summon as much *"revolt, freedom and passion"* (the words and the italics are Gerzon's, and applied eulogistically to "this generation") as expressed by that unswerving arrow of rebellion, we drew blanks. Oh, there were always those who resented this catering (mine, and that of others) to the functional illiterates, there were always those who both understood Sisyphus and were willing to confront his joyful agony—and those were the very same who later discovered some Mentors: Brown, Goodman, Orgone therapist Wilhelm Reich, Summerhill founder A. S. Neill (with only Goodman and Neill, as I recall, provoking sustained and profound interest).

One cannot play the spiritual assumptions of the elders and the elites as those of even *college* youth writ large. Thus one must recognize, for example, that when Gerzon informs us that existentialism, the theater of the absurd, Kafka, Lenny Bruce, Feiffer, and on, are properties of "this generation," he is projecting the spiritual possessions of those who, in his own words (echoing those of Kenneth Keniston) are the "most articulate, energetic, educated members of the generation," those who are most likely to have committed themselves, been frustrated, yet continued to roll the stone. As likely, he is referring to another generation entirely, as, in passing, he cites the white elephant of the Peace Corps as evidence of "youth's commitment" to cultural relativity and involvement. The delusion doubly intensifies when we are offered, as a "proof" of the pervasiveness of the spirit of existential absurdity among "today's youth," the long Broadway runs of absurdist dramas. Unfortunately, Gerzon is serious, which perhaps demonstrates that even a Harvard education these days may be an absurdist drama.

If I have dwelt excessively on what may appear to be a minor issue, I do so for reasons both visionary and pressing. First, and looking toward the last section of this collage, which deals directly with the Academy arena in which we are accustomed to confronting large parcels of youth: those whose lives are spent in interplay with young people cannot operate on these elitist images, images which project distorted expectations, and still be effective. The publishers keep truckin' the myth out, 'cause they figure a Harvard kid's representation of youthcult will possess articulation, glamour, and respectability. One has no quarrel on the first two counts, but the respectability may be undermined by our own experience as we discover a significantly different world of youth. If our image of college youthcult is bounded by the projections of Mark Gerzon and the palette of James Simon Kunen, and if we act on that image, then we will either generate frustration or perpetuate apathy.

More immediately, I am concerned with our very notion of "generation," particularly as that lumping concept has emerged from those hyperbolic dialectics of the 1960's. I simply wish to indicate how truly difficult it is to define exactly what we are confronting in that headlined "youth culture" or "now generation" if the artifacts and explanations which are thrust at us have been elitist in perspective. What angers persistently is that the depth reports on Youthcult have been almost exclusively confined to admittedly "small percentages," a phrase the sympathetic reporters oddly hold in common with right-wing pyromaniacs and other more orthodox cacophonies. Were one to concentrate, let us say, on ten "alienated" Harvard students, or six Weather-people (assuming one could locate them under the manholes of Detroit), or thirteen dedicated communards, or a random sampling of Berkeley street people, one would inevitably arrive at a vision of youth that would fit every clichéd analysis that we have been tendered to date and so desperately want to believe. And once one perceives the deep and shattering effects of such images on young people themselves, one develops a far more nasty and cynical analysis of the process by which the images are wrought. That's for a few pages hence, the "parliament of apologists." But crucially, now, some hopefully intriguing data leading to some exploratory notions on the very definition of our current generations of the young.

2

An Account of a Survey, and the Notion of Sub-Generations

As interested in the gravitational fields as in the cores, I wished to fathom how far—in time, in space, in spirit, in quality—these extended. Indeed, I wished to verify the extent to which the equation of youthcult with the multifarious spirits of counter culture and counter politics was justified.

The small facts, then, of a strange form of personal odyssey. In the spring of 1971, with the aid of friends in the Academy and elsewhere, I ran a depth survey on a more or less random sample of college-educated young people between the ages of seventeen and thirty-two. Why the college-educated? And why the particular age brackets? First, our conglomerate image of youthcult seems to have emerged from the universities. One would assume from both slick and underground media that any movement toward cultural and political alternatives would spring initially from the general Academy, student division. If so, then a survey would reinforce the popular image; if not, we turn elsewhere and explain, right? Too, I felt that if one was to unveil a high degree of awareness of the presumed prime elements of youthcult, the discovery would take place among the relatively educated (although college attendance is never any guarantee of either education or awareness). By this time, as well, such a large parcel of American youth had attended college at one time or another that a broad sample of that group, as I have previously noted, would *not* produce an elite. Still, to check, I engaged a number of wanderers, working young without the college experience, and "street people": neighbors in a working class section of Brooklyn, hitchhikers on the Northeast interstate circuit, hangers in small upcountry New England towns.

On the age brackets: Only the downside was inevitable, that is, one would not expect to find too many college students under the age of seventeen. There was no *a priori* up-side limit: Thirty-two just happened to be the age that turned up, and, as we will note, thirty-two was a very coincidental age in 1971.

Segments of this survey had been run, in roughly the same form, among my former students at CCNY since the fall of 1968. In each running previous to the broadly designed survey of 1971, the information gathered was for the use of the students in a number of writing-course projects. But in extracting the data from these previous runnings, I became disturbedly aware that there was something going on, something that didn't exactly mesh with what we were reading in either the slick media productions or in the academic exegeses and apologias for youthcult. I confess to not vaulting into this survey blind, then; but I simply sought to certify that I was dealing in neither isolated incidents nor too-broad fictions.

Thus a questionnaire (most of which is reproduced in the Appendix, along with nearly all the raw data). But not your insidiously abstract sociologist's questionnaire. None of that "circle-one-of-the-five" business that fits so neatly on the keypunch operator's side-table and never captures nuance. If there are five choices, there must be twenty-five, or the number of options floating around this world is frightfully limited. And not one of those galluping ten-question forms for threshold literates, forms which produce nothing but simple and stale water.

Rather, get it all at once, as much of it, and in as wide a spectrum of manifestation, as possible. Ask for descriptions as often as you provide them. Leave plenty of white space. Be outrageous! Encourage comments—indeed, hope for them. And at times, the audience was dearly obliging.

Now, some really dull facts for the squeamishly minded, which others can skip—and turn back to only when they start questioning the data. A brief obligatory description of methods of administration, the questionnaire itself, the group sample, and the data chosen for reproduction—all prerequisites for what emerged: the criteria for sub-generations of youthcult; the underpinnings of the distinctions between cores and gravitational fields, and thus between hard counter culture and counter politics and the inchoate urgings, sympathies, and stirrings that dance around the cores; some harder criteria for judgment of academic explanations and apologies; and finally, some basis for analysis and prophecy.

The questionnaire was distributed with the aid of friends teaching in colleges and universities of all types and sizes in ten states, and to and through friends and acquaintances in those and others. I worked with roughly 530 responses to the seven-page questionnaire and interviewed, usually informally, approximately 12 per cent of the respondents. Unstructured discussions accounted for perhaps seventy or eighty memorable individuals beyond those who filled in the questionnaire. Twelve colleges and universities were heavily represented in the 530 responses: CCNY, Brooklyn, Douglas (Rutgers), Vanderbilt, U-Mich, U-Ill (Chicago Circle campus), Saginaw Valley College (Michigan), Simpson College (Iowa), Northwestern, Yale, Columbia (School of General Studies), and Williams. Including those schools of lesser representation, and those represented by respondents no longer attached to the Academy, the Generations survey covered young people educated at some forty-six divisions of American higher education, a hardly deterministic range.

One might complain that, for all my efforts at reaching a "typical" sample, the method of administration was hardly uniform, and that therefore the data is skewed. I had, after all, no control over the way in which my teaching friends chose to distribute, describe, and collect the questionnaires they received in bulk. I likewise could exercise little control over the way in which other friends chose to distribute and describe the questionnaires they funneled through to their acquaintances. One group, however, was tightly controlled: thirty-five of my students at City College (and approximately 200 former students of the years 1968–70 who had taken previous versions of the questionnaire). As this group ranged in age from seventeen to twenty-nine, I garnered a fairly decent indication of whatever discrepancies might turn up in other returns. The discrepancies never appeared.

One might also object to the random and loose sampling on

ideological grounds, to wit: that, for example, the heavy counter-culture, drug-culture, or counter-politics people would resent the mere idea of a questionnaire, particularly when its source was anonymous (and regardless of how amateurish the physical object appeared; but paranoia has reached such a pitch that the appearance could always be considered an FBI ploy), and would simply not return them. Therefore, it would be argued, any assertion I make concerning the relationship of youthcult to counter culture, for example, would have its authenticity precluded. A *priori* I would be tempted to jab at that objection as a form of blind escalation apologetics by people who have grown so accustomed to the most favorable of fictions that they deeply resent the disturbance of their slumbers. The form of that criticism, the tortured shill, ironically turns up quite often in the rhetoric of those who have been so defensively reacting to the Establishment-soothers: "Not all college students are . . ." or "It's only a small minority . . ." or other such neurotic blah.

But the actual evidence for refutation is substantial. Begging the question for a moment, and seeking refuge in the disquieting rhetoric of either/or, one might counter that it is more than probable that as many "straights" did not return questionnaires as did the "hip." The statistics, though, reveal significantly pervasive *sympathies* for counter culture and counter politics, although a far narrower claim for *involvement* in counter culture or counter politics. For example, if 76 per cent of the total sample indicated sympathies for two or more "new" or "counter" politics groups (question A.26), 44 per cent actually participated in two or more Movement-oriented demonstrations, etc., during the period 1968–71. Or if, on an attitude scale running from 0 (most negative) to 5 (most positive) the mean responses to Earth Day, the Sierra Club, and North Slope Oil were 4.3, 4.1, and 1.9, respectively (question C.1), approximately 24 per cent of the respondents had offered concrete gestures in ecological action programs (question A.16). Or if the mean attitude response to sensitivity training was 3.1 (an only mildly positive index, anyway), only 9 per cent of the total sample had indeed groped-in with group therapy of any genre (question A.11). One might say, in fact, that the questions were designed to touch even the most inchoate of freaks, to brush the concretions of the culture so many believe they exist in, or so we are told.

The questionnaire was divided into three sections. Section A consisted of twenty-nine items designed to determine social and geographical movements, media habits and attitudes, degree of counter-culture and counter-politics involvement, general political attitudes, etc. Only five of the twenty-nine items did *not* present the opportunity for free-form answers. The burden of *a posteriori* category construction was thus mine. The second section consisted more or less of an "examination" of the respondent's knowledge of both popular and general, counter and mainstream, cultures. At the top of each page in Section B, the respondent was advised, "PLEASE DO NOT USE ANY REFERENCE MATERIALS FOR THIS PAGE" (in other words, what's known in the trade as a "take home"). The data for Section B should adequately demonstrate that the respondents held their honor extremely well —perhaps too well. In the quest for certainty, though, those thirty-five CCNY control students took Section B as a formal classroom examination. Their results did not differ in the least from those of the fifty-three other students at City who took the whole under noncontrolled conditions.

Section C, which I describe at length in the Appendix, sought a more intense and specific set of attitude responses. Many of the individual items contained in the one question constituting the whole of Section C* were repetitions of those from the first two sections and thus served as cross-checking vehicles. For example (and as a paragon), is it not curious that so many of those who indicated identification and/or sympathy with the National Organization of Women in Section A (Q.26) responded with either nonrecognition or a neutral attitude to "NOW" in Section C? When the counter-politics claim factor was high, the nonrecognition was all the more telling. Betty Friedan may have to live with the insult for a time, but the sacrifice will prove to be slight if The Culture is at all spurred to recognize its own.

Based on the data reproduced in the tables, there are more than 300,000 possible individual correlations of attitude, knowledge, and involvement categories, all of which would necessitate a comparatively uninstructive centerfold grid of poster dimensions. I pre-

---

* The single question, as worded, with slight variations, on nearly all questionnaire forms: "Would you indicate your response to the following by placing a number ranging from 0 (most negative) to 5 (most positive) in front of each item. If you do not recognize the item, please place an X in front of it."

ferred the resource of language for the correlations and, besides, could not humanly fill that grid and count the pencil blurs. For such problems are computer grants made to prominent members of the Academy.

What I have done, though, is to break down the gross responses twice (although not for all questions): first, by three age groupings we will be describing shortly and, second, concentrating on the 17–20 age group alone, by groupings of colleges and universities. The second breakdown should point to the kind of variances the sociologically squeamish will be interested in, hard evidence a number of previously assumed clichés, and, most important, provide the blocks of information upon which to determine the movement and intensity of the counter culture.

In the 17–20 age group, six groupings of thirteen colleges and universities presented themselves. Combining returns from two or three schools in a single category was necessary were one to lean on an even half-adequate sampling. Once that decision was made, the groupings were largely determined by (a) similarities in raw data results, and (b) similarities in type, size, and location of the institution. (For the record, see page 30.)

Okay. What did we find? First, and most significantly, three distinct *sub*-generations presented themselves on the basis of both raw and correlated data. There were equally matching psychocultural generation groups, but these we'll leave for a moment, as they make a good deal more sense after the facts. Within the 17–32 age group, the three sub-generations divided at age twenty-one (b. 1950) and at age twenty-six (b. 1945). It is perhaps more accurate to acknowledge that the sub-generations *fade into* one another, with the fixed lines determined by the most intense moments of the shift (as well as for the convenience of data columns).

The first criterion—and what, for the purposes of this first section of the collage, will be the paramount indication—is found in the arena of media habits. Respondents were asked a series of questions dealing with their media habits and opinions, to wit:

A.2 Do you listen to radio at all?:
How many hours a day?:
What kinds of programs are you most apt to tune in?:

A.3   What TV programs, if any, do you watch regularly?:

What TV programs, if any, do you watch occasionally?:

A.4   What magazines, journals, underground rags, etc., do you read regularly?:

What magazines . . . etc., do you read occasionally?:

A.5   What newspapers do you read, if any, and how often . . . ?:

A.6   Roughly how many record albums or tapes, if any, have you purchased (or otherwise acquired) in the past year?:

What were the half-dozen or so albums you acquired most recently?:

Whether or not you actually purchased any albums or tapes, which recordings do you think have been the most *influential* or *significant* over the past few years?:

Again, whether or not you actually acquired any albums or tapes, which recordings have had the most attraction for *you* personally over the past few years?:

A.7   What motion pictures have you seen during the past year?:

Which motion pictures have had the most attraction for *you* personally over the past few years?:

A.8   Have you attended the theater (Broadway, off-Broadway, street, summer stock, university, etc.) at all during the past year?:

If so, what did you see?:

A.9   How many concerts have you attended in the past year?:

What kind were they, and/or who played?:

A.10 Which museums or galleries or street art shows, if any, did you visit during the past year, and how often?:

Did you go for any particular show, films, etc.?:

If so, please specify:

A.14 Have you had any training or experience in the visual or plastic arts?:

What, specifically?:

A.15 Have you had any training or experience in the performing arts?:

What, specifically?:

The answers to these questions, along with other obvious information and attitude items from sections B and C of the questionnaire (see Appendix) were used to determine the degree of involvement of each of the respondents in print media,* visual media, audio media, and multiple media activity. Although I shall gradually unfold many of the specific, item-oriented answers throughout, only the raw data tables are of concern here. They follow, with degree of involvement (or "media index") indicated by the symbols + for "significant," o for "moderate," and − for "minimal." The reader will note that I have added separate categories for TV and films under "visual media." The divergence in degree of involvement between those two fields was unequivocally consistent, a fact that will assume greater weight when we later drill the delusions of McLuhan.

A number of radical shifts in media habits are quite evident. The dramatic jump into high print-media orientation occurs at age twenty-six (b. 1945). The most significant increase in motion picture attendance occurs at age twenty-two, although the most significant changes in the texture of the "most favored" film list (see below, "Media and Generations: The Delusions of McLuhan") occurs again at twenty-six. The shifts into high over-all visual media involvement are both plural and less dramatic, but they too occur at ages twenty-two and twenty-six. There is an evident drop in the membership of the audio-media culture at age twenty-one, but a recovery at twenty-six. And the most dramatic immersion into multiple media occurs at twenty-six. On the basis of raw data alone, then, and in terms of age alone, those who qualify for the appelation "The Media Generation" were, in 1971, between the ages of twenty-six and thirty-two. As 53 per cent of that group in the survey was still in school, and as interviews underscored the fact that their involvement with media is probably *less* intense today than it was five or six years ago, one cannot attempt to write off the comparative indices with the sleazy excuse that, as one friend noted in trying to anticipate objections, "older people have more time and money for media."†

Some other facts on those borderlines before the hypotheses. At

---

* Books were purposely omitted from the media question series since most of the respondents were in school and therefore, one *assumes*, involved with books, though usually not by choice. The book issue was taken up in interviews with respondents and nonrespondents alike, and is covered elsewhere.

† Too, the expenditures of the average audio media freak on rock concerts and records is generally at least equal to that signed out by the print-visual people on magazines and motion pictures.

TABLE 1—MEDIA INVOLVEMENT BY AGE GROUP

	Age Group		
	17–20	21–25	26–32
Print media			
+	20.3%	23.4%	55.0%
o	34.6%	38.3%	30.0%
−	45.1%	38.3%	15.0%
Visual media			
+	17.3%	24.6%	33.3%
o	37.6%	38.3%	40.0%
−	45.1%	37.1%	26.7%
Television*			
+	9.6%	6.7%	5.0%
o	28.4%	28.3%	22.5%
−	42.0%	48.3%	57.5%
None	20.0%	16.7%	15.0%
Motion pictures†			
+	19.6%	33.7%	48.7%
o	31.2%	33.3%	31.3%
−	49.2%	33.0%	20.0%
Audio media:			
+	38.7%	32.0%	42.5%
o	36.7%	30.0%	25.8%
−	24.6%	38.0%	31.7%
Multiple media‡			
+	12.7%	19.3%	34.2%
o	32.3%	26.7%	37.5%
−	55.0%	54.0%	28.3%

* + granted for four or more regular shows and three or more occasionals, *or* for a dozen or so occasionals. o granted for no more than three regular shows *only*, *or* two regulars and no more than three occasionals, *or* for a half-dozen or so occasionals. − granted for no more than one regular *only*, or no more than three occasionals *only*.

† + granted for ten or more movies (exclusive of those on TV) per year, o for five to nine, and − for four or less.

‡ A combination index. If, for example, of the three major media divisions, a respondent received two significant rankings (+) and one moderate (o), his index was automatically high in Multiple Media. In less clear-cut cases, e.g., two pluses and a minus, I turned to other sections of the questionnaire for hints as to how to tip the balance.

age twenty-one or twenty-two (b. 1950 or 1949), the following striking inflections also occur:

(1) dramatic rises in counter-culture activity, ecological con-

TABLE 2—MEDIA INVOLVEMENT OF 17–20 AGE GROUP,
BY COLLEGE AND UNIVERSITY GROUPING

	College and University Groupings*					
	A	B	C	D	E	F
Print media						
+	11.8%	14.5%	20.0%	44.4%	23.5%	27.2%
o	37.3	27.2	27.5	27.8	23.5	40.9
—	50.9	58.3	52.5	27.8	53.0	31.9
Visual media						
+	17.6%	14.5%	22.5%	33.3%	14.7%	25.0%
o	41.1	47.5	40.0	36.1	44.1	43.2
—	41.3	38.0	37.5	30.6	41.2	31.8
Television						
+	11.8%	9.1%	12.5%	0.0%	2.9%	6.9%
o	17.6	41.9	20.0	19.5	35.3	27.2
—	50.9	25.4	32.5	52.8	38.2	56.8
None	19.7	23.6	35.0	27.7	23.6	9.1
Motion pictures						
+	15.7%	12.8%	25.0%	47.2%	17.6%	22.7%
o	43.1	41.9	35.0	22.2	35.3	38.6
—	41.2	45.3	40.0	30.6	47.1	38.7
Audio media						
+	41.2%	32.7%	45.0%	44.4%	29.4%	31.8%
o	39.2	27.2	22.5	36.7	52.9	44.4
—	19.6	40.1	32.5	18.9	17.7	23.8
Multiple media						
+	13.7%	5.4%	15.0%	36.1%	5.9%	13.6%
o	37.3	30.9	32.5	33.3	35.3	31.8
—	49.0	63.7	52.5	30.6	58.8	54.6

* The groupings and the number of responses involved:

Group Key Letter and Schools	17–20	All Age Groups
A. City College of New York (not grouped because of the control factor, and also because total respondents here form a sixth of the whole)	51	88
B. Brooklyn College, Douglas, U-Ill (Chicago Circle)	55	66
C. Simpson College, Saginaw Valley College	40	53
D. Yale, Williams, Columbia (School of General Studies)	36	55
E. Vanderbilt, Temple (principally Graduate Division)	34	45
F. U-Mich, Northwestern	44	61

I regret only that representation from schools west of the Rockies was minimal, although it picked up considerably in interviews with passers-by who were not subjected to the questionnaire.

cern, general (as opposed to popular-culture) information
held, and political awareness, and
(2) with less drama, increases in popular-culture information,
and mainstream culture information possessed.*

And at age twenty-six or twenty-seven (b. 1945 or 1944), the following:

(1) dramatic increase in social and community action,
(2) likewise for general and counter-culture information held,
(3) concentration of political identifications and sympathies,
(4) decline in *multiple* drug use, and
(5) manifest increase in sympathy for black groups (among
whites).

Such are a selection of crude basics. It is my contention that
those shifts that define the sub-generations have nothing whatsoever to do with the simple process of aging itself. The correlations
turn up too many curios for that reduction. The media-habit patterns for college group "D" (the "elite" schools), as I have hinted
before in dealing with primitive elitist distortions, are nearly interchangeable with those of the "elder juniors," i.e., those in the 26–
32 age group. More important is the notation that, *regardless of
age*, those with *high multiple media indices* present a combination
pattern of political-social activity and information possessed that
matches the dominant pattern of the elder juniors. That is, he
who is most immersed in *all* media not only possesses a proportionally greater awareness of the world (that much would be expected), but also is very likely to be *actively involved* in that
world.

But he whose media involvement is concentrated *primarily* in
the *audio* is equally likely to be a passive ignoramus. That is (and
I devote a separate excursion to the matter), it was a correlation
of the highest consistency *in all age categories* that he who possessed a high audio media index *alone* was not merely low in
information but also lacking in political and social activity, awareness, commitment, and sophistication, and higher in both drug

* For the distinctions between general and popular, mainstream and
counter-culture information categories, see Appendix, section B.

use and counter-culture sympathies (regardless of low counter-culture information possessed). As to the parentheses, for example, consider: Those in the 17–20 age group (the *eminently audio generation*) who claimed to read nothing but the underground press generally were among the lowest scorers in counter-culture information. I am looking at one questionnaire, in passing, from a nineteen-year-old, in which *Rolling Stone* is perhaps the only indicated medium beyond a heavy audio combination, and although possession of general information is moderate, the following items from section B drew blanks: Originator of the Geodesic Dome (cf. *Rolling Stone*'s Bucky Fuller feature and interview of June 10, 1971), Nicholas Johnson (cf. the *Stone*'s front-page "The Greening of Nicholas Johnson" feature of April 1, 1971), Arthur Janov (cf. all the John and Yoko interviews), Robbie Robertson* (my God!). It is my unfortunate duty to report that correlation, coupled with a minimal indication of political, cultural, and social activity, to be rampant among the juniors, i.e., the 17–20 age group (b. 1951–54). Thus a typical alternate press point of information, such as "rock heads and media freaks are often the same person, despite the polarity of approaches" (Ben Gerson in *Fusion*, May 28, 1971), is only a wishful projection.

Still, there is a community of spiritual interest that *dominates* the entire age spectrum, encompassing affairs and attitudes both political and cultural, a community that allows us to employ the tag "youthcult" with impunity. The manifestations of the spirit seem to be *concentrated* among those born between the posts of 1939 and 1954. The community figured itself forth in the Generations survey primarily through attitude and sympathy factors. For example, if one turns to the third section of the questionnaire and forms two lists of items that received the highest and lowest *mean attitude* responses—regardless of the age of the respondent—one *begins* to define that community. Granting all my errors in construction, granting all the oversights of that limited number of items (fifty-two) for attitude responses, conceding all, the two lists still present a highly defined image. On a six-point attitude scale (0 to 5, negative to positive), the two lists are formed from items receiving *mean* attitude responses of 3.4 and up, and 2.0 and down:

* Lead vocalist for The Band—hardly a minor group in the rock hierarchy.

Honorifics	Pejoratives
Earth Day (4.3)	John Mitchell (1.0)
National health insurance (4.1)	Agnew's criticism of media (1.1)
Sierra Club (4.1)	Timothy Leary (1.4)
Methadone maintenance (4.0)	Billy Graham (1.6)
Al Lowenstein (3.9)	Walt W. Rostow (1.7)
Small business (3.8)	1970 elections (1.7)
Graduate education (3.8)	ARVN (1.9)
Siddhartha (3.8)	Bernardine Dohrn (1.9)
GI coffeehouses (3.6)	North Slope oil (1.9)
"All in the Family" (3.6)	Bob Hope (2.0)
William O. Douglas (3.5)	
A volunteer army (3.4)	
National Organization of Women (3.4)	
2001 (3.4)	

To the spirit of this list, add such measurable factors as those reflected on the political sympathy list (A.26), the relatively high
participation in Moratoria and similar peace demonstrations over
the past few years (A.21), and the pervasiveness of the specifically
marijuana culture (A.18), and that spiritual community is defined
even more clearly. I should add, and not so parenthetically, that
when that *spirit* is betrayed in practice or, more likely, by non-
practice, one writes a book that seeks to understand why and thus,
indirectly, to halt the betrayal.

Within this generation called "youthcult" are three distinct age
subgroups that it is now our burden to explain beyond the mere
data patterns. Among those from whom we have inherited our
definitions of "the youth generation," there has been a considerable temptation to posit a single static age, independent of time,
which will separate the eithers from the ors. The age of twenty-six
seems to field the most frequent and convenient notation. Mark
Gerzon (twenty-two) of *The Whole World Is Watching*, for example, defines the youth culture simply as "the postwar generation," which was, he glibly remarks, "the first to have faced man-
hood in a mass society." In 1971, to be the first of the postwar
generation, to be twenty-six, was to have been born in the Year

of the Bomb, and from that, in some explanations, we inherit the Youth-Bomb Culture. No doubt, extending this logic, the twenty-six-year-old in 1989, born in the Year of the Assassin, will gather together with his peers to form the Youth-Assassination Culture. Even in the far more serious readings of a Kenneth Keniston we meet with the notion of a static 18–26 age group as defining "Youth," as opposed to Adolescence or Adulthood. But is not one always dealing with a particular block of this Youth in a particular moment of history, a block conditioned by a culture that itself will change even as the young do? So that if those who met Keniston's broad criteria for the Youth block (psychological maturity but sociopolitical adolescence) in 1968 happen to have been between the ages of eighteen and twenty-six, there is certainly no guarantee that the same age brackets will hold even in 1978. Unfortunately, in all our media-shot illusions, that grammar school distinction has to be brought to Show-and-Tell.

It seems to me that we have to ask a far different kind of qualitative question in order to determine just where a generation lies. We should be enjoined to ask a series of questions about both the individual *and* the culture, questions directed toward pinpointing the shaping forces of pre-adolescent and adolescent consciousness: What forces, ideologies, styles, spirits permeated the culture during *whatever years* in which the individual psyche remained predominantly malleable, the years before resiliency tipped the balance? And thus, what cultural forces *and* individual responses can both determine and define a community of interest, a dominant sensibility? The forces that bind extend over more years than we have been led to believe. For now that we have gathered the clans together in universities, one can add to the shaping spirit of a generation the dominant forces at work in the Academy during those early years of Keniston's static "Youth." Thus, for example, the sub-generation described in the Generations survey as being born between 1939 and 1945 (the coincidence of the war dates might make for glamorous copy, but is really quite insignificant) was shaped by a series of cultural forces through which they passed until 1965 or 1966. If one considers those forces carefully, I think the reasons for the leadership of this sub-generation in matters of counter culture, and more so of counter politics, will swiftly become apparent.

First, though, turn back to the three sub-generations the survey data indicate, and consider them in light of the kind of question I think we ought to ask. The poles of the generation of youthcult— the juniors (b. 1951–54) and the elder juniors (b. 1939–45)—are highly defined, with the center group (b. 1946–50) blurring in both directions simultaneously. The poles are highly defined in terms of characteristic media habits and attitudes, and political and social activities, sympathies and involvement. The center group leans toward the juniors by virtue of its dominant media habits and consequent dominant modes of communication, conceptualization, and perception (with the attendant social, political, and moral consequences of these—as will subsequently be demonstrated); on the other hand, the center also reaches toward the elder juniors by virtue of a common experience of cultural forces, ideologies, styles, and patterns of historical events during its *social* adolescence. That is, like the elder juniors, center group's *adolescent* consciousness was *not* touched by the violent period of degeneration of American culture and polity of the late 1960's, was *not* bombarded by whirling sets of apocalyptic imperatives. They did *not*, for example, share a high school drug culture with the juniors but did share the new dominance of the audio media, specifically embodied in rock culture. They did share a brief period of political involvement with their immediate elders, but they do not, in the main, share their literacy. Briefly, then, if the confusion associated with psychological adolescence reigns in any one subgroup of youthcult, it is among those who were, in 1971, between the ages of twenty-one and twenty-five.

In this I am dealing with dominant patterns only, not with exceptions or cross-currents. These exist: elites, geographical conditions (yes, Virginia, counter-culture patterns work inland from the coasts, and outward from those evil cities; but as anyone who has taught school in New York City well knows, a kid from the Bronx is as liable to be provincial as the Appalachian who knows only what's between here and yon ridge), ethnic groups in isolated locations, unredeemable squares, and other such hackneyed caricatures. If we have progressed beyond the elitist distortions of a Charlie Reich, I hope we have moved equally beyond the fetid simplicities of a Spiro Agnew.

Intersecting all three sub-generations is that fundamental divide between the small core groups who are intensely involved in "alternate life-styles" or "counter politics" or both, and the wider fields of gravitational influence where young people dabble or sympathize with the core or develop less intense versions and visions of the values and commitments of those at the core. The fact remains, however, that, as noted, the sympathy and/or dabbling and/or variations on themes are expressed frequently enough to justify the notion of youthcult. So much for the exclusionists.

The prevalent *critical* ideology of youthcult is quite simple and has been well accounted for elsewhere: a dissatisfaction (ranging in intensity from mild concern to profound rage) with the hypocrisies, violences, injustices, insensitivities, and down-the-line-of-mainstream sins of America in its unique technocratic age; a growing awareness of the seemingly inexorable venality of power, of a degeneration plan that epiphanied in Vietnam (and in a thousand smaller daily atrocities), although it was shadowed forth long before. That is about the broadest statement that can hold the whole generation together. As I said very early on, it is precisely because I accept this critical ideology that I am not interested in rehashing its details.

The responses of youthcult to the critique, however, are qualitatively multiple: within sub-generation groups, within shared basic sensibilities, within the split between counter culture and counter politics. There is a forest of variables. So much again for the reductionists. What interests us at this juncture, though, is the relationship of the dominant behavioral characteristics of the sub-generations to the type of response they are able to offer.

Look first at the highly defined pole of the elder juniors. A fortuitous entry into the consideration of the fact of their leadership is provided by a very intriguing (for what it reveals of false assumptions) analysis of generational patterns found in a counter-media newspaper. The writer excludes those now twenty-six or older from the "New Life-Styles." The reasoning: This group

> began life in the time from the depression years through World War II and its patriotic penumbra. They finished school before the new ideas began to have much impact on the campuses. Their children are still too young to have influence on their thinking. They have firm roots in yesterday. (Monty Green, in the *Vermont Freeman*, September, 1971.)

A most curious assertion from a staff member of a counter-rag that is veritably run and written by people over twenty-six. Three of the principal writers for the *Freeman*, it turns out, are professional newspapermen between the ages of twenty-eight and thirty-three, to which one adds regular copy from a vacationing lawyer in his late thirties, a Washington-based government employee in his mid-thirties, and a full professor of chemistry at a small private college (who one seriously doubts is under twenty-six). The editor, who weighs in around forty, is a former activist minister now continuing his activism in a full plunge into the "New Life-Styles." Two of these regular staffers are part-time residents of communes.

Disregarding Green's inability to perceive the longevity of those in his own editorial offices, one recognizes the thrust of his analysis to be, "Where were *you* when the revolution was a-borning?"— theoretically, a potentially productive question. Provided one can deal in concretions. For if Green had looked to the roster of certified counter-culture heavies and committed and consistent counter-culture and/or counter-politics followers, he would have found most of them concentrated in precisely the age group he chose to reject as "the ones who probably can be firmly placed on the other side of the much-discussed generation gap."

Some excerpts from the roster of heavies: Ray Mungo (founder of Liberation News Service, twenty-eight); Jerry Rubin and Abbie Hoffman, both in their mid-thirties; Bernardine Dohrn, key Weather-woman, twenty-nine; Tom Hayden (indeed, with the exception of Dave Dellinger, who is well into his fifties, the whole Chicago Eight); all the Black Panther heavies; most of the alternate-film people (Gould, the two Fondas, Sutherland, Nicholson, the Maysles brothers); heavies and ex-heavies of the rock world (Dylan, Hendrix, Zappa, Joplin, Slick, Crosby, Stills, Balin, Clapton, Nash, Young, Pappalardi, Kantner, Kooper, Hammond—just about everyone but the Taylors); and most of the writing staff of *Rolling Stone* (although founder Jan Wenner is twenty-four), the *Los Angeles Free Press* (of late, anyway, as the whole gang split off to their own, *The Staff*), *The Realist* (but asking kids under twenty-six who reads decade-tired Paul Krassner's high-powered verbal satire is as absurdist an exercise as exorcising the Pentagon—shades of the night), and, indeed, most other major alternate media publications. Oh, did we forget the Sons of Los? Let's drag 'em back: most of Nader's Raiders, the law commune people, Stewart Brand and much of Whole Earth company, and many of the leading New Agrarians we'll take up later. Need one continue?

A frequent experience: I pick up any of the counter-culture magazines or underground rags, scan the by-lines, and inevitably uncover someone from what we used to call the East Coast Conspiracy, someone from that well-knit Ivy League-Cambridge-Washington-Berkeley ping pong now turning it on for the kids, the prose impeccable, but with enough hip jargon thrown in to lend the impression that the writer is perhaps eighteen and not twenty-eight, that he's doing a number off the streets and not holding an M.A. in English. Occasionally sad, too, to hear them writing of figures from *their* youthcult. Recall a review of jazzman Charlie Mingus's autobiography, *Beneath the Underdog*, in *Earth*, a very slick youthcult media production. The review was by a uniquely fine writer and multi-instrument blues musician I knew in college, at a time when there were lingerings of an authentic beat culture, during which only jazz musicians and their circle of friends blew the weed. He had done a gig at the Iowa M.F.A. writing program, followed by stuffy, lying days of centerfold copy at *Playboy* for bread, playing blues piano or guitar in Chicago cellar clubs set up for the ambiance of hickory-smoked kids from Northwestern *circa* 1967–68. The writing was still there, but so were the indispensable references for the tale of Mingus's agony, and no one under twenty-six would understand. I guess all of that places him beyond the "New Life Styles."

And another: from the same college class, even did a year or two of law school following, then a series of meretricious media stints, here reviewing *Gimme Shelter* in *Fusion* (Christmas issue, 1970). The article opens in hip dictionary (e.g., "no one is trying to mess your head or lay some heavy trip on you"), succeeded by a similar rhetorical ploy to engage the sympathies of the lower age brackets of youthcult:

> *Gimme Shelter* is bound to be a controversial movie, both because it is so much a part of *our* lives and because of what it is going to mean to the straight community. What grownups think doesn't interest me very much and I'll leave it to those it does. But here are some thoughts for *us*. [Italics mine.]

In the "thoughts for us," though, the writer gives himself away—
unless he is so thoroughly deluded as to believe that the audience
he is addressing here is actually under twenty-one:

> The music in the film is not very good. Jagger is hostile and con-
> descending in turn, and the band sounds tired and bored. . . .
> I don't think we accept the star trip as easily as we once did. A lot
> of us are certainly made uncomfortable by the screaming male
> chauvinism of Jagger's act. We are a lot more demanding as audi-
> ences. So we and The Stones were engaged in a sort of agreement to
> pretend *we were people we used to be*. Since we naturally still
> hoped to realize the *dreams that had led us from Monterey to
> Woodstock* (and since we weren't ready to admit that Woodstock
> really was "the last festival"), Altamont was the inevitable out-
> come of the agreement. [Italics mine.]

The judgments, when compared to samples of average under-
twenty-one student responses to both records and films, some of
which are later transcribed in these pages, are light-years removed
in terms of simple perception, let alone more embracing cultural
analysis. So is the sensibility: I recall seven or eight twenty-year-
old girls who indicated women's lib sympathies on the questionnaire, whose response to Mick Jagger was decidedly positive, i.e., a
4 or 5 on the attitude scale, one of whom, when later interviewed
in a very unstructured rap, was only *forced* into perceiving male
chauvinism in both Jagger's act and in The Stones' lyrics, and
even then resisted. Yet the *Fusion* reviewer, twenty-eight or twenty-
nine, pretends to be one with his readership, assuming that he
and it together had passed through identical reincarnations, since
they all (of course) had been at Monterey.

In the same issue of *Fusion*, a parenthetical comment on *The
Greening of America* as it first appeared in *The New Yorker* again
unmasks the perspective and the age of the bulk of the counter-
media writers:

> 42-year-old Charles Reich often writes like three 14-year-olds. His
> Consciousness I and II—frontier and corporate impulses—are sep-
> arated out as they really haven't been in history. (Vietnam being
> the perfect blend of the two.) And his evocation of Consciousness
> III, sweet as it is, should only be read aloud at the Fillmore East.
> It's hard enough for non-adults (a group happily getting older and
> older, as fewer take the option of becoming adults), to define their

lives and their relationship to their country without being alternately excoriated as vermin and canonized as saints. There's already enough self-righteousness connected with the "youthculture" to sink any movement. *The New York Times* financial page, by the way, reports that Reich is "required reading for worried businessmen." Pepsi helps to green you on . . .

. . . as do the legal and legalistic columns in the counter-culture press. An editorial in one of the more irregular and ultimately ephemeral rags took up the worthy but worn liberal issue of consumer protection, laced with quotes from McLuhan, Joseph Wood Krutch, and the State Consumer Fraud Statutes covering "assurance-of-discontinuance." No doubt a helpful column to those who can actually read it, just as the *Fusion* comments on *Gimme Shelter* and Charlie Reich were articulate decompression chambers. But to pretend that such analyses express the involvement or comprehension of "youth," i.e., "postwar generation," 18–25, or what have you for a demarcation line, is sheer hallucination. When one begins to look more closely at declarations of intent on mastheads, the notion that he who is *writing* counter-culture copy is more culturally significant than he who is—supposedly—reading it becomes both more intriguing and more plausible.

And where, returning to the question, were so many of Monty Green's roster people when the "revolution" was so inchoate? Precisely at the place he bars them from when he asserts that "they finished school before the new ideas began to have much impact on the campuses." If one accepts the Beats as authentic precursors of counter culture, one must acknowledge that the attraction to them ranged beyond the avant garde, and Ginsberg's *Howl* or Ferlinghetti's "Junkman's Obligato" spoke as closely *out of class* to the budding recognition of the American wasteland as Eliot did in the classroom. Corso's readings to jazz improvisations, Lenny Bruce's "Religions, Inc." routines, Mort Sahl's diatribes at the plasticity of the American flag—these were all components of a spirit that began to mold sensibilities so that they were later prepared and comprehending. If one examines the book list or favored film list of this generation, the pre-eminence of the anti-hero, from Colin Wilson's *Outsider* to Godard's *Breathless* Belmondo, needs no elaboration. The rule of the literature and film of alienation is a legitimate concept applied to the elder juniors.

The drug culture arrived late, SDS was founded only in 1962, and it is generally conceded that the first college graduating class to have experienced the beginnings of an overt counter culture was that of 1964. That, of course does not mean that so many college graduates of the early 1960's skipped right off into mainstream jobs. Graduate education was in a period of high promotion, particularly at the big twenty or thirty, plus all those little elite places. So if one is talking about the college-educated *only* in, let us say, an age group now running from twenty-six up to *thirty-five*, one will swiftly discover a fairly high proportion holding advanced degrees and/or currently in school (the combination reads about 75 per cent of my sample, but undoubtedly that is high). So many of these people were on the academic beach when the counter waves came ashore in force.

If any one sub-generation *grew into* and reeled with the forces, ideologies, styles, and spirits that have developed into the sensibilities of counter culture and/or counter politics, it was a generation that had passed out of the narcotizing effect of adolescent faddism by the late 1950's. Artlessly reconstruct the 1960's, I doom you: Through the heightened political-social awareness that came (justly or not) with the Camelot years, to the first great national trauma since Pearl Harbor, to the arrival of that little pill and a new order of sexuality at a moment when the elder juniors were either in college or about to enter, to the total break with the old jazz culture through folk to folk-rock and off it flew, through the shifting dialectical tides of the black revolution—the elder juniors rang all these changes at a psychological time of intense awareness yet lingering malleability. They were not born into these in the same sense that, for example, their juniors were "born" into television.

And thus, I hold throughout, their commitment, where it existed, ran deeper and for the longer distance. The Culture was something they found, not assumed. They were presented with real choices, whereas rare is the seventeen-year-old in 1971 from any area of America other than the backwash who finds the choice of counter culture and/or counter politics as difficult as it was in 1965. The media have made it a lot easier. They were not hyping alternative realities in 1965.

More than being presented with a choice, the elder juniors not only discovered it, but, at times, created it. They seem to have possessed a far higher degree of perception-conception-will fluency than that evidenced by their potential successors. Who was it, after all, who initially propelled what has become identified with youthcult? Where did the ideas, the energy, the talent come from? And why, now, do so many of the early sympathizers feel that the whole community of interest has been betrayed? And particularly betrayed in the realm of counter politics? For the current 26–32 group never committed itself to counter culture as much as it did to the politics, preferring the projection toward the Other to that into the self. If the directions are shifting now, an explanation must surely lie in the political exhaustion of a *sustained* period of involvement. All the tears have been taken away.

To so many of these, the betrayal of counter politics lies in the two directions its "activism" has taken more often than not: theatrics and radical back-slapping. On the one hand, counter politics became content with Abbie & Jerry translations of McLuhan and Artaud to the extent to which peace-ins and be-ins and street theater and days-of-rage became media without messages. On the other, some tattered note paper from the University of Chicago Center for Continuing Education reminds me too poignantly of what happened to the New University Conference (the SDS graduate organization). From the Plenary Session of NUC in March of 1968, some scattered scribblings:

Academic as resources for local community
Take 1–2 years off to work & live in a project
Democratize classroom—way one teaches an ex. of political org.
What we do off campus gives credibility & moral force to what
   we do on

It took no more than eighteen months for the NUC *Newsletter* and organization meetings to be either dominated by tell-me-how-radical-we-all-are group-reinforcement peristalses (including monthly show-and-tell reports on "My Trip to Cuba") or chained to intricate ideological debates on the relative importance of—ideology. If that was the core of counter politics for the elder juniors, its community of interest swiftly dwindled. Those idealistic scribblings directed toward projects beyond the convenience of the academic community (note: I did *not* say "campus") remained just scribblings. The definition of "the people" to whom "all power" was to be given thus contracted to the breadth of Telegraph Ave. To pretend that what remained was constructive "action" was the most ludicrous of delusions. Of those I knew around the plenary tables in March of 1968, not one remains.

There are other factors as well that have driven away the initial community of interest in counter politics among the elder juniors and moved them toward active counter-culture commitments. However, true to the original spirit, they gravitate toward those of the counter-culture Ways that involve organization and social consignments (i.e., Free Schools, community service communes, alternate media groups) or to those counter-cult ways that involve the long-distance cultivation of individual crafts and trades. It is for them that the new string of alternate society media productions has arisen, and the statement of intended audience in Vol. 1, no. 1, of *Mother Earth News* points to the collective spirit of this sub-generation. The new publication is

> edited by, and expressly for, today's influential "hip" young adults. The creative people. The doers. The ones who make it all happen. Heavy emphasis is placed on alternative life styles, ecology, working with nature and doing more with less.

It's gone from social activism to personal activism—but activism still. And the people who are doing and creating are not twenty-year-old ex-Hashbury streeters now out on the agrarian lam or audio media freaks currently or recently swilling around in an Academy which, more often than not, shields them from the imperatives of creation.

We'll have a short causerie on the death of the will later on, but having indicated the contrary spirit of the elder juniors, the idea enters now as a way of returning to the problem of generationalizing. Here Kenneth Keniston's analysis, along with the realities of our youngest group, afford a landing place in what will be a continuing spacing in the sub-generations.

The diction has to be rough here in defining the contrary pole. The juniors (b. 1951–54) appear to be lacking—and not by mere virtue of age, either—in basic perceptual, conceptual, and expressive abilities, in fundamental will-energy, and, despite all the contrary hoopla, in breadth and depth of emotive life. So little of so much amounts to the spiritual betrayal of the whole generation, and, as I said, the task of documenting and explaining these potential tragedies occupies much of the following pages—so that what is now potential ruin will never be fully actualized.

To a certain extent, the juniors do fit Keniston's euphemized definition of the psychological state of adolescence as

> characterized by an absence of enduring commitments, by a continuing focus on questions of philosophy, morality, and ideology, by a lack of readiness for work and intimacy with others, and, above all, by a preoccupation with questions of identity, inner intactness, and wholeness. . . . It is a time of turmoil, fluctuations, and experimentation, when passing moods and enthusiasms follow each other with dizzying speed. The adolescent has little lasting sense of solidarity with others or with a tradition, and little ability to repudiate people and ideas that are foreign to his commitments [*Young Radicals*, 259].

To a certain extent. I am not wholly convinced that our current crop of juniors focuses all that much "on questions of philosophy, morality, and ideology," since they seem to be missing the basic abilities to perceive the concrete facts from which such questions arise, let alone to conceptualize the issues by abstraction or to express much understanding in personal response to those issues. Nor am I convinced that the mass of psychological adolescents in the youthcult gravitational field have "little ability to repudiate people and ideas that are foreign to [their] commitments," if by "ability" Keniston encompasses mere rejection. For the Rhetoric of the Pig speaks quite eloquently, in its anesthetic way, precisely to the abilities of a sub-generation to dismiss—albeit mindlessly— all life-styles other than its own. Certainly mainstream adults haven't aided that ability too greatly with their bosh fixations on hair, pot, and order in the death-trap high schools. But to notch the sins of the fathers is to waylay consideration of where the reactions of the children are leading us. Once again, that is not to say that the fathers have not sinned the 491st sin. Both, though, should banner Blake's aphorism: "One Law for the Lion & Ox is Oppression."

As an indication of protracted adolescence—and assuming the balance of Keniston's definition to be reasonably accurate (though not inclusive)—the question arises as to when one normally expects this psychological state to terminate. We might very well be verging on what Jacob Brackman, writing in *Esquire* on his generation (the elder juniors) in October, 1968, hinted at as a "new notion of generation." The question arises in light of the continuation of the pattern of adolescent psychic proclivities defined by Keniston (as well as some of the behavioral patterns the Generations survey unearths) by college students and others into their early twenties—in fact, in not a few cases, into their mid-twenties.

For example, if the media-habits statistics reveal a drop in audio-culture immersion in the passage from the juniors (17–20) to the center group (21–25), the data also indicate that that vacuum was only partially filled by increased immersion in other media cultures. Too, the percentage of those in the 21–25 age group whose media habits indicated high or moderate audio only and its attendant patterns of non-involvement does not measurably depart from that of the 17–20 group (28.2 per cent v. 22.6 per cent), although it drops radically (to 8.7 per cent) among the elder juniors.

Keniston repudiates the notion of "protracted adolescence" primarily on the evidence of his subjects. But his subjects were precisely at the other pole, the elder juniors and their younger doubles in elite groups: in *The Uncommitted*, alienated Harvard students of the late 1950's and early 1960's; in *Young Radicals*, not merely workers in the Vietnam Summer Project of 1967, but leaders. Not merely leaders, but those who had "spent at least one year during which their primary work involved community organizing, civil rights work, peace work, or some other Movement work," i.e., long-distance runners. Their ages are instructive in terms of the patterns recorded for the less selective group in our 1971 net. For in 1967, Keniston's subjects fell in an age bracket ranging from nineteen to twenty-nine, with an average of twenty-three. Translated into our age rubrics, that means people who are now twenty-three to thirty-three, with an average of twenty-seven.

"Protracted adolescence" or "prolonged psychosocial moratorium," Keniston maintains, are concepts that involve descriptive inadequacies,

for both refer to states that are supposed to *end* with precisely the kinds of psychological, political, group, and historical commitments

these young men and women [the young radicals] have already developed. In addition, both concepts suggest a limbo-like waiting
period of withdrawal, preparation, and continuing self-exploration.
But with these young radicals, while self-exploration is important,
waiting and withdrawal are not. And if theirs is a protraction of
adolescence or a prolonged moratorium on adulthood, it is one
that is increasingly taken by others and one that often lasts a decade. And it is preceded, rather than concluded, by the development
of a basic outlook on the world and sense of oneself [*Young Radicals*, 263].

I see we're back to elitist distortions. Armed with this confusion,
it is nigh impossible "to relate to" students flowing through classrooms, cateterias, offices—unless, perhaps, one is working with
young people at one of those "generally academically excellent,
highly selective liberal-arts colleges or private universities" from
which Keniston's young radicals came. Indeed, Keniston's notion
of "youth," an *emergent stage of life that intervenes between
adolescence and adulthood*," applies foremost to those who, in his
own words, are "the most talented, thoughtful, principled, sensitive, or disturbed of those who have an adolescence."

In terms of my analysis, the stage of "youth" is available to
those who have been able to settle their identity problems first,
and who possess the will for commitment, the conceptual tools
for the authentic creation of alternative structures, whether cultural or political. Among the majority of the elder juniors, the
other pole, that will has been tested in active wrestling with
mainstream society, and the conceptual tools have been honed
in the struggle, producing, as by-products, heightened knowledge,
discriminating abilities, reflective capacities. Listen to Keniston's
own subjects in *Young Radicals*, reflecting a tension between action and reflection born of wills and perceptive powers which
had escaped being smothered in the late 1960's only because they
had been somewhere else first:

I'm [now] spending a great deal of time in basic political writing
and thinking about American class structure, the dynamics of the
productive system. I feel that's a great lack of mine. I feel that I
really have been operating without much of a theoretical understanding of what I am doing. . . . People used to ask me, "What
are your politics?" I couldn't tell them. . . . I plan to do a lot

of reading, writing, speaking. Let other people do the organiza-
tional things. I have to begin to define the parameters, instead of
accepting the parameters that other people have put together [175].

Issuing from one who spent well over a year principally engaged
in Movement work, such a statement does not cover a cop-out. It
reflects a willed drive for informed action. And another:

> I need things that would give me more perspective to help me an-
> alyze what it is I've done and what it is I need to do. I need to
> know more about economics. . . . I want to do more reading in
> history. . . . I think if you have a radical perspective, you really
> should. I just don't have those things [175].

Compare a couple of people I spoke to on the way to this thing,
two nineteen-year-olds who *claimed* to be into counter politics:

> *What are you going to be doing?*
> I'm going out to this underground radio station in California,
> and do some heavy numbers on pig society.
> *Do you know where this station is and what their bag is?*
> Ah, I really don't know exactly where it is 'cause this dude who
> told me about it said he's being hassled by the pigs. And I really
> don't know what particular thing they're into, but I know I'll get
> a chance to get into a heavy head trip.
> *When are you going?*
> Soon as I can get it together. I mean, like my head is pretty
> fucked up right now, and I think I've got to cool it before I split.

Three months later he was in the same place, "putting his head
together," no doubt. And another, even more indicative of a
habit one comes to refer to as "politibullshit," the principle of
which involves utilizing a "radical" political line to cover one's
own lack of commitment to counter politics while simultaneously
moving into the penumbra of counter culture. The subject was a
New Communard from Darien, making the courageous move to a
farm in southern Vermont:

> I'm really into a lot of things right now. Like vegetarianism,
> which is very important to the revolution because it frees your mind
> from the meat the pigs live on.
> *Anything else?*
> Well, like we're going to build a dome, too. And that's really a
> break, you know, like from oppressive building styles.

In other words, building a dome is a revolutionary act?

Very definitely! You gotta see it indirectly, like it's a really heavy political trip.

When are you going to build the dome?

Well, we're thinking of starting late in the summer if everyone can get his head together first.

Uh-huh. Have you looked at any of the dome design books, and figured out your materials and things like that?

I really grooved on the *Domebook*. All those poly-plastic things, and neoprane tapes and stuff. Oh, yeah, we're going to get it all figured out. And one of the brothers down on the farm is heavy into geometry, and he's going to figure all the dimensions and angles out.

How old is he?

About 30, I think. But he's cool.

Neither of these conversations is contrived, although these and so many others from the interview tapes read like parodies. But, as one of my former students who admitted to "real contentment in a state of total apathy" noted with a far greater degree of awareness and candor:

> I have to come to my own defense: how about people who are realistically and definitely into nothing? There are a lot of people who say they're into this or that, but in fact they're into nothing. I myself am into nothing, and consequently I stay in college—doing nothing—because it gives me the chance to be while I'm into nothing, as opposed to working, and being into the work partially, and fucking up my head, at least I have the atmosphere of college, of a whole lot of people not knowing where they are.
> *What about the political people?*
> Oh, that's bullshit! That's just a game for them. They don't know where they are either. I have no reason, by the way, to be into nothing, and no reason to be into something—other than the fact that I don't like being into nothing.

At this juncture, the entire company of the communal rap going on was in a state of mild hysteria (read those statements aloud, and see if you can last):

"Is there something you'd like to get into?"

"He's too far into nothing."

"Have you made any attempts to find something?"

"Not that much, really, because I'm not that unhappy."

Excerpts from this conversation will be resumed further on, but the issue here is that if the psychological state of adolescence expressed in the tape-outtakes is carried full-bodied into the counter culture, that alternative culture is doomed to failure in the womb. Thus, for example, the ephemerality of so many communes, illustrating the contradictions between the ideal of "getting together" and the fact of the fragmentation of shifting allegiances, quasi-commitments, and lack of real "intimacy with others" (the phrase is Keniston's, the documentation will come), a fragmentation which undercuts the assumed (or at least announced) political-social vision of the candidates for counter culture.

The counter culture itself has offered us a prophetic vision of the encounter between these opposing spirits of sub-generations. The film was the apocalyptic *Easy Rider*, one of the most simple-minded, polarizing, myth-projecting caricatures of the larger conflict of generations and life-styles in America since Hollywood's last great parade of plastic and nonexistent American families. But *Easy Rider* is an unsuspecting cultural document. Its fantasies are most attractive to our juniors (see Appendix, section C, and the sub-generational film lists under "The Delusions of McLuhan"), who cathect into the cardboard Captain America and Sidekick Billy, and regard Jack Nicholson's ACLU-type Southern lawyer, George Hanson, as (one former student wrote) "really a nice guy, but a small-town square until he turns on." The two principals, invulnerable, protective of self, and only half-capable of perceiving the Other, heroes of hedonism, are yet totally bewildered when Hanson, turned on, sculptures elaborate UFO fantasies. He is an elder junior, in a way, from another culture. Although the sympathies are shared, the perceptions and the vulnerabilities are not. There is no indication that Fonda-Hopper desire either perception or vulnerability; and the tragedy of the film lies as much in their rigidity as it does in the rigidity of redneck America. How that rigidity emerges from the very media habits of the young, from the stunted perceptions their language allows, and thus from the invulnerability that comes with "being into nothing," are the subjects of the following excursions.

3

A Parliament of Apologists

Among explicators of the counter culture there is a pernicious operational hierarchy. With variations, its dynamic runs thusly: The slick media, hungry for marketable copy, present an image that confuses core counter culture with gravitational youthcult and conveniently mixes sub-generations to fit the leveling simplicities America—no matter what length of hair is at issue—revels in. Above the hucksters sits a class of academic apologists and euphemizers. They jump on the elementary confusions, generally add an elitist distortion, and seek to explain youthcult to us in palliative terms. Not surprisingly, their hundred reversible exonerations—ranging from classic Freudianism to visionary fictions—result in a modicum of complacency within youthcult itself. Running parallel to both the slick media hucksters and the academic apologists are the shills of the counter-culture press whose job it seems to be to hype all the myths, which will later be presented to the mainstream by the slick media and rationalized away by the academics. From *Rolling Stone* to the *Los Angeles Free Press* to Jerry Rubin's *Do It!* and on to more ephemeral mimeographed productions, runs a line of filtered down *apologias*. If the average youth in the core counter culture does not pick up from the counter-media the ready-made excuses for whatever it is he is or is not doing, his counterpart in gravitational youthcult will certainly have no trouble finding his own reality euphemized in productions more "respectable" to the mainstream. The moral, political, and cultural consequences of what winds up as an all-encompassing false hype are only beginning to be felt.

This is serious business, particularly if one wishes to believe that firm and lasting Alternatives must be established. So let us begin at the top. How, for example, has the absolute (and decidedly false) identification of hard-core counter culture and college students arisen? One greatly fears presenting an explanation that would sound like a taped Agnew address, but the dangers to the possibility of the counter culture itself are too great to allow that syndicated rhetoric of certainty to run unchallenged. A number of exemplars for the gravaman in the case of the irreversible counter culture–students equation arise fromg the slick mainstream media.

Esquire, for one, whose every annual college issue since 1966 has discussed universities strictly in terms of the most theatrical. *Esquire*'s 1969 college issue devoted itself entirely to trashing, counter politics, and the eternal question of who was co-optable and who wasn't. Want a sample of the "Unco-optables"? Hone close for the elitist distortion: leading off with the standard expectancies of Janis, Eldridge, Bobby Seale, Hesse, Mothers of Invention leader Frank Zappa, but following with (and these are presented as college heroes) Nobelist and peace advocate George Wald (I'll lay some serious odds that a mere recognition factor on dear, stood-up George would run about 1 per cent of those who were in college in 1969), Daniel Cohn-Bendit (maybe about 5 per cent for Danny the Red), blues-soul singer Laura Nyro (in 1969?— that's some thirty-year-old avant-gardist at *Esquire* laying his own trip down), and Carlos Castaneda (interviewer of Don Juan, the peyote medicine man), who, from a strict counter-cult party line is eminently co-optable—assuming one knows who he is.

The 1970 *Esquire* college annual opened with a dramatic and sensitively wrought portfolio of Harvey Dinnerstein illustrations, "Dink Stover in Hell," a portfolio that nonetheless, by the rhetoric of its very presence in the issue, defined the college scene in terms of Black Panthers, moratorium vigils, Young Lords, Hare Krishna people (whom, for example, nearly 20 per cent of those in the Generations survey could not even recognize), Kent State, and confrontations with the military. The issue continued with a functional dictionary of counter-culture alternatives to Dinnerstein's portfolio—communes, New Agrarianism, Free Universities and other educational experiments—and wrapped up the whole with a review of the activities of some members of what was presumably the first college graduating class ('64) to dip into the murky waters of the New World. The members, of course, were drawn from Harvard; and if that elitist game hasn't become familiar enough by now, *Esquire* gave an instant replay in its 1971 college issue, in which samples of counter-cult stylists into Alternatives from cab-driving to candle-making were drawn primarily from Berkeley. The latest slick media pronouncement to all of us, then, was that college had metamorphosed into the counter-cult Ways, and that therefore "the Big Trend Is No Trend."

It helps to understand the role of those media above sea level, *Esquire* as a topoid here, in bringing that very trend about. The operation is the same as that which the Mad. Ave. pitchman employs: If the reality does not exist, or if it exists only in part, you bring it into existence by convincing everyone else that *that's* where it's at, baby. Lead everyone to the wagon by holding out the carrot stick. Only when one is dealing in counter-cult, one presents a variety of garden vegetables. In the 1970 *Esquire* college issue such a counter feast was paraded that by 1971 it could all be writ large with impunity.

The total configuration of this garden basket results in what economists called the multiplier effect: The kids down on the campus think that this is where it's supposed to be, *ergo* that's where it goes, while the academic apologists up in the library carrels figure that this is where it's at, *ergo* it is explained with jargonistic respectability. When the kids arrive at the Alternatives, then, they can always turn to the academic apologists, perhaps filtered through the counter-media, for the explanation that fast becomes an absolving blind.

Two other media productions may prove instructive in examining this first (not necessarily in time, but in extent of real influence) stage of the hip reality multiplier effect. The first of these productions shadows forth under the title of *The Underground Guide to the College of Your Choice*. In what one cannot seriously consider a *parody* of Barron's Guide, the presentation of each university assumes that eighteen-year-olds are interested solely in where they can smoke dope and ball freely, sit in and trash, and rip off the anal Academy by copping credit for courses in macramé and astrology.

The assumption, no doubt, is growing more authentic, along with the reality; for the more kids expect colleges to conform to an image like that which *The Underground Guide* presents, the more they will seek to recast the Academy as a series of fragmented jokes, no more constructive than it is now, and no more human, as the Academy will simply come to institutionalize sprinting whims. The greater the success of this transmogrification, the more the truly Ice Age forces outside the Academy will seek to close it down. And to the degree that reaction succeeds, the Academy as a place of uterine freedom will die.

Whether or not the demise of the higher Academy may be a welcome development and how best to control that demise constructively are for later consideration. But there are a number of more immediate issues, not the least of which is the irony of a sub-generation that does not believe language can create a reality being manipulated through the agency of language by members of a sub-generation that does hold to a belief in the power of the linear media. A noted case: Jerry, Abbie & Co. can shrill that "words are bullshit!" but can entice their broods to *Do It!* only through the print-linear complex. And if the rhetoric of hip, unmitigated in such mainstream media productions as *The Underground Guide,* does not reflect present realities, it will certainly bring future realities into existence. Language remains a creative force even in a culture that denies its viability.

Examine, then, the headings for each descriptive section under each university in *The Underground Guide:* "Sergeant Pepper Section" (how many students, what it takes to be admitted); "Academic Bullshit" (key Relevancy courses, popular professors, experimental programs); "Bread"; "Brothers and Sisters" ("ratio cats: chicks," who wears what, where they hang, what kind of dope they are into, local going rates for grass by the lid, what kind of politics people are or are not into); "Political History" (basically, who trashed what and when, issues that linger); "Survival" (if and where one can score some dope, obtain "BC pills," abortions, etc.); and "Environment" (weather, architecture, the subjects of small talk).

Isolate the headings alone, and the rhetoric foists not a mere image, but a desired reality of an institution in which there is nothing to do. Thus there becomes nothing to do.

A single review from *The Underground Guide* should demonstrate not merely the reality gap but more important the way in which the myth-type creates reality by manipulating an adolescent constituency. Again, no one could assert that the mainstream is any less subtle and noxious in its manipulative techniques (particularly in the matter of what Marcuse refers to in *One Dimensional Man* as the process of "desublimation," the procedure by which mainstream culture allows primal energies to be released, and exploits them simultaneously in the very fact of release so as to mitigate potential internal opposition). But the issue of manipulation has to be confronted, primarily because the counter-cult pitchmen have claimed such moral purity, and secondly because the academic explicators and formal myth-fabricators of Consciousness III concepts have provided the literate of youth-cult with their theoretical statements of edenic posture.

The individual case is that of the "review" of the University of Michigan, chosen fundamentally because both students and younger faculty participated in the survey and conversations from which these notes spring. One opens with the elementary strands of myth: "Popular classes are 'Psychology 454' (a T-Group) . . . The Free U offers courses in 'Communal Barbering,' 'Phenomenology of Sexuality,' 'Macrame,' 'The End of the World,' and 'Astrology.'" I sincerely doubt that the U-Mich respondents to the survey were overly linear (indeed, in the section of the questionnaire dealing with attitude responses, sympathies for mainstream items were comparatively low, while counter-culture sympathies ran fairly high). Still, almost no one in the sample claimed to be into "T-Group," Astrology, or experimental education in any form. "People around here become very excited about the concept of Ex ed and do-your-thing courses, but they're really conventional in their actual choices," a junior faculty friend at Michigan remarked, then recalled an Ex ed program in which classes were held in dormitories, "just about wheeling the kids in from bed in their pajamas, and they still didn't show up, so if the involvement is around, it must be with the street people. Commitment to anything, let alone Ex ed, for those students is in somebody's head. It's not real." And if Psychology 454 is such a popular course, is not one rather surprised to find the average attitude response to "sensitivity training," for example, at 2.5 for U-Mich students seventeen to twenty years old, a wholly neutral rating, and far below the 3.3 average for the 17–20 survey group as a whole? (See Appendix, section C.) If that question smacks of non sequitur, it is, by the admitted fallacy of imitative form, appropriate to the type of myth it is responding to.

And another: "Dates are taking in the flicks." If so, a good half of the 17–20 age group didn't "date" too much, as that proportion presented minimal indices in motion picture attendance. Or the expected drug-boast: "65 per cent smoke dope regularly." One has to assume that the author of *The Underground Guide* has a peculiar and felicitous access to the drug culture; either that, or the notion of "regularly" has undergone some semantic surgery. No one pretends that the pot culture is not ingrained in the Academy, but the percentage of both "frequent" and "occasional" users of grass and hash at U-Mich in the Generations survey fell closer to 35 per cent than to 65.

And in case the contradiction escapes the malleable reader, the following two statements exist only a few paragraphs apart: "People are more into the environmental-political thing as opposed to the socially-conscious political trip." "[Dominant] environment—mental: People are talking about politics." The first statement would hold for the whole of the U-Mich group in the Generations survey, but the second seems more of a rhetorical exercise as applied to those in the 17–20 sub-generation. As another junior faculty member clarified:

"To talk heavy politics you go to the graduate students or the street people. Oh, everyone goes to moratoriums, but there isn't too much to talk about that since it's all been said. There was a good deal of 'political'—you have to put that in quotes—rapping during the rent strike, but that was something that touched people's wallets more than their ideologies. . . . The avant-garde is always there: in the newspapers and rags, at the Radical Education Project in Detroit, at scattered free schools for their kids, but they aren't what we normally see around the school or over the house."

The avant-garde image, though, the major variation on elitist distortions, is what is most frequently proffered in the media-myth-hype; and in more formal academic releases, the same blind surfaces. Subliminally, the avant-garde image is a cruel hoax. That is, the elite or vanguard is presented as the typical, and all those poor kids who are *not* psychological adults try to emulate the behavior or opinions presented and are sadly lost. In a metaphor, the correspondence columns of *Rolling Stone* brim with accounts of one rock or pop festival after another, mostly at small campuses, and written up by students who evidently wish to reassure both themselves and the vanguards that things are hip where they go to school, too. It's depressing, in a way, to drift thickly through these nearly identical running précis (same rock groups, same media events, same dope, same phrases, same attitudes, same judgments), but if one drifts far enough, the depression turns delphic with despair. For the process of media-hyped vanguardism is not merely a case of social sadism. Rather, as I hope will be keenly evident when we come to consider the cultural consequences of the activities of the whole parliament of apologists and hucksters, the hype has resulted in behavioral patterns in gravitational youthcult that will preclude any possibility of a stable and affirmative set of Alternatives.

The process of vanguardism might also, and more piquantly, be illustrated through one of its typical vehicles in the Academy, the "relevancy reader." The Relevancy Reader is produced by the college text divisions of the publishing houses—usually through one of the corporate shadows of a large multi-media operation. It customarily flows through the office of the College English Editor, and is directed either to composition courses (just to add a smack of formalism as a reason for being) or to the topical Relevancy courses that seem to be offered, to a great extent, by college English departments.

Now there is no doubt that if one is to utilize models in the teaching of the writing of English, the models should be relatively current, since no one runs around talking like a *bourgeois gentil-homme* of the eighteenth century any more. And as fine a stylist as a Swift or a Lamb may be, they are totally unsuitable for basic training in the mid-twentieth century. Usually a sop is thrown to Orwell or Lawrence or Forster, but they aren't really "relevant" enough and, besides, Lawrence was a fascist pig, Forster should have stayed on that boring ship, and Orwell was one of those tired old socialists, right?

We'll be dealing with the relevancy aspects of the Relevancy Reader again, but here one should understand what happens to a thirty-plus-year-old in the education business who is seeking to satisfy the imagined desires and concerns of the young—but in *his* terms. He obtains the Relevancy Reader by choosing a single topic, e.g., war, racism, violence, eco-catastrophe, women's lib— whatever happens to be the latest addition to Movement quiddities and simultaneously considered marketable by a generally cautious publisher (Gay Lib, for example, doesn't make the topical list), and presents an edited collection of essays (and sometimes photographs, poems, rock lyrics, cartoons, music scores, excerpts from fiction or drama, advertisements, collages) centering on the topic. More often, since the single topical reader won't provide enough flexibility, the multitopic Relevancy Reader emerges. After all, too, a publisher never knows when what is quintessential this year will become heretical, or fade altogether in the memories of the uncommitted.

Initially the concept was productive and profitable; the market is now stuffed with these relevancy texts. As a good friend who was one of the coeditors of the first of the successful readers noted, they're becoming more bizzare in form to attract what dwindling market is left. The gimmicks surface hard, and one of these latter entries, which posits a deceiving gimmick, is at post position to illustrate the process of vanguardism. It is secularly entitled *student voices/one*, and if one believes that both the content and case of the title is a democratic expression, wait on.

The premise of this particular hustle is that students should read other students on the relevancy topics. Theoretically, no objections! So all the articles are billed as being written by students —well, as it turns out, at least by people who *were* students (and *perhaps* undergraduates) within the past three or four years. What is initially at issue is not the premise, but rather the reality of who is doing the writing. For the editors (faculty at the University of Michigan) make the sloppy Con II mistake of identifying the writers by college (where applicable, since not all of them are in college). Thus does the typical student voice emerge, to wit: Of the fifty pieces in the book, twenty are written by students out of

Ivy-League-quality universities, four of which are excerpted from books (Ivy-League kids having first call on many editors who were thwarted in their previous academic incarnations); eighteen emanate from three quality state universities—Michigan (a concession to the editors' convenience), Texas, and SUNY at Buffalo. Twelve pieces are left. Three are anonymous or otherwise political fliers; three are excerpts from the counter-cult press; one is by an unidentified black; one by an unidentified high school student; and, as a concession, it seems, four are scattered among students from Bucknell, the University of Kentucky, and Queens College.

Regard the impression of the whole. Claimed by its very title as a representative piece, *student voices/one* turns out to be hardly that at all. The attitudes and issue-concerns of what are most likely "the most talented, thoughtful, principled, sensitive, or disturbed" (Keniston) and consequently most alienated are passed off as all student voices, or at least the dominant student voices.

But that fact does not trouble a leaf as much as the media multiplier effect, i.e., assuming some threshold literate out in the boonies reads this thing, he figures, "Hey, that's where I'm supposed to be at, 'cause I'm a student, too." But even the editors imply, by the very condescending nature of the "study questions" that follow each essay, that the average reader of *student voices/ one* does not possess the conceptual equipment to be there. E.g., following an excerpt from *I Ain't Marchin' Anymore!* by Dotson Rader (decidedly a nonstudent, and Columbia when he was):

> Is the profanity here necessary to the overall effect? Does the answer to this question depend on the context in which the words occur? Consider what you have heard said about profanity, especially in connection with definitions of morality.

What happens to the kid to whom such relatively Dick-and-Jane banalities have to be directed, what happens to him in his effort to reach the core of counter cult or counter pol is that he becomes a tool in the hands of far more sensory, immediate, and skillful manipulators than the unintentional editors of this book (e.g. Abbie Hoffman, who, in *Steal This Book*, ingeniously succeeds at ripping off his own brood).

The deleterious and sometimes tragic effects of this process of vanguardism may well lead to the noxiously delightful paradox wherein *student voices/one* and its ilk become the last books read by those not in the vanguard. A questionable assumption? Check one of the "representative" student pieces pulled from the underground press. After four pages of literate jargonese and counter-pol allusions, explaining why the writer doesn't dig left-wing student organizations like SDS because they are inimical to his preferred politic of "tribal communism," the writer concludes,

> I could go on at great length about all of this because for the first time in my life I feel that I am beginning to understand where I am in this mystical universe. But words and rhetoric are bullsh**t [*sic*].* I have faith that those who are capable of understanding what I am trying to say will pick up on it the same way I did. And those who do not understand me will understand only in retrospect, if ever.
>
> F**K the leaders and their
> "correct line"
> Power to the people—the
> tribal youth of the world [54, 56]

The manifesto is undiluted Yippie (despite the verbal control, explaining its choice by a couple of English professors for a cautious, dipping-in-toe publisher) but is as guilty of elitist exclusions and vanguardism as it asserts the contrary. The writer disposes of the need for the political organization, rattles off a list of heavies with whom his audience (whether in the underground rag or *student voices/one*) is hardly familiar (in fact, on the basis of his analysis, it is rather difficult to believe that he himself has studied Marcuse or picked up more than a slogan or two from McLuhan), then proceeds to write off the very medium through which one presumably becomes acquainted with the heavies, and concludes with the flip arrogance of smug bourgeoisie disposing of the proletariat: "Those who do not understand me will understand only in retrospect, if ever." The counter-culturally deprived kid, who passion-

---

* One is not sure exactly who is responsible for the scatological ellipses: the courageous editors of *student voices/one*, the anal-retentives at the publishing house, the underground paper, or the writer himself. Probably not the last two. A sanitized version of youthcult vanguard, the editorial contradiction speaks for itself.

ately wants to belong to this tribal revolution in which he does not have to read or organize or use the language, will slip—at the hands of this nasal grandee—into the narcoleptic state of manipulable will-lessness and illiteracy.

But the frustrated reader of vanguard productions who follows the easiest route to the vision of the golden apples should not feel guilty. Indeed, he will inevitably be absolved. For on the second level of the myth multiplier effect hierarchy stroll the academic rationalizers and explicators. Their function seems to be to explain away the contradictions of youthcult or to offer large historical propositions into which the letter of what's goin' down becomes euphemized, and thus fictionalized. They bring with them the true complacencies of the Academy in the conviction that whatever those to whom Keniston referred as "overprivileged" and "over-endowed" are doing or thinking must represent the avant garde of a movement that will envelop the entire social order. Any of the baffled ghosts of nonvanguardists who follow become conveniently sucked into the sweeping fictions. Accepting these visionary tableaux, the academic explicator must embrace the Crusade, in fact, assist in its creation, with nary a critical perspective on its destination. It's off to Acre, and whether we're going to be able to hold it for long is a question we will deal with on the sands.

Thus, when a contradiction arises among youthcult activists, the academic rationalizer, already tied to a jargon that euphemizes with latinates such as "adolescentization," excels at excuse-mongering. When he is forced to deal with the contradictions between what his avant garde says youthcult is supposed to be doing and what, in fact, the *less* "talented, thoughtful, principled, sensitive, or disturbed" kid in the gravitational field is *not* doing or thinking, he outdoes himself in subtle and compassionate *apologias* for lethargy.

As a generalized case: One of the more prominent set of cop-out apologetics centers around the notion that since counter politics is irrational it can only be explained irrationally. Aside from the plain evidence that many paths of the Movement are rooted in at least a pretense of rationality, such apologetics smack of an extreme reliance on the pathetic fallacy and are as guilty as so many counter Ways themselves of abandoning confrontation with the existing world. If, too, the rejected reality (the "mainstream") *is* irrational—the society of moon launches, stuffed Korvettes, and government by remote control—then to resist the irrational with the irrational certainly offers no Utopian possibilities.

This shopworn apologism of irrationality diverts attention from the weighty fact that, by the very phenomenological status of the notion of "culture," the confrontation between counter and mainstream culture cannot lie in that too-easy either/or, rational/ irrational reduction. The same genre of apologism also deludes youthcult itself into believing that its spiritual content radically diverges from the values of its parents on all possible occasions. On the latter: The claim of a non-academic explicator, Jeff Nuthall, in the preface to his 1968 *Bomb Culture*, that the disaffiliated "youth movement" is "a reaffirmation of life by orgy and violence," may represent a paradigm of the shape of shilling offered by more formal rationalizers. For orgy and violence are perhaps more typical of mainstream American culture than they are of counter culture. One strongly suspects that when youth opts for orgy and violence it is simply picking up on the back pages of its parents' lives. And have not those who have been attracted to mainstream American culture admired the visceral style, the anarchic individualism, far more than the Utopian vision? Have they not been drawn to the nonconceptual rather than the linear-programmatic? It should not astound any observer to discover the cultural parents in the children, to the extent that when one spades around enough in the Ways of the core counter culture he will unearth forms of nonconceptual nihilistic individualism only thinly pomaded with the pretense of left-wing ideology in which they are paraded. And has not the "reaffirmation of life by orgy and violence," whether practiced by parents or children, mainstream or counter culture, so often turned into a death trip? Such qualms seem fairly simple, but one must acknowledge that the form of Nuthall's euphemizing (and that word itself is a tragic euphemism) has considerable respectability and following among voyeurs of the youthcult procession.

Weigh, now, a classic piece of advanced generalized youthcult rationalization from John Hersey, written after five years as master of Pierson College at Yale and in the context of an otherwise poignant reportage on events in New Haven leading to, and on,

May Day, 1970. *Letter to the Alumni* was a much-needed statement; but in debunking one politically motivated myth, the reactionary posture, Hersey offers another one. Students, he tells the
Old Blues,

> hope to become, through universal experience, Everyman, Every-
> woman.
>   Because the impossible is impossible and one is driven to avert
> the unwanted and keep the unknown wants down in the dark re-
> gions of the psyche, one must purify oneself by accessible experi-
> ences, or by fantasies about them—by making and hearing music
> that throbs like a bursting heart, by mind-blowing through drugs
> or by mind-numbing through drink or through watching the tube
> or flicks, by running (if possible, alone, without competition) in
> long-distance races, or in metaphors for them, by screwing, by film-
> making, by writing poetry, by defiance of Authority and its Rules,
> by being or imagining being thrown in the pokey, by helping others,
> by meditation, by breathing, by fasting, by transcendence, by
> sleeping and dreaming, and perhaps, alas, by attaining the sleep
> that has no dreams—by death and transfiguration and some claim
> to a modest, symbolic, martyrlike immortality [34].

The poetic pitchman strikes, and one is simply dumped glottal at
a philo- psychological apology, which has more to do with someone's dreams of the real than with the real itself. About the time
Hersey arrived at Yale, someone had to save us from being so
bored with our own redundant claims that we were stretching for
universal experience, save us because we knew we were full of shit.
He who is into rock or screwing or trashing does not really require
a false psychological prop offered from above by people who
should perceive more differentially.

Hersey plunges ahead from these feeble fustings into the increasingly familiar analyses (the Roszak archetype reinforced by
Yippie spirits) of "intellectualism" *v.* the emotive life, with students asking why universities and their faculties don't feel: "Why,
students ask, can't universities offer more courses that open windows to feeling—more film, more music, more writing, more art,
more photography, more doing, more helping?" [36]. Hersey conveniently passes over a number of key issues here, not the least of
which is the paradox of institutionalized feeling. Does he mean
to suggest that the average nineteen-year-old is incapable of nat-

ural feeling unless he is offered some syllabized version of it? If so, then youthcult has inherited and accepted one of the most destructive cultural values of their parents: that the school is the center of the society, that all talents—even feeling—must be "certified" by the Academy. If so, then indeed we are dealing with a generation that has been numbed into passivity. If so, then to imply a generation whose primary value is the active emotive life is an egregious and hollow accolade.

But one is not startled in contemplating Hersey's dubious assumption that Yale is America. Some of his first qualified peaen applies, but the juxtapositions suggest so much of a study in oxymoron: filmmaking, writing poetry, "mind-numbing through watching . . . the flicks," meditation, transcendence—after a small surveying, one has justification in denying these as ontological properties of Middle America in college. Thus, at so many of those institutions where courses offering windows to feeling and doing have opened (as they should be, but better come naturally, without the mongering), few have been willing even to gaze out the window, let alone expend the effort to break through to the other side.

I am told, for example, of a course in media at a major public university, a course in which students were encouraged both to review and to create films. This will be an old story by the time the whole song has reached coda, but they resented the fact that they had to deal with the motion picture at all. There were nine students in the class, eight of whom chose to review, not create. Half of the reviews turned out to be clumsy plaigiarisms of current film reviews, and not one of the authors had actually seen the films in question. On the occasion of the screening of the sole creator's work, the audience consisted of five, including his girlfriend and the course instructor. *Res ipsa loquitur.*

An obvious anomaly exists, too, in the attempt at feeling by a youthcult numbed by that series of desperation moves Hersey himself cites in the "universal experience" shuck. The desperation tactics themselves are not likely to prove genuine windows to feeling, certainly no windows to the honorific emotions that Hersey finds so lacking in the mainstream: "love, kindness, generosity, forgiveness, trust, praise, encouragement." The rock-drug window has led to the suspension of the soul itself, or the hard anger or reds-laced-with-wine, which (among less ethereal factors) closed the physical arenas of the rock-drug culture—the Fillmores and the festivals. The sex culture window has dragged us to the grotesqueries of rock drag-queen Alice Cooper in full flagellatory feathers and the alluring slime on the back pages of the *East Village Other* in which the grand emotive life is played out in codes, e.g.,

> Gnrs. & groovy W/M, 25, bi,
> seeks sngls & cpl.s for fun,
> watch or join . . .

American onanism will play its final gig in such column inches, and *if* youthcult is queuing up, only academic jive can transform its motivations into the emotive life.

Hersey thus unhappily comes to represent a particularly nauseating trend among youthcult pitchmen, a trend that dubs the new suspension of perception, conception, and will "Romanticism," that asserts with flip assurance, as if it were an academic cliché, "but of course we recognize in all this irrationalism significant roots in the romantic tradition."

What revenge do these pretenders think they are taking for their own sterility? Anyone who offers, with library face, even the slightest analogy between the *de facto* rejection of mind, will, and emotive range by the Cultists and assorted Cop-Outs of core counter cult and its gravitational field with, for example, the deep conceptual and emotive criticism of the fallacy of infinite mind and will in *Moby Dick* either requires an academic seeing-eye dog or deserves tar and feathers. And anyone who pretends that Blake's visions are "irrational"—whether they pretend out of sympathetic assumption or hostility—and goes forth to assert a similarity between Blakean vision and counter-cult "prophetic innocence" desperately needs the doors of his perception cleansed.

So Coleridge, while acknowledging the "poison of my life," junked himself into retirement; Novalis sorely tempted by the easy slippage into the sweet world of "the sleep that has no dreams" (Hersey); Hölderlin plunged into madness—and all worked in fragments, as later, for a not-so-offhand example, did Wittgenstein. Are these fragments irrational? Do they express the staying of the feeling and meditative soul? The fragments reveal not only the most powerful and detailed perceptions of outer reality but also the most intense and detailed expressive reflections of the vineyards of the interior. Baudelaire degenerate? Certainly! But which "Why-don't-we-do-it-in-the-road" acid ballad even begins to approach the rich verbal forest of his medium, a forest capable of capturing the dark complexities of degeneracy? The drive of counter cult to simplify emotive experience has carried over into the gravitational field in the very refusal to confront the thicket of feeling, both aided by the euphemizers who inform us, in effect, that the back pages of the underground press have their origins in Romanticism. That argument has the substance of the genuflection of a drunken Alexandrian whore.

Witness the critique that assumed counter-cult guru Marcuse himself implies in response to the "Romanticism" gambit of the youthcult euphemizers. Marcuse is not merely an impeccable source, but a man who understands Romanticism as a humanist, and not as a hip sociologist. Let him speak for a while on "desublimation":

> The way in which controlled desublimation may weaken the instinctual revolt against the established Reality Principle may be illuminated by the contrast between the representation of sexuality in classical and romantic literature and in our contemporary literature. If one selects, from among the works which are, in their very substance and inner form, determined by the erotic commitment, such essentially different examples as Racine's *Phedre*, Goethe's *Wahlverwandtschaften*, Baudelaire's *Les Fleurs du Mal*, Tolstoy's *Anna Karenina*, sexuality consistently appears in a highly sublimated, "mediated," reflective form—but in this form it is absolute, uncompromising, unconditional. The dominion of Eros is, from the beginning, also that of Thanatos. Fulfillment is destruction, not in a moral or sociological but in an ontological sense. It is beyond good and evil, beyond social morality, and thus it remains beyond the reaches of the established Reality Principle, which this Eros refuses and explodes.
>
> In contrast, desublimated sexuality is rampant in O'Neill's alcoholics and Faulkner's savages, in the *Streetcar Named Desire* and under the *Hot Tin Roof*, in *Lolita*, in all the stories of Hollywood and New York orgies, and the adventures of suburban housewives. This is infinitely more realistic, daring, uninhibited. It is

part and parcel of the society in which it happens, but nowhere its negation. What happens is surely wild and obscene, virile and tasty, quite immoral—and, precisely because of that, perfectly harmless.

Freed from the sublimated form which was the very token of its irreconcilable dreams—a form which is the style, the language in which the story is told—sexuality turns into a vehicle for the best-sellers of oppression. It could not be said of any of the sexy women in contemporary literature what Balzac says of the whore Esther: that hers was the tenderness which blossoms only in infinity. This society turns everything it touches into a potential source of progress *and* of exploitation, of drudgery *and* satisfaction, of freedom *and* of oppression. Sexuality is no exception. [*One Dimensional Man*, 77–178.]

If one wishes to perceive—and accurately, without clouds of euphemisms—the social status and function of so many counter-cult expressions and multiplied gravitational trends, one has to recognize rampant desublimation. Not merely the obvious classified ad pages of the "Alternative Media," not merely the sexual and political fantasies of Phreak Comix, but also the nomadic and individualistic life-styles of those who choose an "Alternative" Way, the primitive capitalism of New Agrarian ventures, the double-jump suburbanism of the rural communes, the cult of relevancy in the Academy which wishes to certify its own intellectual hedonism—these are hardly instances (as we will later observe in detail) of an entitative revolt against the established Reality Principle. They are in league with it, and they exploit and bore and repress in turn, for they desublimate the opposing Romantic dream.

If the Alternatives of core counter culture lie so far from essential Romanticism, the general suspension of mind and will that accompanies (though not in a causal relationship) broader youth-cult's acceptance of the myths of the apologists lies even further. The great Romantics never asked for the negation of perception and cognition; indeed, they could not have survived in that void. And, too, at the omphalos of the Romantic tradition is the act, propelled by the will acting in its self-reflexive capacity as *voluntas*. It was the act that expressed the inner being, the subjective self, a self that was a complex of thoughts, emotions, and volitions. And reflective consciousness expressed was the highest form of act. An endless gaggle of slogans is not the expression of reflective consciousness, individual or collective. Perceptions that cannot stick with the minute particular but must move irritably and impatiently to the level of the generalized and stereotyped do not bear any relation to the Romantic insistence on symbol, on the world in a grain of sand. And when emotion reaches the deafening and deadening monotonous pitch of the primal electric scream or the total intermittance of drugged consciousness, one is not dealing in the complexity of inner vision of a *Howl* or a *Nausea*, a *Weekend* or an 8½, a Klee Rorschach projection or a Tanguy humanoid mass, let alone a "Kubla Khan."

Yet the academic apologists persist. Well, if it's not the Romanticism shill, it's a variation. Consider the immediately preceding, and a note in *Rolling Stone* of June 25, 1970:

> "A Legal Assembly," a multi-media event at the University of Santa Barbara produced by a freak-genius named Frank Goad, ended in an unplanned but thoroughly satisfactory way when, to a background of a taped peyote chant and a live rock band, several couples got onstage, danced, took off their clothes and finally fell to fucking behind the speakers.

Men in high places have termed this indicative of "the new psychic reality," a very accessible rug under which to sweep such scraps of youthcult. The attendant contradictions of what has become a standard nostrum are perhaps accounted for by what evidently is the academic rationalizer's distaste for phenomenological dialectic, and this despite the existence of such an epiphanic notion as Consciousness III. One will grant that counter culture, as opposed to counter politics, is rooted in psychological concerns. Roszak claims that for the youth culture, "building the good society is not primarily a social, but a psychic task." But when he continues euphemistically,

> What makes the youthful disaffiliation of our time a cultural phenomenon, rather than merely a political movement, is the fact that it strikes beyond ideology to the level of consciousness, seeking to transform our deepest sense of the self, the other, the environment [49],

we despair that this explication, filtered down, has itself deceived youthcult into the death trips of the soul like that recorded by

Rolling Stone precisely because the task of "building the good society" was couched in the terms the elder apologists set forth: that either/or, two cultures, Snow/Leavis jazz they wrote the text-books for in the early 1960's. It was either "Reason" or the "non-intellective level of personality" (Roszak).

Just where the non-intellective has now led the more phreaked phases of counter cult can be measured in the junked bodies of the Haight and the former East Village (now returned to its earlier incarnation as The Neighborhood, the Lower East Side), the broken psychic lives of the graduates of Janov and Laing, the drugged requiems of Katmandu or Marrakech, the clown politics of Algerian exile. With the exception of the first, of course, we're dealing with a small number of people, many of whom are *not* under twenty-five, but who tried to play as if they were, seeking the fountain of youth in a fatuous self-delusive acceptance of the junta of media manipulators.

And the distaste for the exegetical dialectic, a distaste that has merely reinforced that delusion, reacts back on itself to the extent to which we can be told, almost simultaneously, that kids "have a deep skepticism of both 'linear' and analytic thought" (Charlie Reich) and that those who migrated to the Haight in the late 1960's came out of a "youthful revulsion toward all private prop-erty, ecological rape, the bomb and the war in Vietnam" (William Hedgepeth, *The Alternative*).

What is so disturbing in the juxtaposition of those two state-ments, and what do the two of them together have to do with the deceptions of *apologias?* On the one hand, Reich in effect has accepted the same dualism Roszak *et al.* were trapped in, failing to perceive that "Reason" or "both 'linear' and analytic thought" are not the only cognitive processes. It is quite possible to disdain linear thought and still deal in perceptions, concepts, and expres-sion, all of which are "intellective" in the broadest application of that sadly wallpapered term. Even the presented Alternative of the emotive life has usually been perceived, conceptualized, and expressed. Indeed, the daemonic subjective struggles of poets and artists have monumentalized the possibility of perceiving, con-ceptualizing, and expressing the "non-intellective" life *without* desiccating its energy.

The juxtaposition is quaintly instructive, for come Hedgepeth in the realities of the Haight, describing a sub-generation which has rejected not merely "linear" thought but nearly all conceptualization (including that of the emotive life), and ascribes them quasi-conscious motives.* Hedgepeth, twenty-nine in 1971, issued from a conceptual culture in which the very notion of motive is strong in the consciousness. His juniors do not; nowhere in the Hip Dictionary is there a set of terms that even confronts the idea of motive. Motives are "heavy," a "hassle" to contemplate, and are often referred to as "hang-ups," i.e., neuroses. And whether read by youthcult or not, Reich simultaneously absolves the Con III brood from dealing with motives at all, and absolves them under the juggernaut of a false dualism.

Emanating from a most pervasive gravitation to the apology, a gravitation made respectable by both academics and mainstream media tantalizers, are three other forms of rationalization: Guru-recruitment, in which fragments of high theory are employed as sanctions for both life-styles and psycho-social longings; historical apologetics, in which the cultural forces in operation during the adolescence of one generation are transported into the adolescence of another generation to account for the behavior or non-behavior of one with the historical realities of another; and the escalator's rationalizations, which beat around any contradiction in youthcult by upping the explanatory ante into realms of absurdity. This last, the hysterical rhetoric of the escalator, becomes the logical and final chapter in the cosmic blowout of excuse-mongering, which has removed us so far from the realities of young people that we have become accessories to the crime of their stagnation.

Some brief marginalia, first, on the Use of Gurus. It should be obvious that the more reductionistic the thought of the guru, or the simpler the structure of his advocacy, the more vulnerable he will be (in most cases, unintentionally so) to recruitment for excuses. On the matter of sloth, here's Paul Goodman unintentionally excusing it: "My own view is that people cannot be 'de-

---

* Hedgepeth belies his age too cheaply in the motives chosen. The Bomb was a concern of *his* late adolescence. Russell, Pauling, and SANE were unknown to the Hashbury Generation *circa* 1969. And if the ecological motive was so prominent, what apologetic strings do we pull, Bill, to explain the environmental rape of the Haight performed by the inmates?

humanized'; they can just be made unhappy. Their apparent docility and conformity simply mean that, for the time being, they have no available alternative." (*Earth*, August, 1971.) Or Alan Watts, conscious, however, of the tendency of counter-culture candidates to cite the "profound mystical contemplation" of Zen to cover "the most ordinary lethargy." From Goodman it is too easy to adapt the ideal of "withdrawal and simplification" into the rhetoric of "finding my head," a rhetoric which, in turn, is ordinarily used to cover removal from both self and community. The combination of that passivity and Goodman's genuinely informed "anarchism" open him to co-option by those who think they are doing something about injustice in a rural commune. He who terms the coming regroupment and reformulations of social institutions "disorder" is serving a strange god who holds that when things are let loose, they will eventually fall into place. Unfortunately, the worshipers of that god are living an opium-dream existence that holds no promise of reformulation or regroupment at all.

Bucky Fuller, too, counsels "disconnecting from the switchboard" for a time, and anyone who wishes to rationalize away his preferred position in a disconnected situation can draw on Fuller. Those, too, who desperately wish to do away with words also have the convenience of Bucky's account of his own period of disconnection in the late 1920's, here from the *Rolling Stone* interview (June 10, 1971):

> I had been victim of the ease with which human beings can make it: to sound words like a parrot and not really know what the effect of those words on other human beings might be. So I went in for a functional moratorium for two years. My wife had to talk to people for me. I could not be completely free of words but I hardly spoke for two years. I did not want to make any more sounds until I was pretty sure I knew what those sounds meant and why I wanted to use them. I had to make a complete disconnect and start really doing my own thinking and I had to really try to find out what man has and see how it could really be used for the advantage of other men.

Now, that's an adequate excuse in itself for not reading Fuller and for knowing only, as a group of rural communards I spoke to agreed, that "Bucky says we're not going to have to work and there's going to be no more property and we can afford to do our thing, and that's a groove." The key elements in Fuller's World Game, the building blocks of synergy, ephemeralization, vital trending—these are of no concern. Somebody *else* is gonna do it, and make it possible for us to do our thing which we're gonna start doing now, anyway, to get ahead of the game. And Fuller's persistent judgment that the reformation due is to the environment and not to man himself, removes—at the hands of those who are so inclined—the responsibility for inner change. It is not surprising, then, that Fuller himself explains away all sins, even those on the order of Mylai or Kent State, in terms of "inertia," i.e., they are morally neutral, and the inner self never has to answer to them. From that it is even less shocking that Fuller's World Game winds up in a cosmic fascism: We surrender ourselves up to super-visionary design-scientists who run the spaceship while we sit back and "do our thing." The kids who are trying to get ahead of that game now, citing Fuller as a resource, will move us toward that state faster than they realize.

One picks and chooses from his preferred guru, of course, and Fuller is no exception. The new primitive tribalism advanced by another overused guru, Marshall McLuhan, and hyped by the more phreaked phases of counter-politics pitchmen, is decidedly at odds with Fuller's analysis, e.g. (in the *Life* interview of February 26, 1971), that "racism is the product of tribalism and ignorance." By that analysis, our new communards are contributing to racism (as indeed they are by jumping the cities), so Bucky is simply ignored on that count.

Moving toward the escalators, but still within the realm of guruism, is the convenience of R. D. Laing's reductionistic politipsychiatry. An obvious area of potential absolution, dovetailing neatly with the rhetoric of the Yippie escalators who gangrene everyone to be a "political prisoner" of some form. By holding that mental illness is really a social judgment applied to individuals as an instrument of political oppression, Laing provides another escape hatch for every laggard who wants to run away from himself, who would rather sloganeer at somebody else than perceive his own inner being. It becomes a glorious honor to cult-in among the schizophrenics. The *reductio* possibilities are delightful: From the *legitimate* black power, gay power, woman power, we can now move on to power to psychotics, power to necrophiliacs, power to ulcer victims, power to terminal patients. All of them, after all, are oppressed, exploited seventh-world peoples, no?

We enter historical apologetics under the aegis of Roszak, who, in *The Making of a Counter Culture*, while acknowledging the very disheartening possibilities for guru-recruitment, *euphemizes away the very rationalizing tendency!* His case was the use of Zen, and, in the course of the following, recall how Alan Watts himself judged the misuses of oriental mysticisms by a new culture in which "hardly anyone dances at the Fillmore; they just sit." Roszak's refusal to confront the concrete realities:

> The great advantage Zen possesses (if it can be called an advantage) is its unusual vulnerability to what I have called "adolescentization." That is to say: Zen, vulgarized, dovetails remarkably with a number of adolescent traits. Its commitment to a wise silence, which contrasts so strongly with the preachiness of Christianity, can easily ally with the moody inarticulateness of youth. Why do Zen masters throw their disciples into a mud puddle, asks Kerouac's Sal Paradise in *The Dharma Bums*. "That's because they want them to realize mud is better than words." A generation that had come to admire the tongue-tied incoherence of James Dean and which has been willing to believe that the medium is the message, would obviously welcome a tradition that regarded talking as beside the point. Similarly, Zen's commitment to paradox and randomness could be conveniently identified with the intellectual confusion of healthily restless, but still unformed minds. Perhaps above all, Zen's antinomianism could serve as a sanction for the adolescent need of freedom, especially for those who possessed a justified discomfort with the competitive exactions and conformities of the technocracy [134–135].

Latinates tend to euphemize, and "adolescentization," a turgid sociological abstraction, is intended to describe the reality of the desire to remain in a state of presumably joyful limbo, a desire encouraged by mainstream institutions that simply cannot cope with what was *once* the energy of young people; so simply extend adolescence to remove them for a time in *largo*. Ironically, Roszak is not deluding himself when he refers to the "moody inarticulateness of youth," if we conjure the image of a society of twenty-four-year-olds who cannot speak beyond the vagueries of the hip dictionary. The evidence is strong, however, that Roszak is *not* referring to those who are twenty-four, but rather to those who are sixteen, and therein lies the tragedy of the apologist's inability to transcend his own mentality and perceive more than a combination of academic theory and media-hyped image.

For "the generation that had come to admire the tongue-tied incoherence of James Dean" is not composed of young people now in college, or even those in most colleges when Roszak wrote (1968). James Dean was a hero—*on reflection*—to the inchoate counter community of the early and mid-1960's, to people who were teenagers when James Dean was alive. Most of these people are now approaching the thirty-yard line, if they have not already passed beyond, and they are precisely *not* the people who have blunderbussed language from human reality. For them, Dean fitted into a pattern of moody flick antiheroes that included Bogart and Brando. That triumvirate of posters on dormitory walls is now vintage—except to those who wish to impose *their* antiheroes on another generation.

More generational confusings for the sake of expiation are evident in the linking of the admirers of James Dean's "incoherence" with those who had "been willing to believe that the medium is the message." I hope to make it rather clear that the anticonceptual movement, dovetailing in time and metaphysic with the antilanguage movement, did not arrive at its maturity and influence until McLuhan's theory could be advanced as an excuse for ordinary mindlessness. And since McLuhan had to have some time to filter down to mass culture (as a college junior in 1970 remarked, "I never heard of him until 'Laugh-In,' and even then I didn't know who he was"), the generation that has been willing to embrace that theory as self-justification has only recently emerged in the mass, and includes precisely those who were *not* among the James Dean-as-silent-brooding-hero fans.

Guilty again of this mixing of sub-generations, here for promotive purposes, is Mark Gerzon, who extends himself to elaborate and self-contradictory lengths to explain the Bond and Bogie cults in terms of the "total involvement" (read Hersey's "universal experience") youthcult is presumed to venerate. He explains both cults in terms of the ideal of detachment, which ought to seem remote to a generation that was—we have all naïvely assumed from McLuhan—so totally involved in the emotive life of television. Thus James Bond was attractive because he

> was fantastically successful with and fantastically attractive to women, both characteristics which men are socially patterned to feel that they lack. But Bond's magic quality was not only physical but psychological: he managed never to become emotionally involved with any woman. . . . Here was the ideal personality in all its unreality; he could get others involved but he could stay detached; he could see through others, but they could not penetrate him. He successfully applied capitalism to his emotions: maximum profit with minimum investment. . . .
>
> He had achieved the traditional behavior which the young people of McLuhan's electric age found so difficult to master [*The Whole World Is Watching*, 87].

One has to follow the twists of this argument quite carefully in order to appreciate the extent to which such promoters torture basic perception. The Bond phenomenon is linked to stroke books and the porn biz to indicate both lack of involvement and sexual inhibition, both of which, Gerzon holds, are ideals embedded in the art of the surrounding culture. The sequitur in the inevitably ensuing revolt is a contrary insistence on the dissolution of the "division between emotional commitment and sexual involvement." The realities of the crash pad and its mainstream imitators, however, reveal precisely the reverse: the counter-cult image of the Bond ethic. As Alan Watts meditated, " 'Love' has become 'fuck.' " The sexual expression of the group-grope hardly expresses total emotional involvement, but Gerzon is so intent on informing us that free-love societies express youth's dissatisfaction with the separation of involvement from sex that the contradictions slip through like spilled seed.

As one would by now expect for this type of promo, the whole is wrapped in the incandescent big statement, the pretentious language that convinces the academic theorists that they are accurate, and the media hypers that they've got a market:

> Young people have clearly begun to disdain the external image and to be concerned about the inner man. They are interested not in where a man got his degree or in what his income is, but in

whether he is fulfilled in his marriage and if he can feel and love [89].

This statement, mind you, presents itself as a *sequitur* to that flight on free love-societies. One does not question for a moment the rejection of external images, at least the images of the fathers. But one must seriously doubt the extent to which the assertion that youthcult is deeply and intimately concerned with the internal man can be justified. The solicitude usually boils down to "finding out where one's head is at," and there ain't too much finding out goin' on, 'cause the very language in which the concern is expressed is constitutive to our inherited set of apologias for the cop-out. "Hey, baby! Can you dig, feel, love?" "Yeah, man!" "Far out!" If that expresses concern with the inner man, then it is also a shield, for the inner man may be nothing more than a blast of psychedelic lights or, at most, a stale backwash of decaying suns, a solipsistic image, incommunicable, hence unknown beyond the generalization of assent: "Yeah, man . . . right on . . . heavy."

Finally, the escalators, the most prolific among the in-house operatives of youthcult. The escalator's technique is a logical extention of the combination of persistent rationalizing and the limited perceptions allowable by the hip dictionary. As an indication of how facilely the professional apologist can turn escalator, listen to Roszak, writing in *The Nation* (April 1, 1968), offering poignant and sensible advice to the young, but unable to resist temptation in the last sentence:

> This is the point at which the young, who are offering, I feel, a great deal that is good to work with, need the help of mature minds, in order that distinctions can be drawn between the deep and the shallow, the superstitious and the wise. It is important to discern the underlying connection between the inspired seer on the one hand, and the side-show charlatan on the other, and to recognize that the skeptical en bloc rejection of both has been a prime disaster. That much the young have seen. But between the seer and the charlatan there is also an all-important difference, and it is apparent only upon reflection. *But who, among the alienated young, constantly on the lookout for the narks, has time for reflection?* [Italics mine.]

Roszak's exercise in absurdity is perhaps more the exception than the rule among the academics, but the spirit of that exercise runs thick in the literature of youthcult pitchmen. To draw on a distinction offered by Oxford philosopher J. L. Austin, what might be legitimate and convincing *justification* is transformed into mere *excuse*; and excuse (here I depart from Austin), born of weakness, too often detaches itself from reality. The euphemizer becomes the Yippie demagogue, and the *political* fantasy enters. Witness some aphorisms of Rubin, first from *Do It!* (one of the few cult books on the 17–20 age group list, as you will recall):

> We are all Eldridge Cleaver [241].
> The war on campuses is similar to the war in Vietnam: a guerrilla people's war [215].
> [in the mid-1950's] while a car radio in the front seat rocked with "Turn Me Loose," young kids in the back seat were breaking loose. Many a night was spent on dark and lonely roads, balling to a hard rock beat [19].
> The yippie political strategy is to ally with Billy Graham. Keep the word "fuck" dirty! At the same time we yippies fight for the right to say fuck whenever we want to. It's a contradiction—but in contradictions like this lie the genius of making a revolution [111].

and from the more aphoristic *We Are Everywhere:*

> Housewives are political prisoners. / Children are political prisoners. / Secretaries are political prisoners [159].
> Dope is political because it is our sacrament [158].
> The choice is revolution or heroin [118].

Far more frequent, and centered in the counter-cult press, is the tendency to wash this political tone on every conceivable youthcult happening. A smug *Rolling Stone* piece suggested that after the firecracker series of Cambodia–Kent State–Jackson State, record sales declined, *ergo* youthcult was boycotting records as a mode of political protest. Again, in a review of the unlimited-access disaster that was the 1971 Newport Jazz Festival in *Boston After Dark* (July 13, 1971), the reviewer opened by pointing to the "aimlessness, belligerence and half-baked ideology of the audience," and, a number of paragraphs later, shilled that those "who tore down that chain-link fence were tearing down the iron curtain between capitalism and communism, between a free festival and a rip-off."

Aside from the obvious, that nobody 'round here ever heard of a communist jazz-rock festival, aside from the commentator's casual notation that "a large number of these people were totally stoned out," who the hell is he kidding? Somebody goes beserk, doesn't give a shit about the music, and there's always a drooling dude waiting offstage with varnished fangs and some political banner for it.

I have found no better example of the range and process of escalation than that in an article on Drop City by one Bill Boyd.* The analysis should indicate the pernicious effects of the entire parliament of apologists, as it moves through a dialectic (such as it is) embracing exoneration, euphemizing, rationalizing, and promotion. The first stage of this dialectic is the counter-statement, i.e., that since "the whole structure of American society was rigid and oppressive . . . the only way to physical and spiritual freedom lay outside the established system." Despite the either/or, grant a degree of general agreement with the principle. The apologist still feels the counter-statement is too general, so plunges into a bed of euphemism, and rephrases the initial call to the Drop in terms of the culture of art:

> The artist's "life" as a member of industrial civilization has rarely become "art." The nature of his activities alienates him from the mainstream capitalist society and its market values, because the production of art is not inspired by consumer demand but by cultural necessity. When the necessity of survival forces the artist into participation in society, the contradiction in values destroys the man to preserve the artist; it often destroys both. Art has ceased to be a natural function. Although the work of art springs from inner necessity, the format of the work and the environment in which it is created and displayed are remote from, and antagonistic to, its purpose in the world. The artist in society must live with this absurdity and exploit it to gain his livelihood [158].

Here, I suppose, if one desires to sound "counter," he is obliged to take a pot shot at capitalism as quickly as possible. It's an entertaining rhetoric, one which we'll listen too quite frequently among the counter-culturists, and it contains a logic that is both exclusive and naïve. To hack an old argument, one must suppose

* "Funk Architecture," in Oliver, P. (ed.), *Shelter and Society* (New York, 1970).

that art, as Boyd conceives of it, flourishes in all those puritanical socialisms he so admires. As folk-rock singer, composer, and lyricist Leonard Cohen realized when he returned from a visit to Cuba a decade ago, he was "exactly the kind of enemy that Fidelistos were describing: bourgeois, individualistic, a self-indulgent poet," a description that would do no great injustice to Boyd's hidden notion of the artist. Of course, if one considers social realism the only form of art, and if one is willing to produce and hence live art for the state, then perhaps we can hold with Boyd that art is a "natural function." And if the state is to be equated with "inner necessity," then it is indeed surprising that Boyd's state can possibly extend beyond the bounds of one person. The borderline intelligibility of Boyd's paragraph adequately testifies to the utter putrescence of the tortured shill that inevitably winds up in a contradiction. For, when boiled down to the individual as state (the logical extension—if that phrase can apply—of this second stage of Boyd's "dialectic"), we are presented with a *reactionary* form of anarchism—not an infrequent politic for counter-culturists, as we will later find.

Indeed, the robber-baron instinct of the totalitarian child of technology reveals itself a paragraph or so later in the ascending justification:

> These values are the spontaneous response to a technologically perfectable world, over which we have total domination: a world in which we are capable of manipulating our environment to a degree that demands creative decisions of extreme subtlety. The works of art we envisage are total, vast.

By this self-serving utterance, any activity that is the spontaneous and free choice of the individual becomes art: "All activity is creative activity. All creative activity is done for its own sake, without ends. All noncompulsive activity is art."

It's like, "Hey, you wanna be an artist? Well, man, you're an artist." Beautiful! In consideration of what transpires on the six acres of Drop City, located in the middle of one of the most depressed areas of the United States in southern Colorado, shit by any other name still stinks. It's the same mentality (and I cite here another Drop City huckster writing in the *Domebook II*) that screams about oppressive corporate Amerikkka, and five minutes later, into dome-building, recommends the use of a silicone rubber adhesive put out by GE and Dow, the former unquestionably one of the most reactionary corporations in the country, the latter recognizably of napalm fame.

Okay, so now we have some rudimentary justification for Drop City, in which all workers are artists, in which even a "depression of nothingness," also known as a downer, is art. We're driving for "inner security," the goal defined by encounter group ethics. Very altruistic.

Somehow that is an inadequate expiation, so Boyd escalates twofold again: first to defend the commune idea out of the burden that we're all "immigrants" to a new land, and thus have "to band together to save *energy* [italics mine]." Hang around a while in Drop City and similar places doing nothing, and you can always claim that you're "conserving energy." Besides, you're an "artist," right?

Secondly, because even this panegyrical fodder fails to address the problem of the oppressions of the outer world, a gesture toward re-engagement must be made. It is ready-made:

> The only thing that will allow each of us to create his or her Utopia is praxis—and the pooling of our resources to free each of us to pursue our individual activities and strengthen the autonomous boundaries of our free communities. For there must be good men and women in the mountains, on the beaches, in all the neglected and beautiful places, so that one day we can come back to ghostly cities and try to set them right.

Oh, ye poor suffering bastards in the City, sleep sweetly knowing that the beautiful "artists" are out there "saving energy" in all those "neglected places," doing something which may, in the final years of this our Kali Yuga, actually help you. In fact, they may be coming back around that time.

SOME CRITICAL EFFECTS OF EXPIATION

To understand the cultural effects of the work of the hucksters, the euphemizers, and the pitchmen, one must enter that very slippery philosophical vapor on the line between morality and politics.

The distinction between political/legal motives and moral ones entered counter politics after the first flush of victory in 1963–64. Participants were forced, primarily by a temporary lacuna in political/legal tasks, to look both within and without themselves. Politics contracted into mass morality; issues came to be defined in moral and not political terms. The process took some four years, jelling under the impetus of the noumenal madness set in motion by the Vietnam war. The move was away from liberalism; the mainsprings for action were defined in terms of the relation of the individual conscience to the Other and not in terms of criteria external to the self. In its shift toward libertarianism, then, radical counter politics unconsciously created its own genetic soup in the possibility of counter culture.

The morality that ultimately served as a decompression chamber for counter politics demanded self-consciousness, an old Socratic connection. And thus, barely audibly, the movement toward "consciousness raising," a movement oriented toward the self, and *not* toward the Other. What happened, though, in too many cases was that the Other was forgotten completely, and youthcult invented the hip line, "putting my head together," to rationalize away its self-centered inability or unwillingness to act. A phrase such as "I can't relate to it" served the same function.

The media hypers, academic theorists, and counter-press pitchmen have played an extremely negative role in this process. The cults have come on, have been heavily exposed and advertised, and have provided myriad Ways Out under the name of "consciousness raising." Their overflow into counter politics putrifies altogether like acid the moral sense from which it sprang.

For example, if one adopts the Yippie line of put-on politics, if he holds that "all is theater," he has provided a cover for himself that vitiates the moral sense. He never has to stand before consequences; he can always excuse effects. He thus is only a pretender to the fulfillment of existential awareness, an awareness which comes with answering to the act, with bearing witness in oneself over oneself.

The collapsing of ethics and epistemology which reflects the original impulse to provide an intimate connection between morality and self-consciousness is an honored philosophical tradition mirrored in the development of language itself. As Hannah Arendt has been fond of noting, Athenians and Romans alike did not distinguish between consciousness and conscience: The Greek *syneidisis* and the Latin *conscientia* served both meanings, and, when broken into their morphemes, signify "to know something *with,*" to know myself *with* myself. Out of the very language, then, the Socratic ethic that instructs: "rather at odds with the world than at odds with myself." If, in response, one slogans "Right on!" and thinks the original philosophical martyr can be gurued into use to apologize for the act of nilling that theatrics often express and the political solipsism of the counter culture confirms, he should seriously consider the intense moral consciousness that the Socratic ethic demands, and, simultaneously, the lack of possibility of moral consciousness he would embrace, for example, in Artaud's life-as-theater metaphysic.

The ethic born of the euphemizing habit becomes a form of radical, libertarian-conservative, moral anarchism under which the individual is free to act in his radical uniqueness without ever having to answer *to himself*. The posture and the reality diverge so abruptly that one must express bewilderment that the critics, let alone the shills, have been incapable of perceiving it.

The extension of the alibi mentality that leads to the preclusion of moral responsibility has also led to the preclusion of political responsibility. The collapsing of psychology and politics, epitomized in the reductionistic work of R. D. Laing, has yielded a radical innocence that refuses to treat social problems. For to administer, one must partake of some form of active collective government, and the sterile rhetoric of counter cult and counter politics alike has conveyed to youthcult the distinct notion that all government is fascistic, repressive, or whatever the refrain may be. Therefore, one does not confront social problems for reconstruction unless one wishes to run the risk of becoming a fascist, repressor, etc.

Anarchic style alone, from the flower children to the Weathermen, has not proved an effective alternative to government. America remains on the verge of being wheeled to the terminal patient ward. Somehow, the radically effective alternative of becoming Chief of your Local Constabulary has rarely struck the counter culture. And for good reason. I refuse to write it off to the "impatience of youth" or to some other nauseating cliché of the apologists. It's radical sloth, plain and simple, which finds it easier to chant meaningless slogans, pass out flowers wordlessly, or trash. This is not an expression of energy, nor, and pardons to Norman Brown, is it an expression of the accommodation of life to death.

It's not easy to establish a dynamic and effective law commune. It's not easy to redirect working-class sensibilities so that they are sympathetic to Movement concerns. It's not easy to establish working alternatives in education. It takes perception, conception, expression, and will-energy commitment. It takes long-distance runners. And within the Movement itself, particularly on that large field where counter politics and counter culture uneasily blend, the forces arrayed against producing the *mass* of long-distance runners we so desperately need are formidable indeed.

Instance again: The hyped illusion that all crimes are political crimes, or that all life-styles, all individual acts, are subject to political judgment, has insulated a significant portion of a generation not merely from reality (that would be a mistaken and trite notion anyway) but from the means to heal what it so desperately wishes to heal. Thus the paradox: The assertion of total political reality yields an abstention from political decision and government altogether. The means to heal rest on an analysis that accepts the responsibility of the individual will to act in relation to other wills, accepts the responsibility to effect courses of action that will materially affect other human beings.

It is oh-so-unfortunate that courses of action realize ideas, and if one does not have to deal with the idea realized, then one certainly doesn't have to think too much about the idea. If one had to deal with an "idea" such as "free all repressed third world peoples," or "off the pigs," or "free all political prisoners," why, the idea might prove to be an elusive vapor if one tried to implement it. By merely sloganing the idea, though, one absolves himself of both political and moral responsibility, since he never has to bear witness to his own functional ignorance.

We are not speaking here of those whose dedication to counter politics is unalloyed and informed. We are decidedly not thinking of Keniston's elite young radicals. We are concerned with the political counter-culturists, those who have inherited a fairly formidable set of academic resources which they can handily employ to cover the cop-out, the resources that claim a rampant set of power relationships in American society that renders all government irrelevant, that offers the despairing notion that the car is out of control and a change in drivers would make no difference. So we are offered the handy idea that the distinction between John Mitchell and Ramsey Clark running the Justice Department is negligible. Suggest Huey Newton running the Justice Department, and the answer comes conveniently structured in the assumptions of the ideology of the academic resources: "Then there wouldn't be a Justice Department." Oh, really?

The good Saint Nicholas Johnson, our sole defender on the FCC, did the commencement address gig this past year. On at least one occasion, under the title "Working in a Corporate State: Tactics for Survival and Reform," he offered a celebration of the individual will which he naïvely thought would be interpreted as an invitation to engagement. That portion of the exhortation which was remembered sounds innocent enough: "Once you really *feel* the reasons why you don't want all that material fluff junking up your life, you find that you can get along on a lot less income, and that there are then a lot more alternatives for life." By dint of the demoralizing political absolution of the times, Johnson becomes the unfortunate victim of those who bear all such sensible statements to never-never land. An utterance such as this is used to justify all forms of disengagement—and that's not what he meant at all. That's not it at all.

But that is precisely what a couple present remembered when I spoke to them later in their weedy New Agrarian paradise, "putting our heads together," 'cause engagement "is not our thing." One celebrates the power of the individual will at great risk. If one is addressing an audience to whom the assertion of the individual will means "doing my thing" in the backwash, then a reformist's social conscience is badly misplaced, and his celebration dangerous, for every mindless self-server will utilize it to justify his bag without thinking of consequences.

The fragmentation that this trend encourages foredooms a viable *political* alternative for America. The chaos of what would be a Fourth Party Convention is now a fit subject for a rock festival movie, and, indeed, one has occasionally seen the previews. As long as the baggie people split to their corners under the cover of what has been made academically respectable, as long as the perceptually and conceptually illiterate are encouraged to remain so, as long as the hip dictionary is around to provide the easy ineffectual gesture toward the Other, power will remain in the hands of the technocrats, and in the remnants of an older order than that.

A REVIEW OF AN INTERVIEW: CHARLIE REICH AND *ROLLING STONE* (February 4, 1971)

Well, here's the evangelist, exhaling the exasperation of a decade, doing some backtracking. The revolution isn't doing very well, he says, primarily because

> there's so much to be learned. . . . We know only the most elemental things, like how to play the guitar, how to sit around in a circle in a room and listen to music. But learning to do medicine, or law, or architecture in such a way that it is non-alienating, rewarding and good for the person that does it, good for the people you do it for—we haven't learned any of that. We have to help each other, we have to learn from each other.

Contradictions have a way of working themselves out above the heads of the apologists and senior resource theorists. What Reich overlooks in the very situation of the *Rolling Stone* interview is the process by which *he* is being used by a culture that does not particularly care to expend the energy to "do medicine, or law, or architecture" at all, regardless of who is benefiting, or the degree to which alienation can be overcome. They do not will to do, and Charlie has, in effect, said that since their first task is to find their heads, which "is not an 'ego trip' but a radical subjectivity designed to find genuine values in a world whose official values are false and distorted [*Greening*, 202]," they are not required to do. It should not astonish to come across Reich here rationalizing all drug use but that of heroin in some naïve terms as, "They're good as the use you make of them or bad as the use you make of them." By that criterion, any zonked-out kid can cop an apology from Charlie by hyping his use of drugs as a truth search. Hey, man, I'm Allen Ginsberg. My roach-holder you are!

Or, in another context, as the interviewer noted, "I just met a fellow who said 'I'm reading *Greening of America* and thinking maybe I should drop out of Law School.' " Perhaps our educational system is so deadly that a law student possesses such minimal conceptual equipment as to accept Reich's effluvia unquestioningly. Self-conscious Reich replies:

> Well maybe he should—maybe that's not his trip, maybe he went to law school because his parents wanted him to go. But there are some people who love law, though, and only the people that love it should do it. The biggest problem now in the new consciousness is that most of us haven't learned how to do most things in a new way and so we're in a moment which in some ways seems almost a moment of despair. In a sense we've exhausted, for the moment at least, the possibilities of just hitchhiking and playing the guitar in the streets, just wearing groovy clothes. [If Reich thinks those activities are the sum of counter-cult consciousness, he must be joshing, or terribly myopic, or tripping, or holed up at Yale, or all four of the above.] When you get into that for two or three years, when you've been through the drug thing for awhile, you begin, it seems to me, to want to start functioning on a level that is personally satisfying. That means a different thing for each person—for some person it might mean being a doctor, for another person it might mean working with handicrafts, for another person it might mean design, like architectural design. But I could never be happy just sitting on a beach the rest of my life, much as I love beaches, because I have abilities in me that cry out to work.

But of course you have those abilities, Charlie. You're committed, and, if a bit in orbit, still capable of literacy. The problem is that you fail to observe the effects of your own analysis and advice. For now, you see, any freak can say, "I'm getting my head together," or, more appropriately translated, "I'm finding out where my consciousness is at," as a self-serving slogan for the abdication of all will.

Then, too, ponder what happens in five or six years when the current microboppers who are into this fecund notation you and others have so blindly provided, ponder what happens when they enter even an "alternative" society. They will be unable to do law, for example, will be unable to love it, because they won't be able to read it, let alone perceive the "facts in the case" under the aegis of any medium. Because, Charlie, you and the league of euphemizers have shut the doors to them. Not the doors to a venal and programed society. Those doors need to be barred, and they will be. But doors to elementary inner acts, like the perception of the Other, wide-ranging feeling, thought, and expression. You have told those in the gravitational field that those at the core are *"whole"*—and the italics are yours—while performing neat surgery on half of the soul. Every core kid who has ever wished a "respectable source" to quote-out on now has one, and *Rolling Stone* and Random House and *The New Yorker* become agents for carrying the message to the field. As the kids grow content with your mythic structure, more power will be left to the technocrats and those now preparing to succeed them. Charlie, I am interested in an Alternative that has power, 'cause that's the only way it's going to survive. And you are not preparing the kind of people who will make possible the survival of the Alternative.

Even when *Rolling Stone* inevitably arrived at the music questions, Charlie revealed not only his woeful ignorance of the very culture he pretends to hype, but the dangers of advancing a misunderstood theory that ignores its own consequences:

> The new music is, first of all, incredibly important because it's the chief language and means of communication for the people of the new consciousness, particularly young people. The kids have discovered a new means of communication, like extra-sensory perception. We don't have to send each other messages through the mail because we have a magical network of communications, and the chief vehicle of that is music.

One is never sure whether Reich is witting or not, but such an utterance thoroughly convinces the mastodons of the field that they don't need to talk to each other. When someone walks into a room, just sludge over to the stereo, lay something on, sit around gaping "Groovy!" and "Far-out!" and Reich's "ultimate sign of reverence, vulnerability, and innocence," "Oh wow!" and let someone else do the communicating.

A number of prophecies arise: Keep that one up long enough and the order of people who were around to raise Reich's consciousness initially—the Beatles, the Airplane—will no longer be found. There won't be anyone left to write the lyrics for "I Am the

Walrus" or "Wooden Ships." If Mad. Ave. and the White House
have kicked language to death, Charlie will preside over the last
rites; and with that, the last rites of the will to communicate, and
the range of emotions, perceptions, and thoughts which are subject
to communication. A universal silent order of monks descends.
Hey, kids, Charlie says you don't have to speak any more, and,
allied with McLuhan and Artaud (gurus you can pick up on, if
you wish, by stealing Abbie Hoffman's book), has rationalized
away the very idea of meaning. Thus a student named Jack I
once knew, and of whom we shall hear yet again, could assert of
his pissing in the street, "I'm saying something."

Reich repeats the nondiscriminatory when he leaps into *Rolling
Stone* ideology and informs us that, in the '50's,

> The very first thing that began to happen when rock came in on
> a mass cultural level was it started to say, "We feel lonely and
> alienated and frightened" and music had never said that before.
> [Whoops! So we backtrack:] Blues always said it, I'm not talking
> about the black consciousness. But white people were told how
> happy, how romantic, how nice, how smooth the world was. And
> that didn't reflect the truth.
>
> Then all of a sudden there was Elvis Presley singing about
> "Heartbreak Hotel" full of lonely people, and he said no matter
> how full it is, when you get there you're lonely because none of
> those people can communicate with you and you can't communi-
> cate with them. You see, the first step toward the new conscious-
> ness is to acknowledge your own misery, your own loneliness and
> alienation. If you can't be honest with yourself about where you're
> at, how are you going to get anything better? So the first truth of
> rock, the first big communication was to say things aren't that
> good. In an early song like "Lonesome Town," Rick Nelson sang
> about loneliness.

As usual, it is difficult to determine the most felicitous moment at
which to plunge into this barrel of rot. Why not open with
Charlie's radical-chic elitism? He obviously never listened to the
lyrics of bluegrass or Country & Western, or, as a posturing radical,
would not admit to it because that stuff is produced by all them
redneck, Billy Graham-totin' dupers 'n' greasers. All Charlie really
has to look to is the Beatles' derivative C&W piece, "Act Natu-

rally" (the song which, in 1966, you bet someone a tenspot that it was the Beatles singing, and you won) to understand that Hank Williams and his ilk from the Opry were into broken men, lonely lives, and ironies of defeated innocence, existing side by side in checkered counties with black blues—and all in the roots, roots of a unique experience in America that Reich now wants to reject in favor of a new ethnocentricity.

Secondly, let us not allow the contradiction to escape: Reich is analyzing music, his new communicative mode of the new consciousness, in terms of *lyrics*, not in terms of musical forms. Charlie is still a product of the print culture but desperately wants to dump it. He should. After all, in his rage for an apocalyptic order he has choked himself away from talking about nonverbal aspects of music. It would probably be more therapeutic for him just to sit down and drop something heavy or far out on the turntable, groove on it, and say, "hey, dig this . . . oh wow!" Just point, even though no one knows why you're pointing; but given the persistent habit of escalating apologies, one can project Reich skirting the dilemma of noncommunicative pointing by asserting an extra-sensory communication system available to those who have raised consciousness to the third power.

Reich is a Stoned Age man caught in his own contradictions. His welcoming of the *Rolling Stone* interview spelled self-consciousness on that score. After all, and despite appearances, he is no fool; as much as he may believe that his Con-II—bound critics didn't understand his winnowed simplicities, he is more than ready for the continuing defense of a thesis that advocates the introverted lethargy of consciousness-raising while waiting for the Revolution to arrive, and simultaneously absolves itself from the Cop-Out. How strange for a legal mind to become bogged down in a very convoluted defense of that advocacy:

> I'm advocating that you strenuously and with a great deal of hard work and self discipline and struggle [If that isn't a Con I mentality, I don't know what is.], that you change your own life, that you live according to the way you really believe in and that when you are ready to begin to help other people live their lives differently, then that's the revolution as I see it. *That's not doing nothing. I think that is doing a great deal.* There was an interview I read somewhere with Ken Kesey in which he said just this. They

were asking him what he was doing to free John Sinclair.* He said, man, I'm doing a whole lot. What he meant was just this, that he was working on his own life and helping other people live theirs. *And that's no cop-out* [Italics mine].

A prayer meeting of department store managers. Tell that to John Sinclair, who was ultimately freed by activist lawyers.

What is at issue here are the practical effects of the apologist's theories, particularly those that create a cosmic mythic circuit board into which everyone is plugged at one resistance point or another. Reich starts with Con I without the competition (basically, as we'll propose when we come to the practices of the counter-cult core, that's what Con III boils down to—and even then, the possibility of competition lurks). But his formulation is so embolistic that Con III becomes a grab-bag of excuses for the abolition of the will itself. That emulsified Con I tint which governs the above, that "hard work and self-discipline and struggle," becomes a sad, head-shaking joke. Even were Reich coherent, the dangers of the exonerating use of his theory would still abound.

Charlie typifies the either/or paranoia mentality which expresses itself in crescendo toward the counter-cult core. The world is observed in terms of a very simple choice: a "police state" or the New Consciousness (a leading tone to Hedgepeth's volcanic prelude in *The Alternative:* "The only choice . . . is between dropping out to mold an entire new counterculture or going underground to master the manufacture of explosives.") The pervasiveness of that mentality itself testifies obliquely to Reich's own hypocrisy when he (rightly) accuses the corporate state consciousness of fostering mass ignorance in America, aided and abetted by the media: "And we go on deceiving ourselves and we are willfully deceived by those to whose advantage it is to deceive us." Running true to either/or, however, Reich replaces one deception with another. If, for example, "we are in a race between the police state and the new consciousness," and if "it's a nip and tuck race," why the hell are we hanging around trying to free John Sinclair by grooving on the Airplane? But undoubtedly the mere

* Former leader of the White Panthers, and motive force of the first of the politirock groups, the MC5, out of Detroit, who was framed by an undercover agent, and sent up for 9½–10 years on a charge of possessing *two joints* of marijuana.

fact that Charlie's brood is simply hanging indicates that we're not really in an either/or situation, that an apocalyptic night of long knives is not upon us. Reich, however, has been so taken in by the simplistic sloganeering he accepts as the sole expression of reality that he can let pass analysis of the *use* of his work.

4

The Death of Language I: Some Basics Prior to the Apologies of McLuhan

"Like there's this cat who lives in back of me and our heads just aren't together at all."

"What do you mean?"

"Like we just can't relate our heads. He comes over and lays down these heavy raps."

"Like what?"

"I don't know. Like he just comes in all the time with this really heavy stuff and I don't understand his experience and he doesn't understand mine. Like he comes over when he's tripping, you know? And he puts down this very heavy number and his mind is so fucked up and I just get very uptight. The vibrations are really heavy, you know, and negative. We're just not together at all." (Opening of conversation with a twenty-four-year-old counter-culturist, female, college grad, now living in rural Northeast, intermittently doing "things.")

As I've said before, we're dealing with an increasing tendency—particularly in the gravitational fields of youthcult—that runs far deeper than the mere death of language. The either/orists would have us believe the singular efficacy of the cognition-emotion, rational-irrational, linguistic-gestural divisions. If the facts of the case seeped no farther, only the propagandists themselves on both sides of the either/or should be concerned.

My basic plaint is that expression is the only indication we have of the inner life, and through language alone have we comprehension of the complexities of the inner life. When language is purposely primitivized or when expression dies altogether, we have no evidence that the inner life still exists; or if little evidence, then the inner life may be nothing more than a vapid Haiku so abridged as to preclude the very presumed ideals of counter culture, e.g., the perception of the Other as the indisputable prerequisite to "togetherness." One cannot "get together" if he is incapable of perceiving the detailed uniqueness of the Other, conceptualizing the detail, and expressing his similarly particular and hence communally meaningful response to the Other. Language functions at each stage of this process, and if it is unavailable, one sorely suspects that the process itself cannot exist in the plenum of its humanity.

The new non-languages have drawn their inevitable group of academic explicators and rationalizers. We are told, for example, that youthcult language is primarily gestural, with occasional words in a supporting role, and that this circuitry reincarnates a genuine form of primitive telepathy. One can only describe the communicative function of such gestural rituals as the rolling and cleaning of the weed, the precise moment for the roach holder, etc., as a 1970 version of Nick Adams at the Big Two-Hearted River. The small acts are wholly sensory, not experiential, and require a working vocabulary of no more than two dozen idioms. That "universal experience" John Hersey told us was the goal of youthcult is impossible when one operates wholly on the level of the simple sensory: for simple sensation is certainly not experience.

What about complex sensation? Assuming for a moment that language is the most accurate reflection of the spirit of a culture, look to the new hip dictionary. Adjectives, indeed, all qualifiers, those signals of complexity, are minimal, and when they do exist, it is as vagueries: "heavy," "up-tight," or "bad." The explicators will now escalate: No doubt the qualifiers are substituted for by gesture, including grunts and groans and primal screams.

In fact, a swift reading of what I take to be a fairly accurate production, Eugene Landy's *The Underground Dictionary*, reveals a preponderance of nouns, a political paradox for a culture that extols its movement away from things, objects, coherent events. The verb is dead altogether, again strange for a culture that claims to action, conveniently supported by the Reichian thesis of the constitutive "energy" of youthcult. What verbs remain? Sample a reasonably full list: cop, off, con, freak out, cop out, hassle (the last three, however, usually used as nouns), turn on, trip out, rap (again, often used as a noun). In fact, most cult verbs are not single words, but phrases built around the nominal, e.g., "do a number on." By this time we should be able to predict the next stage of excalating explanation, to wit: Youthcult has developed gesture to replace verbs. The act replaces its description. But to borrow that phrase again from James Herndon, if the total quantity of acts hammocks softly in "nothing to do in here . . . nothing to do out there," then certainly even the new gestural language is limited in communicative potential.

Let's take another blood-sample of youthcult vocabulary, one which should direct us back to the problem of perception itself:

super-uptight	laying a trip on
his cool	scoring
had a thing about	into (anything)
vibes	the property thing
karma	bummer
getting it together	downer

What is particularly noticeable is the dominance of *generalized* perceptions, abstractions, and vague phrases—all of which can convey only the loosest of meanings. In fact, after periods of continued use, they all degenerate to the same sodden level of interchangeable meaning. Thus, in the Generations survey, we were told that "off" meant "stoned on smoke" or "shooting up," that "up-tight" meant "in need of money or drugs," that "heavy" indicated "a great sound or group," that "smack" was "another word for mesculaine" (*sic*), or that a "toke" was "something given to a person as a reward." One twenty-three-year-old provided an epiphanic flash when he defined a fourth of the vocabulary list in terms of one of the few youthcult qualifiers, "hassled":

> **rip-off**: hassling by theft
> **up-tight**: hassled by things
> **cool**: unhassled
> **hang-up**: constant hassle

It was a fairly consistent and expected phenomenon, however, that the greater the degree of print *and* visual culture involvement and/or mere presence among the elder juniors, the greater the recognition of the comparative meaninglessness of the hip dictionary. A twenty-four-year-old U-Mich grad student in history evidenced such self-conscious recognition in defining

> **fascist**: originally a practitioner of a particular political system, now a pejorative epithet directed to any one in authority
> **far-out**: what you think is great—or what you think your peers will think is great—or merely an expletive signifying (falsely) thought

And a twenty-one-year-old junior at Northwestern, with high print and visual media indices, after commenting that most of the terms were "meaningless," sarcastically remarked of "heavy" and "far-out," "I know what they mean, but a paraphrase that would catch every shade of use is beyond my humble power."

The serious issue is that for those who did *not* emerge from a print-visual culture, such a dictionary so levels language that perception, thought, and communication become impossible. The monotony of technocracy and its accompanying abstract liberalese is replaced by another meaningless and leveling totalitarian language, *no less abstract and dehumanizing than that offered by the cultural mainstream.*

In fact, more so. Look again at that second verbal blood-sample list. There isn't one concrete perception on it. The case can rest on such a frequently utilized phrase as "had a thing about," "thing" being a word that youthcult substitutes not merely for all objects, but for events, emotions, inner processes, ideas, institutions, movements, in fact, for most potential noun categories in the phenomenal world. The heavy use of "thing" itself expresses the refusal to confront the particularity of both inner and external environments. Couple this with the death of qualification as expressed in phrases of comparison such as "super-uptight" or (an exemplar from the counter-cult press) "vibrationally the highest," and one ceases to wonder at the inability of even the youthcult hucksters to recognize their own.

"To Generalize is to be an Idiot," Blake marginalia'd at Sir Joshua Reynolds, and added that the man capable of perceiving minute particulars alone was the true genius. The ability to perceive detail coalesces with the ability to discriminate in conceptualizing, let alone thinking. A culture whose language rests on phrases that express generalized perceptions will also be a culture given to abstract categories. If the technocracy categorizes through the keypunch hole, at least one can say that the number of its categories is significant. Compare to the limited categories of "brothers" and "pigs" (and their precious few synonyms) into which politicized counter cult of all intensities stuffs human beings on the most flimsy evidence (flimsy, too, because the youthcult dictionary does not allow for perception of detail). One wonders at times whether counter cult is not ironically competing with the ignorant, zealous gymnastics of simplification used by harassing government prosecutors in "conspiracy" cases.

One school of our ever present exonerators will undoubtedly counter that, though the perception of outer detail may be passing away, the perception of the inner self, the "raising of consciousness," has made significant advances. But revolve the youthcult vocab of the inner self: "getting my head together," "bad karma," "up-tight," "hang-up," and the ever flexible "vibes." Expressive gesture is grand enough but, without language, limited in its ability to communicate, even if one is a professional mime. There were no fascist pigs around when Ice Age man began to articulate his grunts, no corporate state in the societies of the earliest codified languages. The death of language, then, is not a noble regression; it is, rather, a mutation in evolution, a perversion that has to be reversed before we arrive at the horrific antiseptic world of Kubrick's anti-Utopian satire. By either route, technocracy or its vaunted "alternative," we're now headed for the silent interstices of 2001.

It was philosopher John Wisdom who offered the metaphor of language as a net. We fish in the sea of this fallen world, a sea filled with an infinite variety of fish—objects of knowledge (feelings, thoughts, objects, events), some of which we can know. Each of us fishes with a different net, the net of his language, and what he ends up knowing or feeling or thinking is what comes up in the net of his language, not what is in the sea. When you've got a large chunk of a generation out there fishing with a twelve-inch net (i.e., a very limited number of warps and woofs over a large area), it ain't gonna know too much, or feel too much, or think or perceive too much. The only token one can salvage is the recognition that youthcult at least declines the insane blasphemy of those who attempt with extremely fine nets to drag up everything in the sea. (It might surprise the either/or reductionists and their youthcult following to discover, though, that it is not the technocrats of the corporate state who possess such fine net. It is the poets.)

Hard by these elementary observations on the demise of language lies an extremely fertile ground for our new false comforters: the growing acceptance of the idea that language is not necessary at all. Into what debate exists on that vanguardist poseur's question we might insert some observations arising from Paul Goodman's delightfully instructive causerie "On Not Speaking" (*The New York Review of Books,* May 20, 1971). The act of speech, of language itself, Goodman observes, recognizes the existence not only of the Other but of all phenomena. There is a type of silence that is *purposefully* gestural, e.g., the disgusted silence of "no comment." And there is a type of silence that is Nirvanic.

To be sure, language and silence are contraries necessary to human experience. Blakean Goodman puts it thus:

> Thus, not speaking and speaking are both human ways of being in the world, and there are kinds and grades of each. There is the dumb silence of slumber or apathy. The sober silence that goes with a solemn animal face. The fertile silence of awareness, pasturing the soul, whence emerge new thoughts. The alive silence of alert perception, ready to say "This . . . this . . ." The musical silence that accompanies absorbed activity. The silence of listening to another speak, catching the drift and helping him be clear. The

noisy silence of resentment and self-recrimination, loud with sub-vocal speech but sullen to say it. Baffled silence. The silence of peaceful accord with other persons or communion with the cosmos.

The epistemic problem lies in determining which type of silence is at issue; for behavioral inference from silence contains a wide margin for deception, an old philosophical hat. Think, though, of how convenient this hierarchy is for those on its lowest rung, those of "the dumb silence of slumber or apathy." They can and do explain their silence—when pressed—by picking up a rationalization from somewhere up the ladder, e.g., "I'm grooving on the Far Out" ("the silence of peaceful accord . . ."), or "I'm putting my head together" ("the fertile silence of awareness . . ."). But without expression of *any* sort—verbal, gestural, musical, visual—it is impossible to determine the content of the soul. Not to express is more often a choice than a need. It is the paradox of negative choice, nilling.

The absence of expression presents a youthcult conundrum particularly in the matter of the emotive life. In a culture that presumably values feeling to the exclusion of cognition, nonexpression is self-contradictory. As Goodman notes:

> It is precisely consumatory experience, whether joy or grief, that we finite creatures often cannot contain. We are made anxious by too much excitement or even feel that we are going mad, and then our human way of coping with our feelings is to say them, for example in poems of praise or lamentation.

How lamentably naïve of Goodman, whom counter cult picks for what it wants—but not this. To him they oppose the order of a William Hedgepeth, whose ceaseless shillings for the new consciousness justify the death of language even in emotive affairs ("Growl to Me Softly and I'll Understand," *Look*, Jan. 13, 1970):

> No one translates deep-felt feelings into language and says it like they [youthcult] sense it.
> Probably because most often they can't. And because they can't say it, they can't imagine it being said. And because of that, if somehow, they were able to, the chances are they wouldn't—at least not right off. So, as it turns out, there's a whole vast range not only of emotions but of newly grasped sensations that seems doomed to lie locked up, unwordable, in our heads. Our language,

in its present shape, just can't handle it, and people—particularly young people—are slowly becoming aware of this flaw in their tongue.

They're becoming aware that—as a vehicle for conveying new sensibilities, perceptions of consciousness and the huge input of new ideas and formation—straight English is inadequate. And because, at present, it's untrained to operate in this dimension, people are feeling around elsewhere for ways to express the new reality in words (or in wails, grunts, growls, shrieks, or sounds no one's heard yet labeled).

Hedgepeth's is a highly sophisticated proposition, which, when used as a source for excuses, eliminates the necessity of all expression beyond "wails, grunts, growls, shrieks," et cetera. Are these vocalizings presumed able to handle that "huge input of new ideas and information"?

And what is this "new consciousness" that is presumed to lie beyond understanding and expression? If, indeed, it is the mystic's consciousness, then let the claim rest there, and no one will object either to silence or to ejaculative cries. But the claim of the youthcult apologist never rests, and Hedgepeth drives beyond the mystic to "new sensibilities." If one believes that such a rainbarrel of a phrase refers to the emotive life, recant! For whereas not everything that can be *perceived* or *thought* has yet been perceived or thought because objects of both perception and cognition can lie beyond the boundaries of the self, and there are doubtless objects and processes we simply have not observed as yet, everything that can be *felt* has, in fact, been felt at one time or another in human history, if for no other reason than the essentiality of the emotive life to the subjective self.

Perhaps Hedgepeth thinks he provides an ineffable understanding of this "new consciousness" and its inexpressibility in ordinary language when he notes that

> there are important new realms of the mind, of interpersonal involvements and levels of perception that defy its ability to convey or communicate—or even to conceive. The whole business nowadays of people talking about ineffable vibrations they receive from this or that suggests the existence of dimensions of reality beyond the outer limits of our language's vocal range.

I seriously doubt that Hedgepeth designed such a statement as a

parody on the ontological argument, but that's what it turns out
to be. The mere fact that some revered street freak runs around
talking about vibrations "suggests the existence of dimensions of
reality"? Oh, when are we going to recognize this bullshit for what
it is instead of paying such blind homage? The street freak simply
cannot talk about what he sees or feels, and there is no sequential
de facto case that a reality not subject to expression exists. The
very practical notion that we're dealing with a sub-generation of
functional illiterates who are simultaneously stoned into uncon-
sciousness but nonetheless clever at the art of running for cover
under the kind of primitive rubrics that he himself encourages
doesn't seem to strike Hedgepeth at all. If Janis Joplin wails, well
now, that's a new language expressing the "new consciousness." I
treasure Janis's wails, but I wonder what one does with the old
R & R wailers of the early 1950's. How does one fit Chuck Berry
or Little Richard into this schema? What does Hedgepeth do with
the exuberance of the jazz scat-singer?

Look, and this needs to be worn thin: When someone talks to
me about all those "ineffable vibrations" he is receiving, he is
making a generalized perception that results from the refusal to
confront, i.e., perceive, an object, person, whatever it is, in its concrete particularity. There are words to express that particularity;
they've been lying around, perhaps unused, for some time now. To
use them involves a multiple act of will, actualizing perceptions
from the blur of "vibrations." When one excuses an entire generation from the elementary acts of perception and expression by
resting his case on the presumed existence of an imperceptible,
inexpressible order of being, one has simultaneously killed off the
conscious will altogether.

Adolescent jargon has always existed. There has always been a
subculture idiom. But never, I am willing to assert, has expression
been as leveled into nonexpression as it is in the pervasive use of
youthcult vocabulary, or in the substitution of *someone else's*
music for the *expression* of one's own feelings, or in the claim,
which becomes more burlesque by the day (though it is a logical
extension of the mythologizing of a Hedgepeth or a Charlie
Reich), that ordinary involuntary bodily functions are purposeful
statements, e.g., in a variation, pissing or screwing as political acts.

Not to deny that expression is subject to political judgment.

—

Quite the contrary. The distrust of language is understandable in us all, and from a political point of view. We are too keenly aware that the hypocrisies of statesmen are couched in words, words that often serve in place of action, that mask reality with a vicious frenzy. Orwell reminded us long ago that the ordinary political uses of language amount to so much impoverished inanity; but his invective can apply as easily to the nonsense of radical sloganeering as it can to the blandness of technocratic platitudinous propaganda. But again, why that reductionistic either/or mentality? Why in reaction to one set of uses of language do we have to abandon language altogether, an option that Reich, for example, hypes into reality? Why not refurbish? Oh, but that's such a drag. That means exercising the will, along with the perceptual and conceptual faculties of the inner self. It's so much easier to piss in the street.

Come back now to Hedgepeth's convolutions, and grant, to begin with, my favorite fragment from Wittgenstein: "To imagine a language is to imagine a form of life." The notion can be extended in a number of directions, but Hedgepeth in effect chooses only the most handy and, not so incidentally, the most misleading, that is, that individual languages are so rigid that what is expressible in one is not expressible in another. Aside from the very questionable assumption of rigidity (language has proved itself as flexible as the human soul that created it), the example feeds right into what a preliterate youthcult, feigning another guru's notion of "tribalization," wants to hear: "The Hopi Indians, for example, can put forth ideas and feelings we can't even think about. The Hopi has a whole conception of time and space that's so far removed from *our* frame of reference it seems the work of Martians." An authentic, if elementary, anthropological notation; but now weigh the *sequitur*: "What this means, in other words, is that there are other ways of regarding reality. 'A change in language,' wrote Benjamin Whorf, 'can transform our appreciation of the Cosmos.'" What Whorf is talking about is not what Hedgepeth is hustling for. Whorf, Wittgenstein, and the Hopi are still sticking with the notion of language. There is no doubt that the Hopi culture has evolved a conception of time and space different from ours, but that conception has been encoded in their language, not in grunts, groans, shrieks, and the other unintelligibilia Hedgepeth feels can somehow handle concepts. Certainly the case of the Hopi illustrates the eternal proposition of Wittgenstein's little maxim; but what it does not reinforce is the notion toward which Hedgepeth's whole article thrusts: that "there are other ways of regarding reality" than that expressed in the *fact* of human speech, unless one is convinced (by what, we'd never know—probably just vibrations) that there is an internal language of the soul that is inexpressible, that passeth even the wise understanding of silence.

As a classic manipulator of youthcult reality, Hedgepeth cannot stop with the Hopi, for the very genre of the hype requires a political rationalization (in this case, for abandoning language and, with it, the will to perceive and conceive). And here Hedgepeth does great injustice to his own quoted sources by failing to distinguish between language itself and the uses of language. He tells us just what we want to hear: Guess what? Our language is *repressive.* As soon as one has uttered the magic froggie word, the ready-made clichés of the new consciousness pour forth:

> Much of our tradition-bound speech is structured in a way that creates a polarity between us and everyone (and everything) else. Our language forces us to conceive so much of life as an endless, goal-focused struggle, a war. And success, even in the most mild endeavors, is depicted in outright battlefield terminology: We grapple with, strive, clash, cross swords, lock horns, tussle, contend, engage, fight for or take the offensive to achieve (with flying colors) a triumph, victory, conquest, a win, a mastery, a put-down, a killing, etc. Roget's *Thesaurus* [an unquestionably accurate treatise on the political status of language use in the mid-twentieth century] devotes 28 lines to "Peace" and 162 to "Warfare." [Could it just be, Bill, that man has been at war with his own kind more often than he has been at peace, and that language is simply reflecting the realities of history, not creating them?] Thus, at a time when we need to be dismantling barriers to human unity, we continue to generate tension as we talk [assuming we are all so cliché-bound as to limit our speech to that rip of old saws you somehow think are rigid staples of ordinary language-use]—and our talk, in turn, influences our behavior. We tend, too, in this way, to use language not as a means of touching souls with others but as a defense, a barrier, with words deployed as little bricks to wall us in and hold other people off.

When Wittgenstein spoke of language as a form of life, when Wisdom presented us with the metaphor of language as a net, when Whorf underscored the transformational vision inherent in the shifts from one set of coded cultural expressions to another, they were all speaking as much about the individual uses of language as they were of the inherited symbology *per se*. Hedgepeth evidently wishes to deny human beings the possibility of individual creative use of language, and thus denies the flexibility of language. He assumes that we are so will-less that we necessarily dominate our utterances with the rhetoric of battle, indeed, assumes that we have no other choice.

But, you see, that's all so very appropriate to the creation of youthcult party line. Reduce all language to the uses of the mainstream. Make it repugnant enough by that political tinge, and you can dismiss language altogether. Do not hint at the possibility of creative language use, because that implies the existence of an active will—the last existence the youthcult party line is willing to accept. True, many use language as a social-psychological barrier; but one is not wholly sure at all that depth-perception of the Other will be served by the poison of slogans and grunts offered as an alternative. Hedgepeth provides his own political contradiction here, for the new universal language that must couple with the "new consciousness" will result in the destruction of cultures such as the Hopi. That, among the contradictions of the youthcult pitchman, is called "getting it together." Well, the hypocrisies of the party line are multiplying geometrically, and they seem to be seeping toward a totalitarianism born of the dismantling of options for the human soul.

Just where the death of language and the attendant deaths of perception and conception, encouraged along by the euphemizers and pitchmen, has led youthcult, core and gravitational fields alike, may be indicated by the function of "language" in counter politics. As an adequate entry, here's a letter to the *East Village Other*, printed on May 18, 1971:

> People: We are all citizens of Woodstock Nation. Some invaders from pig nation have taken our words and symbols (like power to the people and the fist) and are trying to make profits from them. If we are to defeat the amerikan way we must think about this too. An easy solution to this problem is to open up more free stores,

make free music (not like the rip-off Fillmore) etc. WE HAVE
TO MAKE EVERYTHING FREE! ! ! ! THE WHOLE WORLD
IS A LIBERATED ZONE— – –DEFEND IT BROTHERS AND
SISTERS ! ! ! CAPITALISM VS. BOURGOISE SHIT! ! YIPPIE!
LETS STOP THE PIG AND SERVE THE PEOPLE NOW!
WE ARE OUR OWN LEADERS! ! LETS CELEBRATE THE
FESTIVAL OF LIFE! !

                                    ANARCHA PIGHATER

It's like a six-year-old with a runny nose slobbering his drool over
a table and calling it significant, and sure, by this time, that some
euphemizer will pop up and lay respectability on his whining,
thus encouraging others to whine. The multiplier effect leads to a
very simple proposition: Sloganeering precludes revolution; in fact,
counter politics has killed itself with its own slogans. We have
been beseiged by offerings, most often dilletantish, to the gods of
revolution. And the explanations of why or why not "the coming
revolution" have run a murky gamut, the young radicals simplify-
ing, the old liberals obfuscating. The climate of the debate, more
than the debate itself, becomes part of the media hype under
which we come to believe that something radical is occurring and
hurry to jump on the slow freight before it leaves the yards and
becomes an express.

The debate, however, must come to rest on what is meant by
"revolution." "Anarcha Pighater" and his mindless gang certainly do not know, and for that reason, as much as any other,
there won't be a "revolution." Any revolutionary has to combine
high perception, a modicum of conception, and will. If a revolutionary is to succeed, he must be able to perceive *loci* of power
and be able and willing to seize them. But to read or hear the
graffiti rhetoric of the mass of counter-politics adherents, one
cannot believe that these people could recognize or seize power if
they were smoking it. In order to perceive power and to know how
to seize it, one has to be able to reflect and organize, and not out
of the desperation that shouts "Off the pigs!" (by which is meant:
Everything and everybody but me and my "brothers and sisters"*

* The determination of those included in this honorifium rests on "vibrations," a very profound form of behavioral inference which perhaps explains
the comparative success of undercover agents sent by a foolishly paranoiac
"establishment."

go). Marching to Foley Square with clenched fists raised is neither recognizing nor seizing power, but the expression of an aimless will following the easiest route.

Hannah Arendt has observed of "the coming revolution" that

> at the moment one prerequisite for a coming revolution is lacking: a group of real revolutionaries. Just what the students on the left would most like to be—revolutionaries—that is just what they are not. Nor are they organized as revolutionaries: they have no inkling of what power means, and if power were lying in the street and they knew it was lying there, they are certainly the last to be ready to stoop down and pick it up. That is precisely what revolutionaries do! Revolutionaries do not make revolutions! The revolutionaries are those who know when power is lying in the street and when they can pick it up! Armed uprising by itself has never yet led to a revolution.
>
> Nevertheless, what could pave the way for a revolution is a real analysis of the existing situation such as used to be made in earlier times. To be sure, even then these analyses were mostly very inadequate, but the fact remains that they were made. In this respect I see absolutely no one, near or far, in a position to do this. [Interview in *The New York Review of Books*, April 22, 1971.]

What Arendt goes on to term "the theoretical sterility of this movement" is really a euphemism for mindlessness born of the death of language and perception, raised in the cop-out that holds all analysis and theorizing to be "bullshit," baptized in claptrap pieces of street theater. There is no will lying around to form the analysis, let alone perceive its elements in an incisive and discriminating mode. What is lying around is a stoop pile of blurred perception, anticonception, and lumping thought. The result is as much incantation as it is sloganeering. Indeed, in the more mystical ways of counter *culture*, universal apocalyptic jargon is the parallel.

If one were really driving into revolutionary politics, into the analysis that must precede the act, he would have to be able to get his mouth around all those latinates: imperialistic, chauvinistic, colonialistic, militaristic, revisionistic and, further, would have to know what they meant. That just might require the confirmation of all those Thomistic battles over just who was being chauvinistic. From this perspective, and in light of the dominant perceptual habits of the whole range of youthcult, think for example of the efficacy of the word "pig." Come the new zombies who don't know how to talk and are told they don't have to know, and "pig" can serve as a substitute for any and all of those big bad words. And from the Generations survey, some definitions of "fascist" from self-styled and attitude-confirmed counter-politics juniors: "Anyone who doesn't agree with me," "capitalist," "conformist," "pig, any pig."*

Pick up some lesser counter-politics slogans and their contradictions. Start with "third world peoples," used with such abandon to indicate not merely anyone who isn't Caucasian, but anyone who isn't of European extraction. Such people are "oppressed" by definition. The phrase actually embodies a racist and elitist notion employed by those very people who vaunt their desire to eradicate racism and elitism. How elitist? By using the phrase, adapted from the rhetoric of European socialism of the 1930's, counter politics is accepting an ideal based on the perspective of European and American colonialist impulses. Why is it the "third" world? Why not the "first"? Why foist an obsequious and deferring position on the "third world peoples"? Because the half-begotten who bandy this one about in their slogans have not stopped to think about the perspective the phrase speaks from. It's that of the imperialists, whether in Moscow or Washington, looking down their navies at the unspeakable uncivilized.

The phrase also expresses that lumping tendency of the generalized perception that leads to frighteningly simplistic political analyses that cannot but end in frustration. The effect of the slogan, for example, would be to tell the Indians who have been expelled from East African countries over the past few years that they were really the "brothers" of the people who threw them out. I'm sure those glad tidings would be deeply appreciated by some exiled Bengali. It's the same nondiscriminating totalitarian mentality that Hedgepeth presented in advocating a universal language for the "new consciousness," the effects of which would be to kill off Hopi culture, for instance. But if we have a generation within which whole battalions carry a nonlanguage that cannot

* The author of the last also said that Sam Hayakawa was a Senator (which is known as a right-wing reality plugg), and that Yukio Mishima "married John Lennon" (guess they all *do* look alike).

penetrate beyond the simple-sensory or the slogan, we cannot reasonably expect it to think of causality in terms other than the absolutely immediate. Thus an Abbie Hoffman is taken perfectly seriously by the more intense segments of mindless counter pol when, in *Steal This Book*, he advocates a "monkey warfare" tactic that plainly does not look to its consequences:

> By getting masses of people to use electricity, phones or water at a given time, you can fuck up some not-so-public utility. The whole problem is getting the word out. For example, 10,000 people turning on all their electrical appliances and lights in their homes at a given time can cause a black-out in any major city. A hot summer day at about 3:00 P.M. is best.

Think of the "third world brothers and sisters" who might actually die of the consequences of that little joke. When they haul the subway car of trampled and suffocated black people up from somewhere under the East River, Abbie had better be around to pay his dues.

But no one wants to stop and consider such contradictions, short of dismissing them with the battering ram of "irrelevant!" No one wants to stop and perceive particulars. No one wants to ponder the essential difference between that Bengali and his former neighbors in Kenya. In fact, the generalized perception born of the sloganeering mentality leads to a persistent phenomenon in the counter-politics trip, the built-in *reductio*. The burden can rest on the "third world peoples." For if Nigeria is "third world," what is Biafra? If China is "third world," what is Tibet? Do we move on to fourth and fifth worlds, or do we decide that the moment anyone oppresses anyone else he is kicked upstairs to the first world? Or do we write off those oppressed by "oppressed third world people" as in reality, "lackeys and running dogs" of the first world? Jargon inexorably runs to blah. But then again, one can always dive into the convenience of the absolute dismissal of "irrelevant!" and slip from there into an Om-trance.

The man who lives in slogans, Orwell once noted, will eventually talk in bullets. Witness the collapse of SDS at its 1969 Chicago convention: The final confrontation between the factions consisted of an hour or so of crescendoing, overlapped chants, which gave birth to the bombs of Weatherman. The total blank of the soul has no way to cope with the complexities of a world it chooses not to confront, except down to the seas in internal and external violence. The death of language and perception leads to the terminal euphoria of the last speed rush.

Precisely because the slogan generalizes and reduces, those trapped in its mentality are incapable of perceiving the most elementary realities upon which, one ordinarily assumes, political action is structured. An unhappy paradox thus decrees that unworldliness is a political virtue. In talking with some YAWF-ers I once discovered that Israel started the Six-Day War because "they wanted the Arab oil fields." When I asked them just where the oil fields were, they replied "Oh, all around the Arab countries." Persisting naïvely, I asked what countries Europe and America bought all their Arab oil from, and was told that "it doesn't matter," i.e., we don't know, and we don't care. As a point of geographical information, I noted that the major oil fields were located in places like Kuwait ("What?"), the Trucial States ("Huh?"), Iraq, Iran—all on the Persian Gulf, some 500 or more miles east of the Jordan River, and that it seemed quite strange that if the Israelis wanted the oil, they would attack in the opposite direction. The escalation that followed reminds one too poignantly of its models: "Oh . . . um . . . well, they'll get there eventually." "Why didn't they do it right away? I mean, they had the momentum." "The time wasn't ripe." "What does that mean?" "Oh, look, it really doesn't make any difference." And so it goes, in a culture that demands its simplicities in the same way that the Agnix-boosters demand simple answers for the causes of crime or simple solutions to a happening such as Vietnam. As one self-described "anarchist-radical" in the Generations survey noted of the whole second half of the questionnaire: "I don't care who these people are or what these places are because I have no use for the newspaper or television"—the quality of that *sequitur* matching the attitude.*

What is at issue is the simple perception of the world. Throughout the reaches of youthcult—and *not* as a function of the age-that-acquires-wisdom—its existence is minimal. One assumes at

---

* The same gentleman, the very same, indicated that he was boycotting Alcoa because "they make napalm." With a little escalating exoneration, one can always say that the thirty Dow Jones components are interchangeable.

the risk of high naïveté that the more "relevant" the object the more likely it is to be perceived. A weekly column in the *Los Angeles Free Press*, "Ecommando Tactics," once opened thusly:

> Here's a quickie: name me four cities in Alaska.
> Name me three Indian tribes native to that state.
> How about the name of the governor?
> Sitting up there next to Siberia is the biggest piece of real estate in this country. And not one in a hundred of us knows anything about it.
> But we'd better be finding out—and soon.

and later, a curious assumption:

> Because of the wonders of modern communications, we all know about the Great Alaskan Oil Discovery, wherein the North Slope (How many of you actually know where the North Slope is?) was found to contain lebbenty zillion barrels of oil per square foot. And this has led to everyone's knowing about the Trans-Alaska pipeline number.

Match those paragraphs against the recognition and attitude responses to "North Slope Oil" among the college-educated in the Generations survey:

> 17–20 Age Group
> Median Attitude Response: 1.9
> Not recognizing the item: 59.2%
>
> 21–25 Age Group
> Median Attitude Response: 1.4
> Not recognizing the item: 48.6%
>
> 26–32 Age Group
> Median Attitude Response: 2.1
> Not recognizing the item: 14.4%

The "Ecommando" author saves with his pitch: You ought to know, if for no other reason than because it's "relevant" to the spirit of what you think you're up to. The spirit emerges lucid from the data: The attitude response in all cases is negative. But the most confirming factor is that among those who, in earlier sections of the questionnaire, indicated strong commitment to ecological concerns, the nonrecognition percentage on "North

Slope Oil" was not that much lower than that for the respective age groups as a whole: 40, 29.5, and 11.5 per cent.

It is obviously my case that that ignorance arises from both an unwillingness and an inability to perceive the world in concrete particulars, an unwillingness and inability reflected in the death of language in youthcult, the political consequences of which are prophesied in a sloganeering mentality of self-destruction. The potentially grand tragedy lies in the delusions wrought from the slogans.

If, for example, you're going to scream "fascist" at all the little events, what are you going to call the big one? What discrimination in urgency will you be able to employ? If the college dean offers an inadequate answer to some peripheral issue such as twenty-four-hour-dormitory-visiting-privileges-for-fornication's-sake and is called a "Fascist Pig," what are you going to call Ronnie Reagan when he lets loose his promised bloodbath? And if Gloria Steinem, setting a fine precedent, pisses "fascist" at the arrival of the midi, announcing it as the heraldic banner of the impending military and otherwise coup of the Right,* what is she going to call Agnix when they start throwing dissenting congressmen in jail? How significant or shocking will be the cry "Free Ronnie Dellums!" or "Free Bella Abzug!" after years of yelping for freedom, not merely for some unquestionable worthies, but also for every two-bit asshole who happened to get busted?

The point, of course, is that when one kills off language, violence handily presents itself for the larger response. No doubt, in the cases cited, large-scale violence would be not only justified but called for. It wouldn't take the sloganeers to start it, either. They have insulated themselves to such a degree that I am sure they would rush into spirals of rhetoric to write off what would be the Establishment leadership of *that* violent response.

---

* A year later, after the midi had proved to be one of the larger Rag District busts of recent years, hot pants were in, and Gloria *et al.* were running around slapping on "sexist" tags, like cops trying to meet a weekly ticket quota.

I would never argue that dress is *not* among the many significant indices of the spirit of a culture; but to exploit momentary turns in fashion design for this facet or that of one's own political anxieties is a hollow gesture of a manipulative power jag.

The slogan dulls with repetition, like all those TV commercial cartoon pumping stomachs. So we require a vanguard, a group left over from the print-visual cultures who can create more advanced forms of banner language. Here we reduce the world to its manageables and manipulate a younger constituency. The following lengthy and turgid tureen of rhetoric of the internal colony reflects the passionate desire of some white middle-class kids to be an oppressed group, and presents the highly discriminatory results. No doubt there are a good many valid observations in the following series, particularly on schools and sexism; but toward the point at which one must resign, it becomes clear that the bulk of the "oppressions" are born of self-indulgence, nurtured in mindlessness, and schooled in moral abdication. At that culmination, the oppressed becomes his own oppressor:

We, as members of the youth colony, are processed and manipulated from the age of five, which has been deemed the Mason-Dixon line of socialization [So whaddya want? The Wild Child? A Chinese Commune? There ain't nobody from Cain & Abel on who escaped "manipulative" socialization]. We are beset upon by sick, authoritarian teachers, a system of program cards (similar to the mechanism whites use in South Africa against Black people) [the pretensions to oppressive analogy in the parenthesis are an affront to Black people everywhere], bells, meaningless rules, lack of freedom of the press and speech, and they even tell us when we can take a piss. We get cut off from our friends, our hair, our favorite clothes, our leisure, and our individuality [Chicago's Blackstone Rangers, a.k.a. Stone P. Nation, have a highly accurate epithet for the authors of such self-indulgent whining: "white bougies," i.e., bourgeois beasts]. We have to wear ties, or other such nonsense, dresses upon occassion [sic], to slowly prepare us for wearing the uniforms of the future office or of the army [the mere fact that you are able to put this statement into print indicates that, if you possessed *half* a will, you wouldn't wear those uniforms, and do not, in fact, have to do so]. Every day we stand and recite the Pledge of Allegiance. Our books are often racist, always male-chauvinist, in that women are never shown to be anything more than secretaries, teachers, mothers, or traditional roles relegated to women by this society. Women are rarely even shown to be the eldest offspring; that job is left to the male, because he is the one, in our books, who must assert himself and offer leadership to his younger brothers and sisters [it's hard to accept the fact that the same people who were capable of such discriminating, detailed, and poignant perceptions on sexism also produced the rest of this]. We are lied to, socialized, and after going through the wringer, if we are still conscious, they smash us with their cops and rules, dictatorial principles and prisons. Sound like Thailand? We get harassed if we walk the streets after dark—they have a five o'clock unofficial curfew—anyone out later than that is definitely suspicious [five o'clock? The paranoia has gone pretty far]. We tried to hold some of our naturalness and identity through our culture and we're busted [if "naturalness" comes with Speed or coke, Eden must have been a considerably fucked-up place]. Large punishments for dope. Laws against rock festivals. Promoters exploit us with high admissions fees [it's so much easier to whine than to hold your own rock festival. So much easier to slogan than to exercise the will. Go to the groups: ask them to play for the vibes]. They charge us for water in their hot dance halls. We are discriminated against in housing, and in jobs. They sell us shitty records at high prices. They build some of us to be leaders, and then they throw those people in jail in order to intimidate the rest of us [who the hell are you talking about? Jerry Rubin? John Sinclair?]. They herd us into ghettoes like Haight-Ashbury and Miflin Street.

> (*The Red Balloon*
> SUNY at Stony Brook
> April, 1971.)

With the last one, I'm ready to trash the mind of the writer. Here's Abbie Hoffman himself, in *Woodstock Nation*, on the decline of those "ghettoes":

The Lower East Side was disappearing out of my plastic dome. I was sick of starting free stores that ended up garbage cans, and bailing out people who never gave the bread back so we could get others out, and mimeos that broke down. I wasn't the only one getting sick of New York; even the gutsy Motherfuckers had split to New Mexico, Massachusetts and San Francisco. The bikers were shooting each other in the streets and the drug scene was all speed. Cops stopped cars illegally and threw people against walls and somehow nobody gave a shit because the whole scene had been wasted [127].

As anyone who has followed the rise and fall of the Haight is well aware, it and other similar neighborhoods were the creations of the counter culture and were destroyed by the counter culture, with only passing help on either count from the outside.

Hair . . . clothes . . . leisure . . . concerts . . . drugs . . . dance halls . . . records—these are presented as staples of oppression analogous to the concretions of the struggles of Vietnamese peasants and American blacks. Quailing incongruities, and one recalls John Hersey shilling for them under the euphemism "desire for universal experience." The whole, true to its models, concludes with an escalating rhetoric of hysteria outdoing even Spiro the Anguish himself: "1971 should be named the year of a thousand trashings. Seal the People's Peace Treaty with a military alliance! Free Erica! Free Bobby! Bring the war home.

"MAYDAYMAYDAYMAYDAYMAYDAYMAYDAY. . . . !!!!!!!!!!"

The vocabulary that reflects the unwillingness to discriminate in perception leaves its speakers in a state of political nihilism: The man who sees only "the pigs" and "the people" will not know how to act and will, in frustration, seek to destroy all in order to arrive at the ultimate simplicity of a uniform society. That simplicity, after all, will not require any differential perspectives. In that case we will have ironically achieved nothingness, the cosmic void, the silence between spaces, the continual Om. The MAYDAY man will have said, "I do not exist—nor does anyone else," because the leveling, whether performed by the rolling pins of the Left, the Right, the Center, or those "nonideologues" of technocracy or its anarchic offspring, reduces everyone to everyone else. For those who do believe that language can contribute to reality, can create it as well as reflect and express it, consider this a frightening extension of that contribution.

5

The Death of Language II: The Youthcult Bookshelf

Although a direct question about books was noticeably (and purposefully) absent from the media series in the Generations survey, those interviewed in the follow-up were asked which books they or their friends were reading heavily *when they were in college*, whether the books were course-assigned or not. In fact, the campus cult book is that which, though it may be assigned in a course or two, it seems everyone is reading. Likewise for the more general proposition of the cult author. Not merely the breadth, but the texture of the following lists is at issue:

17–20 Age Group
Single works: *Demian* (Hesse), *One Flew Over the Cuckoo's Nest* (Kesey), *Soul on Ice* (Cleaver), *Do It!* (Rubin), *The I-Ching*
Authors: Brautigan, Vonnegut

21–25 Age Group
Single works: *Catch-22* (Heller), *Steppenwolf* (Hesse), *Portnoy's Complaint* (Roth), *The Ginger Man* (Donleavy), *Man-Child in the Promised Land* (Brown), *The Prophet* (Gibran), *The Fire Next Time* (Baldwin), *Growing Up Absurd* (Goodman), *Summerhill* (Neill), *The Autobiography of Malcolm X* (Malcolm X and Haley)

Authors: J. R. R. Tolkein, Ian Fleming, Yevtushenko, Allen Ginsberg, Tom Wolfe

26–32 Age Group

Single works: *On the Road* (Kerouac), *The Stranger* (Camus), *Go
Tell It on the Mountain* (Baldwin), *The Fountainhead* (Rand),
Lolita (Nabokov), *The Outsider* (C. Wilson), *Franny and
Zooey* (Salinger), *The Ugly American* (Lederer and Burdick),
On the Beach (Shute), *Catch-22* (Heller), *Lord of the Flies*
(Golding), *Dr. Zhivago* (Pasternak), *Look Back in Anger* (Os-
borne), *Under Milk Wood* (Thomas), *A Coney Island of the
Mind* (Ferlinghetti), *Walden Two* (Skinner), *The Other Amer-
ica* (Harrington), *The Hidden Persuaders* (Packard)

Authors: Henry Miller, Durrell, Huxley, Greene, Camus, Sartre
(the drama)

Respondents not currently in college were specifically urged to
filter out reflective exaggeration. They were asked, too, to distinguish between what the avant garde was reading and what middle-
camp was reading. Thus other works, though mentioned, could
not and did not receive depth backing and were excluded from
the list.*

One obviously begins by noting the temporal position of the
print culture, and the fact that that position dovetails neatly with
the other data on media habits of the sub-generations. One notes,
too, the progressive elimination of both poetry and drama from
the cult book list, as well as the heavier representation of specifically black works in the list of the group (21–25.) that was in college during the first rush of black consciousness into print.

Having disposed of the obvious, we move by degrees toward
the key group, the kids who, as Updike's Rabbit puts it, are going
to "crowd you out." Only one single work, *Catch-22*, spanned
two sub-generations, and the appeal of only one author, Hesse,
did likewise. My former students in the youngest sub-generation
shruggingly responded to *Catch-22* on the grounds that "it's too
long." Likewise *The Autobiography of Malcolm X*, which they
scanned, and to *Invisible Man*, which I was not able to discuss at
all in a course in urban studies because no one bothered to read

* E.g., *Woodstock Nation* (Hoffman), *The Strawberry Statement* (Kunen),
and *The Autobiography of Malcolm X* from the 17–20 list; *Life Against
Death* (Brown), and *Armies of the Night* (Mailer) from the 21–25 list;
The Tin Drum (Grass), *The Lonely Crowd* (Riesman *et al.*), and *The
Power Elite* (Mills) from the 26–32 list.

beyond the first hundred pages, and our narrator doesn't even arrive in New York until page 150 or so. We are choosing our books now by the number of pages, by the amount of sustained perception of language that can be endured by a generation in which language has died.

But those may be the sour grapes of an old media freak. The more striking shifts in the texture of the three respective lists do not necessarily lie in their length, their generic composition, or the individual weighings of their components. What is particularly piquant is the interplay of the quality of the works themselves and the quality of the *responses* to the works, the uses of books. I concentrate, quite simply, on the list of the juniors, specifically the cults of Brautigan, Vonnegut, and Hesse.

The *Rolling Stone* review of Brautigan's *The Abortion* points to one principal attraction of Brautigan for youthcult. The thrust, in a paragraph or two: "Brautigan really *is* fun to read, unless you're a 98-year-old misanthrope with a testosterone habit." And why is Brautigan "fun to read"?

> Common to all of Brautigan's work is the slow pacing, like an angling brook, that makes it a pleasure to stop and savour each paragraph on the way to the last page. *The Abortion* is an easy book for this reason; it passes quickly, and it leaves you smiling the way you smile after eating just enough ice-cream on a hot day.

In so many words, because it really doesn't take that much effort; and, after all, none of Brautigan's works runs much more than 100 pages of large type. The *Rolling Stone* reviewer claims that he originally intended to write a piece of high pedantry, replete with citations "from Gaston Bachelard's *Poetics of Space* and comparisons to Henry James and Sartre's *Nausea*," as if the average *Rolling Stone* reader, whether strung-out in the New Mexico wilderness or just plain mindless in the Gaza of the campus, knows what the hell he is talking about, but just grooves and smiles on Brautigan anyway.

For the unquestionably elder reviewer, then, the New Jerusalem–radical, innocence-political hype must succeed the planned pedantry, for

> the very best thing about *The Abortion*, the reason I felt good after reading it, is that Brautigan has a naive faith in the ultimate salvation of America and in the ability of its people, given a choice be-

tween good and not-so-good, to choose good most of the time. . . .

    The Abortion makes you remember that this other America is out there somewhere, smelling green and alive under the pervasive odor of blood and money and bullshit. It's a good book to read after the *Grand Guignol* of the daily paper or the evening news.

For some, it is clear that the appeal of Brautigan arises from a sense of political exhaustion. He encourages the desire to abandon both the despair and the hassles of even attempting to deal with "the pervasive odor of blood and money and bullshit" by joyfully pretending that none of it exists. Brautigan himself, on the other hand, is skilled at swirling patches of that odor through some of his more surrealistic fantasies, but those who *use* Brautigan as a prop for the langourous life-style are more concerned with the thrust of the tone. Interviewing some junior potential counterculturists, too, one finds a greater attraction to *The Abortion* and *In Watermelon Sugar* (fairly structured and simple allegories), than to *Trout Fishing in America*. As one, "heavy into Brautigan," drawled, "I just like order."

Which drops us on a second notation on Brautigan's fiction. Those in the 26–32 age group who had read Brautigan indicated a far higher preference for *Trout Fishing*. A generational perception trained in the visual intricacies of Fellini or Godard is quite naturally attracted to the fragmentary and episodic, whereas a generation beyond both visual and print cultures simply has tremendous difficulty in dealing with fragments, particularly the wry, absurdist sexual fantasies that occasionally arise in *Trout Fishing* and *The Abortion*.

To an older literary tradition (if one wishes to investigate Brautigan with high seriousness), the montage of such incidents may invite comparison to the scenarios of Beckett, and simultaneously fit well with spaced-through one-liners from a Mort Sahl album circa 1959:

> After he graduated from college, he went to Paris and became an Existentialist. He had a photograph taken of Existentialism and himself sitting at a sidewalk cafe [*Trout Fishing,* 92].

Cute, no big statement, picaresque without the drive, commitment, or identity of the rogue-hero, and decidedly apolitical:

There was a beatnik sitting at the other end of the bench. He had
his sleeping bag beside him and he was eating apple turnovers. He
had a huge sack of apple turnovers and he was gobbling them down
like a turkey. It was probably a more valid protest than picketing
missile bases [87].

Understated violence runs through *Trout Fishing* and, less understated, *In Watermelon Sugar,* but the euphemizing does create a
tension between the sloppy calm of the narrative voice and that
Western pastoral reality in which people are naïvely vicious:

One of the rocks was kind of strange. It was a flat white rock. Off
by itself from the other rocks, it reminded me of a white cat I had
seen in my childhood.
   The cat had fallen or been thrown off a high wooden sidewalk
that went along the side of a hill in Tacoma, Washington. The cat
was lying in a parking lot below.
   The fall had not appreciably helped the thickness of the cat, and
then a few people had parked their cars on the cat. Of course, that
was a long time ago and the cars looked different from the way they
look now [56–57].

What attracts the under-twentys to Brautigan are the same
factors that are involved in their opting for Hesse's *Siddhartha,*
for example, or Vonnegut or, to a lesser extent, Kesey's *Cuckoo's
Nest.* I save Kesey for a later story, but as long as we're sticking
with the most common unassigned experience our college students
have with the print culture, certainly we can recognize some
equally common factors in the objects and responses.

On the objects. They read like Feiffer cartoons. Shimmering
surfaces, sometimes fragmented, heavily parable-like (though not
formal or weighty enough to sustain cosmic allegory), built
around fairly simple metaphorical situations, and written on a
comparatively low level of diction. When Brautigan's language
bounces a bit in one of his overreaching metaphors ("The autumn
carried along with it, like the roller coaster of a flesh eating plant,
port wine and the people who drank that dark sweet wine."), the
surface does not invite real reading, and therefore one does not
really have to bother with it. Vonnegut is filled with effortless and
hot one-liners; and many students are so intrigued and distracted
with the "so it goes" refrain in *Slaughterhouse-Five* that they can-

not perceive that what they are confronting here, as so often in Hesse (certainly in *Siddhartha*), is a paradoxical mask of innocence as thin and as incapable of enriching their conceptual and emotive lives as it is easily graspable.

That students should respond to these works as allegories and seek to discover "messages" in them—usually phrasable in no more than a sentence or two of hip dictionary—is not dumbfounding in light of the medieval-morality-play atmosphere they project. And project hot so that perception is not required to burn in, e.g., from *Slaughterhouse-Five*:

> "So—" said Billy gropingly, "I suppose that the idea of preventing war on Earth is stupid, too."
> "Of course."
> "But you *do* have a peaceful planet here."
> "Today we do. On other days we have wars as horrible as any you've ever seen or read about. There isn't anything we can do about them, so we simply don't look at them. We ignore them. We spend eternity looking at pleasant moments—like today at the zoo. Isn't that a nice moment?"
> "Yes."
> "That's one thing Earthlings might learn to do, if they tried hard enough: Ignore the awful times, and concentrate on the good ones."
> "Um," said Billy Pilgrim [101–2].

And "Om," says Siddhartha, and so it goes. The *lowest* attitude responses to *Siddhartha* issued from those most heavily involved in both print and visual media. The audio generation is soothed by the simplicities of the Um and the Om. After all, its proclivities for vague perception, unthought, and minimal feeling are reinforced by heroes who have the perceptive abilities of a four-year-old, the conceptual maturity of a pterodactyl, the emotional range of a computer. There can be no real tragedy in these dimensions. McLuhan has iced it. No one wants to face the coool complexities of tragedy. No one wants to confront the complexities of the Other. Like it's a hassle, and who can groove on bad vibrations?

The appeal of Vonnegut, unlike that of Brautigan, is *primarily* thematic. His excursions are structured like the episodic *Trout Fishing*, but he exercises tighter control of coherent "plots," so one is not presented with the numbing task of dealing with frag-

ments. With an overuse of understatement Vonnegut mixes a
satiric put-down of mainstream corruptibility, a put-down that appears to be formed *a posteriori* from every cliché sloganeered on
the barricades of the mind. Vonnegut thus serves the cultural
function of therapeutic reinforcer, and, in the face of blackness,
like Brautigan, offers gentility. It is said, almost as a justification
for their existence as novelists, that neither Brautigan nor Vonnegut could hurt anybody. A qualified "yeah," as long as one
possesses the differential perspective that can follow, for example,
the Beatles' transcendence of their own "all you need is love"
line. For in the dissolution of youthcult urban colonies and at
sweet love-ins such as Altamont, we all discovered the inadequacy of that posture.

Yet the sons of Reich listen too well. Exhausted from the trying
exercise of nilling, they sit down, groove on their own things, smile
at the brothers and sisters, and the revolution cometh. Thus
the Tralfamadore (*Slaughterhouse-Five*) or Mercury (*The Sirens
of Titan*) or other curt sci-fi flights. The New Atlantis. The 2001
man of the print culture who, in his first (1952) novel, *Player
Piano*, matches plant manager Paul Proteus against the monster
computer, Checker Charlie, in a cosmic hop to kingship. Paul is
multiply crowned, natch, and Charlie transfigures in flashes of
psychedelic lightning. As much as one can enjoy such games, a
generation immersed wholly in them will be led by sensibility into
some dangerous regions, as I hope future pages will convince.

The Hesse cult has to be dealt with in a slightly different order,
for the manifest reason that it reaches through at least two sub-
generations. In reflecting on the transformational powers of Steppenwolf's Magic Theater or in alter-ego Harry Haller's execution
into life by otherworldly guffaws, one is superficially reminded of
Vonnegut's planetary gambits or Brautigan's absurdist dreams of
mutability. However shallow and pallid the reflection, though,
Hesse structures himself in recognizable and powerful myths.
Much is a replay of *Faust* in modern idiom, and I think what
power there is is largely transferrable from the source. Goethe
is indeed, by admission let alone evidence, a primary influence on
Hesse, and the image of the flight of the man of pure cognition
into the realms of the human soul which he had ignored, expresses that eternal desire for completion for which men are will-

ing to sell the very souls they hope to find. The fallacy of infinite mind rings clear in an age of computerized wars and cauterized, Levittowned souls.

The common bond of the Hesse heroes is a strong (but not raging, for it's so often difficult to feel the presumed passion of a Hesse hero) desire to break from the static bourgeois life of the mind and the stomach. In fact, they do so, and so doing exert a sometimes cathartic and certainly cathectic effect on those who follow Steppenwolf and Demian down the days of sensual outrages into the primal caverns of the self, to the celebrations of ecstasy in the surreal landscapes in which Goldmund of the spirits triumphs over the self-denying Narcissus.

In the novitiate's view, Hesse's ideology is soothing, paradoxically so in that surreal world of fleshly delights. Soothing in the same manner as is Vonnegut: an anticipation of youthcult partyline put-down. But it is what the novitiate does *not* perceive that is far more revealing: that Hesse's answer to one poison is another, the anarchy that Faust tragically realized whether or not he was scheduled to pay his dues. Consider the inscriptions on the doors of the Magic Theater in which Harry Haller languishes in hedonism in *Steppenwolf*, consider these invitations to destructive solipsism in light of the current offerings of our counter-culture:

MUTABOR
TRANSFORMATION INTO ANY ANIMAL OR PLANT
YOU PLEASE
*   *   *
DELIGHTFUL SUICIDE
YOU LAUGH YOURSELF TO BITS

DO YOU WANT TO BE ALL SPIRIT?
THE WISDOM OF THE EAST

DOWNFALL OF THE WEST
MODERATE PRICES. NEVER SURPASSED

COMPENDIUM OF ART
TRANSFORMATION FROM TIME TO SPACE
BY MEANS OF MUSIC
*   *   *

SOLITUDE MADE EASY
COMPLETE SUBSTITUTE FOR ALL FORMS OF
SOCIABILITY [217]

So stapled to the logic of either/or are the respondents that the possibility of a destructive Nirvana is not countenanced.

Another stage of the dialectic can be added for Hesse, but it is no less an absolute: if the choice is not the enslavement of either Narcissus or Goldmund, it certainly evolves into the infinite peace of Siddhartha's "Om." But if Hesse himself is fascinated primarily by the process, the form of the pilgrimage, youthcult is interested solely in the final resting place.

The bookshelf concludes by winding anecdote. In an introductory survey of contemporary literature two books were once assigned to be the focus of a paper: *One Flew Over the Cuckoo's Nest* and *Armies of the Night*. The topic was wide open, that is, one could do anything he wished with the two books.

Now, Mailer is not on the youthcult bookshelf (Charlie Reich seems to think he is—along with Wallace Stevens!!). If one accepts the notion of a significantly wide gravitational field for the counter culture, Mailer's absence is an anomaly. For certainly no man of letters of our time had so anticipated and transcended the youthcult party line in his persistent critique of the punishment technocratic America visits upon the soul or so clearly offered the formulation of counter-culture ideology in his politics of Left-Conservatism, and much more. That the much more becomes tragically irrelevant may strike one as obvious in the face of the distinct fact that the kids cannot read him. Mailer's sad problem is that he is a craftsman of words, not plots. He is an artificer of pushes and pulls of intellection, of deep plunges into the thickets of the soul—and by thickets are required a plemora of perceptions finely composed, of emotive responses ragingly articulated. Mailer is a son of Los, wielding the hammer of language on the anvil of time, perceiving the world in a grain of sand. For all his sympathy and "relevance," he is thus in trouble in youthcult.

Acid-test Ken Kesey's *Cuckoo's Nest* is a novel that, despite the radical simplicity of its central metaphor, the world as insane asylum, presents the attendant complexities that inspire us to despair and, in the poetic consciousness of the presumably moronic Chief Bromden, the power out of depth from which tragedy is fashioned. As a stylist, Kesey displays far greater polish in this one novel than either Brautigan or Vonnegut—or, at times, Nobelled Hesse as well. There is no graffiti quality to Bromden's dream visions of descent into the hellish technocratic bowels of the kingdom of Big Nurse. The plot may be hot (as is that of Book Two of *Armies*, The Novel as History), the allegory may rigidify at moments, but never enough to overwhelm Kesey's invitation to the perception of detail, never enough to preclude recognition of the depth and centrality of that looming narrative voice. But to do so the perceptual memory must at least be existent, if not operative. For if Kesey's prose is not nearly as thick as Mailer's, it is highly concrete—conditioned by the very identity of a narrator who is incapable of that dense combination of perceptual reflection and intellection of which Mailer is a master. For opposing stylistic reasons, then, Kesey, too, is likely to be perceived half-anesthetized among undeveloped lobes who do not even wish to perceive the concrete.

The responses to these two books ironically illustrate an old saw of Mailer's, one which Kesey shares through the metaphors of lobotomy, shock treatment, and other authority-imposed numbings:

> For years he had been writing about the nature of totalitarianism, its need to render populations apathetic, its instrument—the destruction of mood. Mood was forever being sliced, cut, stamped, ground, excised, or obliterated; mood was a scent which rose from the acts and calms of nature, and totalitarianism was a deodorant to nature [*Armies*, 136].

In the death of language, and in the rise of the generation of numbed TV children turned mesmerized audio media freaks, the range of emotions has been flattened and the perceptive abilities reduced to dealing in the broadest of outlines. Such is the totalitarianism of the forces at work on and within youthcult. Mood destroyed and the eyes burned out like Randall McMurphy's, "smudged fuses in a fuse box . . . the blank, dead-end look," as Kesey's narrator Chief Bromden observes upon performing modified euthanasia on the Big Irishman.

In dealing with *Armies*, most simply took the broad *fact* of the 1967 Pentagon march and spent some time talking about the goals of war protest in such profound and laudable Movement phrases as "standing up and being counted," and then agreeing with the general spirit of the thing. One didn't have to read the book at all for that. Indeed, most found it convenient to dismiss Mailer as narrator—and thus never have to confront the deep significances and resonances of the event. As one succinctly copped-out, "Mailer can fuck-off for all he means to me." That was about it for *Armies*.

For Kesey, a number chose to quote the précis inside the jacket cover, then to run off a series of Big Statements, e.g.:

> However one takes it, this story tells of a revolution. A revolution that was a lot more difficult to stage than the revolution Mailer talked about. [That's the transitional statement, by the way.] McMurphy went against innumerable odds to try for change. Within a very close, tight, restricted system, any type of change is almost impossible to get. Yet, McMurphy proves one thing. If one wants something bad enough, if one is strong enough to persist, and the change is necessary, then nothing should come in your way.

That was about it for *One Flew Over the Cuckoo's Nest* from a junior in college. Not one concretion, and to shill for it necessitates a form of the most deceitful torture. Discussion following receipt of the above:

> "What did McMurphy do?"
> "Well, ah, he got the guys together on Big Nurse."
> "Which guys?"
> "The inmates."
> "Were they all the same?"
> "Well, it really doesn't make any difference."
> "Then why did Kesey throw them in there? As a joke?"
> "He had to have guys for McMurphy to organize."
> "But why these *particular* people?"
> "The inmates—"
> "Can you name freaking *one* of 'em, for Chrissake?"

Euphemistically speaking, we're up against the generalized perception. It's really not a matter of not being able to read but a matter of not wanting to as the perception, conception, and emotive and cognitive responses of reading take time and concentrated energy, and there is carrion in such proceedings.

Robert walked with a disarming braggadoccio. A verbal charmer. He also walked with a tennis racket—and little else, certainly not books. He was also the only student in this particular class to head for D.C. for May Day, 1971. He crashed with a commune for a week or so, "balling like crazy," amplifying:

> It really wasn't a commune. It wasn't because the people in it weren't really together. There was like—Oh God!—so many person-ality conflicts it was unreal. But I kind of fit in between the cracks and I was really comfortable. So I met this chick and I stayed with her for most of the time, but she had to split, so I just lived in the house. . . . But the thing is I really dug it, I really dug the idea of it, the idea of no responsibility. . . . I dug it for a while and then I was glad I had to get away from it. Even when I went back, you know, it's not the same. I don't know if this makes any sense. It's nice to be totally free of everything for a while, and then again, I kind of saw most of their lives as being wasted . . . they did noth-ing but ball, and go out and work once in a while when they needed money to pay the rent. It gets to be a drag. What can I tell ya'? . . . But I'm not really that uncomfortable in being totally apa-thetic.

So Robert was okay, in fact, hardly a soporific. When he did read, the mind was keen, the jaws were tight and articulate, the shaggy split ends jangling. He even stopped to wipe his glasses, alternat-ing between the wit of a fast middleweight and the gravity of cardinal. He was one of those people who could, on occasion, enter gyring into an intense discussion and contribute measurably to it without having the slightest acquaintance with the material on which the discussion was based. It's a marvelous talent, and takes a pro, not a palooka, to expedite consistently and with aplomb.

After a time, though, the energy flagged, and Robert returned to amateur status after the commune experience (May Day being incidental). The candor intensified: "I haven't read this book— I really will, though [eddying chuckles—pause] next week? But I really want to say something here." Beautiful! Even then, we could still get by. The embezzlement, though, came with Kesey and Mailer. More entertaining cajolery, but reminding one too keenly of what lies behind the cults of Brautigan, Vonnegut, Jerry Rubin's *Do It!*, and the *I Ching*:

I could probably go on forever with a thousand different approaches to these two books (that's the biggest fucken lie I've heard in months—it took me three hours to type that first page). So I now shall attempt to list the differences between the books:

Armies of the Night	*Cuckoo's Nest*
320 pages	272 pages
1 main character (who else?)	2 main, 5 subordinate
paper edge is red	paper edge is yellow
$1.25	$.95
picture on rear cover	picture on front cover
by—Norman Mailer	not by Norman Mailer
"interesting"	"entertaining"

What followed was a "Bullshit Page," a personal note, hoping I wasn't "offended by this piece of shit," and assuring that "I plan to finish Mailer's book on my own time—BELIEVE IT OR NOT." Better, in its wry, cleft way, than the Big Statements or the anemic précis, but given the surrounding operational fields of counter-cult, the writer's own experience adjacent to the most recent descendant of The Wedge of '67, one cannot believe that suburban intention.

6

A Short Passage to Marshall McLuhan, the Audio Media Culture Assisting

The most persistent set of correlations in all our surveying was produced by those who, *regardless of age*, generated an index of high involvement in audio media *only*. This group also indicated:

1. low information possession in all categories
2. minimum political identification. They offered either no indication of political sympathies at all, or ludicrous combination claims born only of ignorance, e.g., "reactionary—general leftist," "socialist-conservative," "conservative-Maoist," "anarchist—general rightist."
3. nearly nonexistent political-social activity. While tossing in the obligatory demonstration or two, the demos involved were the most tepid and cautious; and there was no activity on the boycott, community action, radical experimental education fronts, or in those of the counter-culture ways that involve orientation to the Other, e.g., group therapy or communal living.
4. short perceptual memory and emotive attachment. The respondent *tended* to lend most-favored status to whatever records or films he heard or saw *most recently* (see Appendix, questions A.6 and A.7).

5. negative or blasé attitudes toward films—with the frequent exceptions of 2001, *Easy Rider*, and *Love Story*. Two excerpted comments from exclusively high-audio people should indicate this trend: "I'm not that much of a movie freak, and besides, there isn't any picture worth seeing these days —maybe *Easy Rider* (male, 18, Brooklyn College); [finds attractive those films] "that are part of the new romanticism that seems to be returning. I hate depressing films that make me think" (female, 21, Northwestern).
6. slightly higher drug culture involvement (a cliché by now)
7. a combination of positive counter-culture attitudes with minimal counter-culture knowledge, e.g., a number of respondents claimed a Rolling Stones album among those most attractive to them, granted Mick Jagger a 4 or 5 on the attitude scale, and yet could not identify Altamont.

Nearly a third (32.1 percent) of the total sample indicated moderate to high involvement in audio media *only*. Exactly 70 per cent of this group, or 22.5 per cent of the total sample, could, in addition, provide *six* of the seven correlation factors above.* That is a fairly high percentage of concentration over such a range of shared habits. The collection represents, I believe, the most accurate indication of where the dominant spirit of youthcult is at. Loosen up the criteria, add a *moderate* involvement index in *visual* media to a moderate-to-high audio index, and reduce the number of the above correlative factors required for membership from six to four, and I am sure we would embrace more than a hairline majority of the sample.

What do we do with the correlations? Briefly now, the case is that we're confronting not merely the death of language and perception but the demise of the will as well. The McLuhanites will shortly have to produce a hard defense, but contrary to their assertions of "total involvement" electronic media yielding increased activity and energy, the electronic environment in fact has produced a staggering degree of passivity, perceptual and otherwise. Generations become increasingly malleable and manipulable,

---

* The percentages for the sub-generations are not wholly unexpected: 30.4 per cent for the 17–20 group, 17.3 per cent for the 21–25 group, and 11.6 per cent for the 26–32 group.

and the potential political and cultural consequences are indeed frightening. Hopes for enduring and positive Alternatives are extinguished as swiftly as the shower of Leonides.

As Benjamin Demott observed in his anti-apocalyptic polemic, "Rock Saves?":

> The rock experience at its most intense is an intimation of engulfment and merger, a route to a flowing ego-transcending oneness. As fans and enemies alike know, rock sound *overwhelms* separateness, *the mental operations that discern and define here and there, me and not-me.* (Many of the lyrics work symbolically or subliminally toward the same end.) Pounded by volume, riddled by light, the listener slides free from the restraining self and from the pretenses of a private, "unique" rationality. Preparation for the descent is of various sorts. . . . All are alike, though, in their relish for a thunderous, enveloping, self-shattering moment wherein *the capacity for evaluating an otherness is itself rocked and shaken,* and the mob of the senses cries out: What we feel, we are! [Italics mine.]

If the self is dissolved, what then? The mode of dissolution lies in the engulfing obliteration of the entire sensory being. Thus the medium is indeed the message, a total environment configuration which blurs out individual perceptions. Distinctions vanish, and one is prepared for his earthly reincarnation in a single continuous undifferentiated state of being: undifferentiated vegetability. Far more accurate, though, to assert that a *coherent* sense of self is dissolved, not into the Other, rather into the prison of the singular senses five. The only "separateness" that *may* be "overwhelmed" is sheerly physical. Far more likely is a total environment solipsism. If that is supposed to lead to a politic of world community, it does so with a fascistic vengeance.

For the greater the exclusiveness of the audio experience, the ability to make oneself relevant to the Other is proportionally dimmed. And thus another element on the rock highway to libertarian anarchism. If one denies all perceptive channels to the Other save a vague sense of universal identification, one is left only with a half-perceived self. "Where my head is at" is the type of vapid, generalized, and hence meaningless expression of psychological condition that's become a staple of youthcult vocab conceived in the sound chambers. When we're told that this expression and the experience from which it emerges is "existential," we have no choice but to balk. The existential ethic demands perception of I and the Other and our specific relations in a world of perceived and conceived limit situations. For the music-*makers*, perhaps, the term applies. For Janis, for Dylan, for Jim Morrison—but that seems to have depended more on a life-style than on the music *per se*.

Music is unquestionably the most mysterious form of communication. Being nonrepresentational, it is the most untranslatable into any other medium because its conceptual apparatus can only be described in metaphors. In a situation of music, it is *possible* for communication of meaning, usually emotive meaning, to take place, as long as the listener responds to the performance, himself, *and* the composer. The possibility depends on the environment in which the music is presented. When a rock festival grouper rises up to spurt "Right on!" chances are heavy that he is responding not to the *content* of the music but to the performance, the total environment. Shift to the solipsism of headphones, and the conditions of the medium transform, the variables of mass audience are removed, and the content has an even greater opportunity to penetrate the individual sensibility. Under the conditions of the inner room there is a great similarity between audio and print media: The perception can be replayed and, again, it is *possible* to perceive detail, ponder it, respond do it. In respect to the ease of halting temporal sequence, the book and the turntable are very much akin. This preliminary and contingent distinction can be reinforced by one of the more influential of the rock music-makers, Frank Zappa, who, in *Rock and Other Four Letter Words*, noted that "most people . . . really aren't into the music; they are too hooked on the pure theatre side of the music," and added that he who has "enough perspective to sit back and view the whole package" in the privacy of a room, that man would be able to provide a genuine response to the music.

The following is *not* a spoof:
"I'm getting into music now."
"How much are you getting it?"
"Heavy, man, heavy."
"Like what kind of stuff do you do?"
"Funky, heavy far-out funk."

"What does that mean?"

"You ever played?"

"Yeah, piano, sax, some guitar. Those were jazz days, though."

"Well, you know then, we're into polythings."

"Polythings?"

"You know, like I do my thing, and the other cat does his things, and all of us are really together."

"Polyrhythms, maybe? Like you're playing in a rockabilly form, and that's grafted onto, let's say, a series of short chopping arpeggios that the guy on bass is doing?"

"Yeah, that's something like it, and it's heavy!"

In this world of day-glo stagnation there blares a curious anomaly: On the one hand, youthcult seems generally incapable of talking about its own music, and, on the other—following the slippery path of a Charlie Reich—when forced to talk about it, it does so primarily in terms of lyrics. One would assume that audio culture people who riff out a concession to the print culture by reading the rock press should, after a time, be able to employ some of the terms they read and to be able to discriminate and judge. But to suggest that your average twenty-year-old rock head can either discriminate, express, or judge is to indulge in a clunking fantasy. Consider, for example and as a control, some of the verbiage offered by the elder juniors who write the rock copy. A few phrases on audio perception:

acid rock truculence	vocal chicanery
electronic exuberance	lyric-supported timing
dynamic modes	Hollywood lemonade singing
sea-chanty ballad	instrumental anemia
dynamic modes	arpeggio ridden
convoluted intensity	punctuative horns

And, from two of the most prolific and talented rock reviewers, some judicial paragraphics:

> At the peak of their frenzy [they] cross over the gospel line into pure shrieking and screaming. In the controlled doses they administer here, it is very powerful stuff. Such vocal techniques are easily misused. [Jon Landau, *Rolling Stone*, May 27, 1971.]

The group is almost entirely acoustic and mainly mellow, though never succumbing to the kind of soporific (or is it sophomoric?) weak-kneed "mellowness" vitiating so much current music. . . . They don't barge into the back of your skull with ballpeen axes, but neither do they quail in gossamer timidity. [Lester Bangs, *Rolling Stone*, May 27, 1971.]

Now, no one expects the nominal audio head to attain the level of the rock journalism of a Lester Bangs. But one might expect at least a rudimentary attempt to describe the music that we are told has such mythic prowess as an identity card for youthcult. Here's pissing-in-the-street-as-medium Jack again, down on words but up on rock as "the new language." Let him write for a while of *Blows Against the Empire,* an album put together under the direction of Paul Kantner of the Jefferson Airplane, who invited various musicians from the California groups (The Grateful Dead, Quicksilver Messenger Service, and Crosby, Stills, Nash & Young) to a joint venture under the letterhead Jefferson Starship. By the way, the following is entirely *sic:*

The album must be treated as a whole. The idea originates from the song Wooden Ships which deals with escaping the hollocaust when the world ends. The main idea of "Blows Against the Empire" is that a group of people are going to hijack a starship and travel in outerspace. . . .

The first song, "Mau Mau (Amerikon)" expresses the groups thoughts on America. They tell Richard Nixon "Whatever you think of us is totally irelevant, Both to us now and to you." They also tell him "So drop your fucking bombs burn your demon babies." These lyrics show their hatred for what America has to offer its people. They say that their office is in the park and they deal with acid cocaine and grass. The music is standard guitar playing, drums and some piano.

The next song "Baby Tree" takes us back to the folk era. Banjo and voice is all that is heard. It sounds like hillbilly music until these lyrics are heard. They tell of an island where babies grow on trees and people come to select the child they want. Again the lyrics are about some wild idea probably thought up while on LSD. . . .

The next song "Hijack" opens again with the ubiquitous topic of drugs. Some history of our country is then mentioned, two events that could possibly have influenced many people to have feelings against our country. The events being "the 23rd of November" the day J.F.K. was killed and "the abyss of Chicago" in reference to the riots during the 68 convention. Now they reveal their plan to hijack a starship that will start being built around 1980 for use a decade later. They sing "people with a clever plan can assume the role of the mighty and hijack the Starship." Here the central idea being that people of the same ideals can have much power and freedom by living in outerspace away from the horrors of our country. They tell us that "Our babes'll wander naked thru the cities of the universe / Come on—free minds, free bodies, free dope, free music." Four central and new ideas for the musical world to deal with. These four concepts are important to the understanding of Acid Rock. The music is strong guitar playing with short but exactly guitar breaks that fill in on the mood of the song.

The approximations of the last sentence of the excerpt nudge about as close as exclusively audio cult can to talking about its own music. Frank Zappa sadly overestimates his audience: Even in the environment of a single room, audio youthcult can neither perceive nor judge. Thus, when presented with the opportunity to describe his own music, topoid Jack relies on lyrics pulled off an album jacket. And no one who is even an occasional reader of the rock press can accept the apologetic that music is indescribable. The only half-satiating explanation seems to be that those who acned their way through adolescence wholly under the audio culture cannot perceive, do not possess the conceptual equipment to describe what they would perceive if they could nor the discriminating powers with which to judge it. All they can do is summarize the lyrics.

And even then, not with too much ease, since language has been blown out on a loud long-in-dying bass. The hollow and banal invectives that so often fill the letters to the underground press indicate the extent to which audiocult would be tortured by the task of thinking about lyrics. At random, letters to *Fusion* of January 22, 1971:

> Your paper bores me to death. There is never anything interesting in it. The pictures suck. The design makes me sleepy. It's so much middle-of-the-road horseshit that doesn't make sense half of the time. So you recognize a market of hip young people and you're

just trying to be so fucking hip by covering and reporting and attempting to interpret what's happening . . . but you fail.

I don't ever read your rag anymore. Whenever I get a copy I just leaf through to see if you put any dirty pictures in it. But you don't do that either.

It's too bad you aren't printed on better paper. What you use now appears to be re-processed toilet paper. I know because it smells funny.

Gonna play Joni Mitchell & try to forget about you. I don't mind the 35 cents really, but why do you have to depress me (you & Dick & Spiro)?

JIVE, JIVE, EMPTY JIVE (& fuck goldstein too).

Letters from the silent majority to a quasi-liberal newspaper. Or perhaps right-wing hate mail. Thus the inability to perceive the very atrocity of "Blows Against the Empire," an invitation to a mindless counter culture for those elites who can afford to leave the rest of us behind, for those whose wills are dulled into the absolute refusal to grasp for power. The Empire is rather pleased. The political contradictions between rock lyrics and rock style are thus allowed to run rampant; but, as Jerry Rubin yipped in *Do It!*, "Let's not let details get in the way of myth."

The distance between rock musicians and the rock audiences who form the exclusively audio media culture is the distance of cultural sub-generations. For whereas the audio culture itself has been numbed into will-lessness, the will-energy of the giants who made the rock revolution into more than a musical phenomenon seems to emanate from another culture. Rock became a sociological phenomenon when, in its early days, the mode of production of popular music shifted from the corporate fragmentary, with its rigid division of labor, to the organic. The same half-dozen people wrote, arranged, recorded, and, in some cases, distributed and marketed their own music. How unlike the MAYDAY sloganeers who concluded our first excursion into the death of language, wishing for someone *else* to provide the stimulus, demanding that someone *else* produce—and "for free"—even those media events which they regard as essential to their survival. If the will cannot exert itself for those matters which it regards as essential to its survival, let alone those slightly less urgently "relevant," no amount of academic euphemizing, underground hucksterism, or political excuse-mongering can cloak the fact that energy has fled from young spaceship Earth. Man, it's all *such* a drag!

Another, perhaps a more telling, form of the loss of will conceived of the audio media culture may be illustrated by Ivan Illich's observation that "instead of learning how to nurse grandmother, the teen-ager learns to picket the hospital that does not admit her." That is, to act becomes that manner of dealing with a situation which requires the least expenditure of energy, which is dependent on the minimal acquisition of individual resources. It is not rattling, then, to observe that, too often, such "acts" bear little, if any, phenomenological relation to the effects the actor has in mind. The smoothness with which this tendency merges with the sloganeering mentality may be illustrated by a mad anecdote provided by Abbie Hoffman himself in *Woodstock Nation:*

> WOODSTOCK NATION wept the night Ronald Reagan, "the fascist gun in the West," sent the Pigs into Berkeley. Not everyone wept though. Three thousand miles away in the part of the NATION called the Lower East Side, someone tried to firebomb the Fillmore in retaliation. They missed and burned down the building next door [21].

Despite his own internal contradictions, how right on Jerry Rubin is when, in *We Are Everywhere,* he maxims: "SELF-AWARENESS IS TRUTH. THE MEDIA PREVENT SELF-AWARENESS." Certainly the counter-media are not to be differentiated from those of the mainstream on Rubin's score. For they have offered and hyped all the convenient excuses for the cop-out, the mentality that covers the refusal to act at every moment. We'll spend considerable moments later examining the varieties of specifically political tarpaulin in introducing the actual practice of counter cult; but it is essential to note here that, within the audio culture, the tendency to excuse nonengagement on every conceivable occasion on which the inner or reflex faculties of the human being might be willed into conscious and directed act simply perpetuates the cycle of lethargy and prolongs the dive into self *without* self-awareness.

The pseudo-consciousness-raising hype of the audio media culture has also become, in practice, an end in itself. It has become a self-gratifying and wholly private (except in the sense that others share the same behavioral pattern) way of noncommitment. The frequent combination of rock-'n'-drug mind-blowing has led to little except variations on the same vehicles for mind-blowing. Since few in the exclusively audio culture seem capable of perceiving more than the fact of their existence, one is left with a void of both interpretation and judgment of the effects of noncommitment. "Consciousness-raising," at least in this significantly encompassing branch of youthcult, becomes a mere exonerist's tool for the passive acceptance of the absurdity, complexity, injustice, and pain that lie beyond the blown mind. The universe is crazy, so all I can do is find an undemanding niche in which to wait out my time. Is it not ironic that such a vision, and its effects in audiocult, have devolved, in part, from counter-politics reductionism? The master-plots of the Establishment have been presented as so monolithically embracing and overwhelming that the individual is forced into himself out of despair. Cartoon propaganda has thus proved counterproductive to the task of reconstruction. Kids who have swallowed this nonsense have often said, as one hitchhiking counter-culturist shrugged, "Well, since it's inevitable that the Establishment will repress us, why bother to put yourself in a situation in which you have to deal with them at all?" Thus, as we'll see, is born counter culture, not counter politics.

I have often noted that in this series of explorations I am primarily interested in the cup being offered as an Alternative to mainstream madness. What strikes me as so tragic, at times, is the extent to which the only visible culture that might have the potential (the double-conditional itself reinforcing the tragedy) to offer lasting alternative structures is both aborted in the cocoon by the mainstream and buried by its own. Thus the death of language, perception, and conceptualization is initially very much a product of mainstream education, with its insistence on form and programing, its stifling of natural expression. One can at least build from natural expression, can move into a world of perceptions, ordering them, judging them, responding to them with the fullness of the emotive life. Reading well will follow intense and extended periods of encouraged expression. Perceiving minute particulars, concretions, will follow intense and extended periods of encouraged expression. Given the dominant media that are likely to continue enveloping adolescent consciousness in the next decade, a schooling of diagrammed sentences and discussions axed by period bells will produce only more zombies. As John Holt wrote in the old *Saturday Evening Post* (February 8, 1969), the entering schoolchild,

> by paying close attention to and interacting with the world and people around him, and without any school-type formal instruction . . . has done a task far more difficult, complicated and abstract than anything he will be asked to do in school, or than any of his teachers has done for years. He has solved the mystery of language. He has discovered it—babies don't even know that language exists—and he has found out how it works and learned to use it. He has done it by exploring, by experimenting, by developing his own model of the grammar of language, by trying it out and seeing whether it works, by gradually changing it and redefining it until it does work. And while he has been doing this, he has been learning other things as well, including many of the "concepts" that the schools think only they can teach him, and many that are more complicated than the ones they do try to teach him.

The school shuts off this natural flow and, after ten short years perhaps, has killed language in the kid. Then he's off to a culture that will evidently write the epitaph.

The two cultures are equally in heinous league presiding over the correspondent death of the will. The mainstream has no other mode of conceiving of adolescents than that contained by the borders of school and consumption. The mainstream has clearly indicated that it has no other uses for them. When they're seen, they're to be consumers. When they're not, they're to be "at their desks, sitting down." In either case, the passivity ranges high and carries over into the aimless life-styles of burnt-out wills. Leave home and do some extended hitchhiking, perhaps, but to nowhere, and for no reason, and with the expectation of living passively off whoever is running the crash pad. As for the Other en route it's like talking about rock—no one even tries. "Oh," yawned one at a nearby rural commune, "it's really so difficult to establish a whole new set of relationships." Communes are a groove: They serve the middle-class embolisms as surrogate parents, and what do parents do but provide, do things for you and to you without expecting you to do more than be in school and perform? No vocational nonsense, just college prep, and the commune weekenders and occasionals cannot even change a tire or wire a lamp—and don't want to. What's left but the New Nirvanas and Asbolutes? From drug-cult to Jesus-Freakism, they all offer assoiling to the mind, the will, the soul itself.

Two lost road signs. Back in 1969, William Hedgepeth did a piece for *Look* on the life-style of the new family. It was very much a-borning then, and as serious and dedicated as its practitioners were, one might have read the sticks. Prophetic husband in the family, then twenty-nine, says that to discover what his kids were like he dropped acid, producing a conviction in the unmediated or "pure" perceptions of the child. The *sequitur* should now thrust at us with the force of logical gravity:

> As a family, Robb and Pat and the children don't "do" much, aside from an occasional field trip, but no one seems any less happy from this inactivity. Even homelife seems bland, for though they are close-knit, their emotions appear internalized. Hours can pass without words. Outwardly, it's maddening. Each Monday night, however, they flock with hundreds of others to a onetime movie house in Haight-Ashbury to hear a homegrown guru named Steve Gaskin pontificate as to what they're all about.

The wordlessness leads to the passivity, which asks for someone *else* to explain, justify, and fortify. No doubt the children will continue to sleep in this state of wordless "pure" perception. Were it not for their free school, at which "the most important priority is teaching kids to relate to other people," we might project them in ten years as ripe for reinforcement by the audio media culture, with a vocabulary of grunts and groans and therefore a tangle of those internalized emotions which just may explode into the pyre of self-destruction.

Or the other, and now with us: the strange form of freedom that the Jesus Freaks assert—believe in the Word, the Father will provide, and you don't have to do a damned thing. The hip dictionary can suffice for the passage, and, like any other form of sloganeering, all you need is the Little Red Book of the Lord. Predominantly under twenty and thus probably exclusively audio-oriented, the Jesus Freaks have had their perceptions dimmed away from despair. Everything is a groove. Like any other cult, it levels and confines, and, in addition, this variation on "the new consciousness" avoids the deep condition of the Other as much as do New Agrarianism, communing, doming, group-groping, and other counter-culture Ways.

One cannot explain witlessly that, in this age group, we are dealing with a case of political exhaustion. The Jesus Freaks are just too McLuhan-battered into mindlessness, so that the ritual of speaking in tongues is more than appropriate and, in many cases, simply an extension of previous life-styles. Witness an interview with a Jesus Freak in the *San Francisco Good Times* (April 30, 1971):

> I've been in the Haight-Ashbury since I was four [he is now seventeen]. Started doing psychedelics and grass four years ago. Looking for the ultimate. Got into Steve Gaskin. Holy Man Jams. Live food diet. Attained cosmic consciousness behind psychedelics. Waves of bliss. Every trip was like Nirvana. All of a sudden, all my friends started turning to Christianity. I thought that was bullshit. I thought I'd found what others had spent years searching for. Came walking in here one day stoned on acid, liked the feelings of the people who were really into it.

And in case you wonder where such successive conversions will lead us, consider a prophecy based on this bag, from a Westchester teeny-for-Christ: After a string of "far-outs" and "outa sights," he informs us that "poverty, see, is just Satanic stuff. Poor people are poor because they don't know how to pray." And if you do not wish the effort of confronting poor people, if you wish not to perceive the facts in the case, you conveniently do not have to look: No reading is permitted outside of the Bible. After all, magazines and newspapers "lead to negative thoughts, which poison the mind." The undifferentiated, totalitarian, emotive stream of total immersion in the Grand Funk Railroad.

An irresistible coda for a final epiphany, replete with political paranoia. In matching back pages of *The Chicago Seed*. To the left is a large spread of space with a column of words working in white diagonal down the page, a column titled, appropriately for our purposes, "To Be Read Listening to Jefferson Starship 'blows against the emipre.' " The column, in part:

We should have our own starships . . . by any means necessary. . . . *I lie on my back at the predesignated spot in the wilder-meadow. Anesthetic vapor fills the immediate area. My life thoughts, crazed neurotic, insane that they are, drift into peaceful uncon-sciousness. Cryogenic systems lower my body temperature to preser-vation. The Starship is on its way. Twenty-five light years later, I awaken ageless. I go topside and embrace the people I love. We are orbitting* [sic] *New Genesis. Anarchoastronauts name landing zone A: Emma. We are home.* . . . Rudely woke up by the city noise, the stardream is vivid in my mind. Polluted haze and demon's rage return to scream inside. Will we deal with time or be left behind? We have twenty years to decide. I want to go. Those who want further information should get in touch. Telephones are tapped. Can they tap a telepath? Write even. Starship passengers and crews are needed. Apply now, travel later . . . really not too many sun-rises from now.

> Uncle Martin
> Chicago Starship Collective

And opposite that, a purple fading up through blackness into blue starship girl with eyes in her hair, announcing above her the "Mid-west Dope Dealers Assn/Yippie Offensive" and its price list, e.g.: "Yellow Blotters" at "$1.00 to $1.50 per hit . . . $.75 in hun-dreds"; "Red Microdots" at $2; "Synthetic Mescaline . . . Evans-ton Red/Yellow caps . . . a little speedy . . . goes good with Apple Pie," at $2. The paranoia and the Starship in a bundle. We're leaving for that Purple Psilocybin in the great sky.

7

Media and Generations: The Delusions of McLuhan

In all our jaded willingness to hail the new avatars, it seems that we have advanced too much of a dowry to Marshall McLuhan. Oh, we have scratched some of his tantalizing evils, such as the collapsing of form and content inherent in the notion that the medium is the message or the particulars of his historical thesis, but we have still let the effects of our own clinical ado go unnoticed. For while McLuhan has been suffused through Halls of Disputations, youthcult has been picking up his filtered-down scraps, and we have been acting on other unquestioned McLuhan assumptions in such a way as to aid the deception.

The most tragically confusing of McLuhan's notions falls out of his now centrifugated distinction between hot and cool media. Electronic media, television, and the telephone, as examples, demand "involvement in depth," i.e., active participation, because they are "cool," i.e., low in informational content. Why low? Because, instead of sequential presentation of information as one finds in the "hot" print media of the high definition of the motion picture image, "cool" information is presented in an immediate "total configuration" of low definition, a configuration in which the perceiver must involve his faculties in order to comprehend. This is a *neurological* and not a semantic notion of "infor-

140

mation," and, as intriguing as the notion may be and despite its occasional accuracies, it apotheosizes as a filigreed belch.

By McLuhan's reasoning, the "TV child" has been conditioned to immediate total-configuration perception and thus cannot deal with the fragmentary, the staggered, or the remote, or with the idea of the future. How right-on he is. Then, however, he follows with the pulpitry that "the TV child expects involvement and doesn't want a specialized *job* in the future. He does want a *role* and a deep commitment to his society." The logical *sequitur* seems to be that he who is raised on television involves himself perceptually, emotionally, and socially in *depth*, is *active*. The logical corollary is that he who is raised in the culture of hot print media, who is accustomed to confronting "information" in its sequential plenitude, who is inured to receiving information, not creating it, tends to be isolated and passive.

The simple data from our sub-generations, let alone very observable patterns of behavior in youthcult, turn up the contrary on both counts. The TV children are passive and pass into the audio environment (a logical succession), in which their passivity is reinforced. The TV children marching off into the counter-culture Ways define neither role nor deep commitment to a society—unless one wishes to torture the notion of society into the youthcult myth. The New Agrarians, the politidomers, the Krishna-Consciousness people, the nomadic libertarians—these *may* express roles, but not commitment to any society larger than the self.

The print-visual kids, on the other hand, the elder juniors, seem to be the ones who are engaged, active, involved, capable of perception in depth and a considerable emotive life.

Let us stick with McLuhan's classifications of the media, separating television (cool) from motion pictures (hot), which separation, unfortunately, the popular press has kept ponderously hidden, thus advancing the self-serving idea of a monolithic "video generation." While maintaining this distinction, let us argue our case twice: On the first round, granting McLuhan's axiom that television *as a medium* (regardless of content) encourages active involvement; on the second round, inevitably, denying the authenticity of that juggernaut.

I propose a distinction between being born into television and having television enter one's life after the developmental stage at which what the belatedly honored Swiss psychologist Jean Piaget refers to as the ability to "conserve" an *image* is manifest.* That is, the stage at which the perceptual memory can operate from moment to moment, when the child is no longer amused by peek-a-boo (i.e., before he can "conserve" your image; when you duck behind that door, as far as the kid is concerned, you no longer exist—out of sight, out of mind). If the child is planted before the tube prior to his development of this basic perceptual ability, he becomes conditioned to a whirling set of visual images and (to him) unintelligible sounds which he cannot manipulate or respond to (read McLuhan's "feedback") in any way. When one image shifts to another, when program gears into diagramatic commercial, the image succeeded no longer exists for the child and, when it re-returns to the screen, is not remembered. The preconservation child, so to speak, is thus wholly detached from the screen. He is aware of the total configuration of the blur, but nothing more, and active only in this general sense of awareness. As Piaget noted:

> To know an object, to know an event, is not simply to look at it and make a mental copy, or image, of it. To know an object is to act on it. To know is to modify, to transform the object, and to understand the process of this transformation, and as a consequence to understand the way the object is constructed. An operation is thus the essence of knowledge; it is an interiorised action which modifies the object of knowledge. [From "Cognitive Development in Children."]

The child who is born into television, then, is not really acting on the configurations, hardly "involved" with them, because he cannot even conserve them, let alone modify them.

Continuing this speculation, by contrast: When television *enters* the child's life after the development of the ability to conserve images, then the child may assume an active neurological (McLuhan)

* This stage is prior to that at which the child's ability to "conserve" matter and number is manifest, i.e., the later stage at which he moves from intuitive to threshold conceptual thought. Although environmental factors obviously play an enormous role in the speed of the child's cognitive development, the age at which this second and most significant conservation ability emerges seems to be five or six (although the ability to deal with more abstract tasks of conservation continues to develop to adolescence).

or cognitive (Piaget) role with respect to the images projected, with respect to the medium itself. That is, in McLuhan's terms, he combines sensory intuitions in total configurations, demonstrating perceptual understanding of electronic succession. As he approaches the ability to conserve matter (understanding that a given mass may change shape but not quantity), the sophistication of his modifying involvement increases. The later the tube enters the child's psychological life, the less likely he is to be passive before it. And this is particularly the case after the child has discovered and developed the rudiments of language. When the sounds that pass in succession with the shifting electronic visual impulses are intelligible, then, of course, the child is entering a situation of meaning in which, though not the initiator, he plays an "active" role. But he is more likely to present the TV with "feedback" once his linguistic and conceptual abilities have passed beyond the threshold.

The child who has been conditioned by television from his pre-conservation period will, I suspect, never develop an active, distancing response to it, will remain predominantly silent, passive, and manipulable before it. But if television first enters the household when a child is, say, six or seven years old, the outburst of enthusiasm that ensues, though it may last three or four years, still involves distancing through his relatively sophisticated ability to modify—i.e., act on—the image. The ability may be wrought from a differential perspective as the child has been previously accustomed to *other* visual and aural media.

These, obviously, are speculations, wholly theoretical, seeking to account for the patterns of behavior we have been noting for some pages now. Television did not enter the lives of the elder juniors, the sub-generation born between 1939 and 1945, until they had passed beyond both basic conservation and at least threshold conceptual-literate stages of psychological growth. Television entered the lives of our fuzzing middle sub-generation, born between 1946 and 1950, sometime *between* the development of basic conservation and threshold conceptual-literate stages. The third group, however, born between 1951 and 1954 (and within the syndrome of the stages of perceptual development), was born into television.

I am hardly disputing McLuhan's claim for the critical importance of television as a psychocultural force. What I am disputing, reasoning back from the cultural artifacts of the dominant
behavior of our sub-generations now in young adulthood, are the
universally constant effects he claims for it. The ability to perceive
particulars and the will to become actively involved with the environment seem to decline through these sub-generations, and I,
for one, do not believe the decline is coincidental, nor determined
by chronological age *per se*.

Thus the emphasis in these pages on the relation of media-
conditioning to the active realities—though not the general spiritual community of interest—of the sub-generations. Besides, that
relation is critical in accounting for where the key group of succession, gravitational youthcult, 17–20, is headed. The moral and
political consequences of television conditioning in this group are
just beginning to be felt.

Now let's turn through TV again, this time in terms of its "semantic" properties and its relationship to the psychology of the
other media. We are again encouraged to do so in light of the
impressive number of live contradictions to McLuhan's phenomenology of media, to wit:

1. McLuhan explicitly asserts that the "cool" electronic media
move us away from the particular to the general, away from the
specialist to the Renaissance man of skills, away from passivity
and toward active constructions. But at the same time our new
Rennaissance men of skills, the new wholists, e.g., Stewart Brand
(thirty) and *Whole Earth* company, are decidedly *not* McLuhan's
TV children.

The unhappy paradox lies in the fact that the total configuration perception has led and *is leading* television's children toward
the search for new absolutes, universal consciousnesses—the "Otherworldly" Division of core counter culture, a search which may be
informed by a wholistic drive, but since it precludes perception of
particulars does not allow for the Renaissance man of skills. It is
obvious, too, that such a motion leads one away from active engagement in the social order.

2. McLuhan envisions the beckoning sea of the global village,
"the instantaneous world of electronic informational media" in

which cultures are known to each other in all-encompassing simultaneity, and asserts that this global-village effect both results from and is conducive to "involvement in depth." One wonders in depth. Since the global village will be accorded to us *automatically* by the electronic media, the notion itself invites the abrogation of the will, and thus of "involvement." Early on in the evolution of his syncretic "probes" McLuhan played on the slogan "the media is the message" and came up with "the media is the massage," a cutism which his proselytizers have taken (as did McLuhan himself) to mean a massage of information; all media, regardless of content, "massage" us into response. Electronic massages, however, yield a paradoxical effect, which also runs true to the orthodox meaning of the cutism: They relax, act upon, barbituatize.

Theoretically, the global-village effect dovetails with the desire of television's children, conditioned to nonsequentiality, to "want the whole world, and want it NOW." Time is a pain in the ass. So is space. Yet when the global village touches our juniors, they run from it—again into counter culture. The realities of the Other impinge on consciousness, and that's a drag man, y'know? So let's off to places that insulate us from the information flow. McLuhan tries to cover himself here, acknowledging the psychological pressure to flee from the global village as "a self-protective gesture of numbing the extended area, at least as far as direct inspection and awareness are concerned." But, again, how does one reconcile that with the assumed "total involvement" effect of the global village?

3. If depth of awareness was a necessary adjunct to the electronic media, one would suspect that a sub-generation raised under those media would be able to demonstrate that awareness, and in depth. The sad fact, however, is that the TV children who have *not* been immersed in *non*electronic media as a balancing force cannot perceive by any of the five senses save the auditory—which dismisses all mixed media containing the visual (including television and the psychedelic blur of the light show), and, because the audio perceived is usually music without coherently perceivable lyrics, all other audio media that employ language.

4. Consider: Those who are capable of bringing the global electronic village into being are those people who still possess the perceptual and conceptual abilities that the electronic media, tragi-

cally reinforced by our castrating schools, kill off. And these people, as previously suggested, "involved" as they are, are getting on in age, with little succession in sight. 2001, the TV child's film, may have pronounced the coming death of language, but it took men with linguistic abilities to put the film together (more on this later).

So much for some elementary confusions and delusions, which no moments will reverse. It strikes me that there is a basic distinction to be made between the task of combining *sensations*, on the neurological level to which McLuhan restricted media, and the task of combining *images* subject to the judgment of meaning. If we stick wholly with the first task, unconsciously encouraging it through the proliferation of an increasingly totalitarian electronic culture, we create a mindless electronic man, as frightening in the amorphousness of his emotions and the vacancy of his thoughts than even the most calculating of technocrats.

The second task requires the recognition of what we might call the "situation of meaning" in human existence, that confrontation between the perceiver and the world which involves the transfer of information through images, concepts, language. Potential situations of meaning exist at nearly every moment of the individual's psychic life. In the situation, there is an "expressor," a "that which is expressed," and an apprehendor (who may be the expressor himself). Things in the world, whether artifacted or natural, do not possess any significance without a perceiver. In the broadest use of the notion, the situation of meaning comes into existence in the mere act of self-consciousness or in simple perception involving an individual and an object. What is conveyed to the mind in such simple situations, however, is conveyed in image, concept, or word (a successive hierarchy of abstraction from the mere sensory), and until the individual develops mental operations that can transfer and respond to things in the world as expressed objects, he is puzzled and frustrated by turns. So it is with the "what's that?" of children, the question that produces simple image identification by means of language. By being able to recognize the object by image or concept or word, the child has completed the situation of meaning.

If, on the other hand, we conceive of the transfer of information simply in terms of McLuhan's jangling nerve-ends, which media "extend," then we have reverted to an eighteenth-century mechanistic conception of the mind as a bundle of corpuscular vibrations and have precluded the assignment of more complex and profound significances in the world.

If the world were filled merely with simple objects and simple motions, such elementary perceptual statements as "there goes a cow" might be sufficient expressions of information. We would exist on the level of simple sensory intuitions. As a matter of fact, statements that express a combination of perceptions would not exist. Thus, instead of "there goes a cow" we might have "cow go." And if the world of emotive experience were limited and primitive, we would not require any vehicle for its expression beyond the grunts and cries (primal screams, if you wish) that no doubt composed the sum vocabulary of primitive man.

But the world is not so filled, as primitive man himself discovered in eons of watching the successive phenomenon of loud rolls and brief flashes in darkened skies, or after the emotional experience of millennia of tangled loves. And when causalities run deeper than the simple sensory, when the emotive life winds itself into a dynamic sea of conflicting forces, an individual (not to mention a society) who does not have the conceptual and expressive tools to deal with it will be physically disoriented and emotionally frustrated. He will either retreat into a will-less void, avoiding confrontation with sensory experience, or turn to physical anger. Starting to sound familiar? As the group of black artists calling themselves "the last poets" accurately bark in explaining the denomination, "After us, the gun"—a testament of sorts to the staying power of language.

Still preparing for our second turn through TV, two questions arise, not so much in McLuhan's theory but in light of the uses to which it has been put. First, whether it is desirable to express even elementary sensory intuitions, let alone complex thoughts and/or emotions. And second, what forms of media are best able to communicate that expression so as to induce "involvement in depth."

I raise the first question in light of the phenomenon of mindless nillers running for cover under McLuhan. Marsh-Baby is a groovy tool for anyone bent on uttering the Everlasting No, and for projecting around the tasks that offer the possibility for creating a new Yea. It's so easy to say "I don't want to read books" because McLuhan says they are responsible "for all the evils of the past 500 years," or "I don't want to go to movies because they're sequential and hot and therefore I really can't get involved in them." College students in a media course, introduced to McLuhan for the first time, start spouting these sloganistic notions whenever it comes time to go to a movie and talk about it. In so doing they are crucial witnesses to one accuracy of McLuhan's fustings: They *are* children of television, even though they have fallen away from it in adolescence, but fallen away without a differential substitute (the audio media hardly qualify).

When these same children pick up on the parliament of pitchmen and shrill "words are bullshit" (Abbie Hoffman *et al.*) or we're "communicating on non-intellective planes" (Roszak), one can only wonder what information is being transferred, what kind of situation of meaning can possibly exist, and what a "non-intellective plane" is. Even the honorable art of the mime—gesture as language—requires high perceptive and conceptual ability, an operational understanding of the multifarious ways in which the body can and does interpret emotion. In that sense the mime is "intellective." The mime also demands a situation of meaning in which an audience recognizes the significance of the gesture or, in fact, creates that significance in responding to the expression. The communication, then, though wordless, requires an active inner language of the mind.

I choose a high kinetic and nonverbal art (the mime) with great deliberation. For both the counter-cult gravitational fields and the core pitchmen, in their zeal to reject traditional forms of communication simply because they were developed by "non-relevant" and "linear" societies, concentrate against the verbal and for the kinetic. So where is the Marcel Marceau cult? And why is it that such a minuscule number of those who claimed counter-culture sympathies in the Generations survey listed *The Children of Paradise* among the most-favored films? These are facetious and nonsequential questions, one admits.

But the questions indicate that perhaps the most instructive manner in which to enter the labyrinth that produces McLuhan's delusions is by comparing television with other *visual* media in terms of his criteria for "total involvement." Even though print is, technically speaking, a visual medium, I exclude it here, as its sole reliance is on language.

Compare first, the "involvement" necessitated by an object of one of the traditional plastic arts, painting or sculpture. The object stands, cannot be turned off, and by its mere presence demands an active engagement between the perceiver and itself. It demands both wholistic and particular perceptions. It cannot relate to the perceiver in any other way; the perceiver cannot relate to it in any other way. The mind is consciously engaged at all moments—willingly. The distinction between the painting and television, on grounds similar to these, is well noted by former BBC director Jonathan Miller in a *New York Review of Books* article, "TV Guide" (October 7, 1971):

> You can step up to an oil painting and suddenly see the image almost dissolve in the concrete material of which it is made. You can walk up to a painting of Constable's and suddenly the surface of the river and the clouds seems to fly apart and you just see great lumps of oil painting. You can't do this with either a photographic or a television image. You are in the fixed position of viewer. The difference is that the television image or the film image is not an object: it is an imitation of an object. The whole point about painting is that it is an object in its own right which can be taken to be an image of reality as well as an object in its own right, whereas the television image has only one place of existence—as something on a screen. In an art gallery when you, the agent, move your own muscles and come up to the surface of the object, it continues to be Constable, even though the river ceases to be a river and becomes bold streaks of brushwork. But as you advance up to the edge of a television screen, it ceases to be an image but it doesn't become anything else. It simply becomes an electronic cloud with no interest of its own.

The diction of dynamics with which Miller describes the confrontation between perceiver and painting indexes the inherent total involvement that the presumably static image encourages. Television may involve the faculties, but not in depth, and *without volition*. One wills only to turn the set on. After the appearance of the electronic cloud, the will is as naught, and with the will goes the will to perceive, conceive, think, act, and even feel in complexity.

Granted, television declines in importance after childhood (the exception being in blue-collar culture, in which it remains a significant force for parents) and increases again in senescence. That is, at those stages of life during which the individual is either malleable or passive, television is the dominant medium. The coincidence should be rather convincing by now. And when social adolescence arrives, TV recedes *but* is replaced by the psychologically most analogous media factor, the audio.

Another mode of understanding the comparative relations of the perceiver to television, on the one hand, and to a static visual object, on the other, is afforded us by McLuhan's mytho-historical media theory as advanced in *The Gutenberg Galaxy*. His Eden is wholly aural (not visual) and hence "tribal," for the spoken word requires a listener, so social organization is a necessity, an immediate and tactile necessity. The Fall arrives with the shift to the dominance of the visual, first encouraged by the recording of experience in primitive art, and later in the encoding of experience by primitive written language. The visual, McLuhan explains, thus allows for social fragmentation, i.e., the individual can communicate without the active presence of another. What happens once this unfortunate Fall has been pronounced, however, is that McLuhan shifts his attention wholly to print and attaches to it all the venalities of modern civilization. He conveniently forgets the other forms of visual communication. The necessitarianism sweeps aside that to which neither evil nor glory can be attached.

Still, these visual media are assumed to hinder involvement in depth, whereas the electronic media of our time work back toward that involvement, hence toward Eden and "retribalization." But now, as we ponder once again that phrase "involvement in depth," we become firmly convinced that McLuhan could not have intended the phrase to apply to perceptual or cognitive or emotive involvement—at least not by virtue of those media that he feels work against that depth. For it is precisely in the media he rejects that the *possibilities* of perceptual, cognitive, and emotive involvement are the highest. Not the life of mere sensations dangling from nerve-ends, but the life of sensory *experience*. Consider a Brueghel, a Dürer, a Goya etching, a Turner, a de Chirico

—the medium itself (as Miller emphasized), let alone the content, invites the will to involve the faculties.*

That last clause raises a most relevant McLuhan conundrum—that contained in the collapsing of form and content in the maxim, "the medium is the message." McLuhan himself, chastised thoroughly for that slice of nondiscrimination, later repented and allowed that individual styles within general media categories may be more perceptually engaging than others. In his introduction to the second edition of *Understanding Media,* he grants that some "hot" media may, in fact, be relatively "cool," e.g., "the Bergman and Fellini movies demand far more involvement than do narrative shows." But why, then, if we live in an age of cool media, if we live in what we have unthinkingly accepted as the years of "the video generation," do a majority of our TV children have so much difficulty understanding Bergman or Fellini, for example, and therefore ignore them?

When asked, in the Generations survey, what motion pictures held the most attraction over the past few years, the incidence of Fellini, Bergman, Godard, Antonioni, Truffaut, and so on could not even be traced in the 17–20 age group, appeared slightly in the 21–25 group, and heavily in the 26–32 group. Only heavy moviegoers in the other age groups matched their elder juniors, and these younger film freaks also registered high indices in print media involvement.

Look, for a moment, at a comparative list of films most frequently mentioned as holding personal attraction among the three age groups of the Generations survey, with an additional column for those in the 17–20 age group who indicated heavy multiple-media involvement.

---

* Consider how pernicious the TV influence has become even among those TV children currently posturing involvement with the plastic arts: A former colleague of mine once delivered a talk in New York City to a group of junior and senior art *majors* on some problems in interdisciplinary criticism in the arts. In informal raps before and after the presentation he discovered that not one student in the group had been to an art gallery in New York for at least two years and that no one was even aware of the work of leading contemporary American artists—that is, the names drew complete blanks. One does not major in art because law school admissions committees smile on the choice, or because mother said so. One assumes a degree of commitment—"total involvement," if you will.

17–20 (A)	17–20 (B)
*Romeo and Juliet	The Graduate
*Funny Girl	Midnight Cowboy
*Joe	*Z
*Easy Rider	*Butch Cassidy . . .
*Z	*Women in Love
*M*A*S*H	Dr. Zhivago
2001	*Gimme Shelter
West Side Story	Elvira Madigan
*Butch Cassidy . . .	*Stolen Kisses
Woodstock	*Trash
*Patton	A Man and a Woman
*Goodbye, Columbus	*M*A*S*H
*Love Story	
Dr. Zhivago	
Gone With the Wind	

21–25	26–32
*Butch Cassidy . . .	Blow-Up
If . . .	*Five Easy Pieces
The Graduate	*Stolen Kisses
*Z	The Graduate
*Women in Love	The Battle of Algiers
Charley	†"Bergman—anything!"
*Catch-22	Breathless
*Ryan's Daughter	†"Fellini . . . !"
*Easy Rider	Midnight Cowboy
In the Heat of the Night	*Women in Love
A Man for All Seasons	A Thousand Clowns
Elvira Madigan	Lawrence of Arabia
*Little Big Man	Boys in the Band
A Man and a Woman	"Truffaut . . . !"
Cool Hand Luke	*Investigation of a Citizen . . .
Lawrence of Arabia	*Z

* Also films seen most by respondents during the past year (question A.7; see above, p. 27).

† Bergman's *The Passion of Anna* and *Fellini Satyricon* fell on the list of films seen most frequently during the past year. Still, respondents noted simply the director's name (usually accompanied with some form of enthusiastic exclamation) under "motion pictures most attractive to you personally."

Here we are dealing with the qualitative nature of the visual experience and with the dominant texture of these lists, for they are revealing cultural artifacts. Would not one have to admit that the films on the list of the elder juniors are, in the main, more exacting total media experiences than a majority of films on the other lists? Are they not "cooler" by virtue of the total involvement, perceptual and emotional, demanded of the perceiver? The line dividing form and content in many of them—*Blow-Up*, *Breathless*, just about any Fellini—is purposely ambiguous, or, if one prefers, rather thin. Compared to so many of the hot narratives on the 17–20 (A) list, they are not easy viewing. They are fragmented, cubistic, and passionately enjoin reassembling, imaginative re-creation. Thus their communicative bonds with an audience in a situation of meaning are all the stronger. The mere form of a Bergman, a Fellini, a Godard cries out for soul-energy, will-energy, conceptual energy, perceptual energy—they were created in such a way as to send these invitations. For meaning and significance to exist, the expressor's acts of imaginative creation must be repeated in re-creation by the apprehendor.

This certainly is not the case for the simple hot visual line, any more than it is for an eighteenth-century couplet. Fellini, Godard, Bergman, *et al.* work in a world of visual metaphor, in which the tenor is implicit and left to the perceiver to supply. The conceptual principles for viewing their films, then, are not too different from those involved in reading Yeats or Baudelaire, Melville or Joyce, Grass or Genet.

It is not bewildering, then, to find such films—and by McLuhan's own admission there are sub-forms of a medium that may be semantically, and not merely neurologically, hot and cold —holding greatest attraction in the conceptually and perceptually active print-visual culture as opposed to the strictly audio culture. Indeed, the texture of the 17–20 (B) list is far closer to that of the films held dear by the elder juniors than it is to the dominant woof of the other two lists.

"Depth involvement of our faculties" (McLuhan), then, is not found in youthcult to the degree the hucksters, academic and street, would have us believe. But their success in projecting that image has generated a deceptive bull market for the communications industry, the leisure-time manufacturers, and the ever popular Mad. Ave. The market support level is very thin when we're talking about young people between the ages of seventeen and twenty-five.

It has become a cliché of film criticism, for example, that the current attractions among youthcult are either apocalyptic or images of disenchantment, or both. Thus, we assume, the biz of *2001* and *Easy Rider*. The older they get, though, the more they seem to turn to Godard or Fellini for the apocalypse—not the Godard of *La Chinoise* but of *Weekend*, not the Fellini of *Juliet of the Spirits* but of *8½* and *Satyricon*. The true vision of the Last Judgment (witness the readings of Reubens and Blake) is never simplistic, visually or conceptually. The films the younger generations of youthcult opt for in this genre do not require extensive perceptive ability; those who are accustomed to television's "total configuration" leading to generalized perceptions no doubt are expressing their desire for a simplified, made-easy version even of visionary reality. It fits so nicely into the Cliff-Notes culture.

The standard expiation lies in the shuck that, in opting for *2001* and *Easy Rider*, our TV children are expressing an honorific and viable primitivism. Thus *Zabriskie Point* over *Blow-Up*. If that's the case, why not *Weekend*? Because the visual demands of Godard's social-critical metaphors (beyond the admittedly overplayed death-by-asphalt) are too intense for McLuhan's brood.

Here, for example, is the *East Village Other*'s review of Godard's *Vladimir and Rosa*, an admittedly tedious film—but "cool" media nonetheless—about the Chicago Eight trial. I would raise this review later on in discussing the Cult of Relevancy in the Academy, to demonstrate the degree to which any drive for relevancy is a sham in the face of the blow-out of perception and will which the electronic culture, abetted by the schools, has conceived. To cater to the relevancy cult under circumstances such as that expressed by the review is milking a dying dinosaur. I think the medium *is* the message here, and Marshall McLuhan, who're you kiddin'?:

> I went to see *Vladimir and Rosa*, Godard's new film about the Chicago Conspiracy Trial. I walked out when Kunstler was being put down for being bourgeois for quoting the Bill of Rights. I met Mike and we walked back in when Bobby Seal [*sic*] was being made a hero for demanding his right to self-counsel, as provided in the Bill

of Rights. We walked out soon again and played a little stud upstairs and I won all Mike's bread, not much. We walked back in
and watched and I listened to Mike discussing the film with himself, "Godard's an asshole," "What's all this shit," and "Dumb as a
motherfucker." Then somebody in the film said to bar all contradictions that stop progress, and I said I stopped at a lot of bars. We
walked out and a bum asked us for a dime. Sorry.

"What kind of word is sorry?" says he. O.K., we're proud. So he
put the no-no on us, a malediction that will probably fulfill itself
some misty night when the street lamps are dim. . . . Another
bum offered us a couple of dollars for a cigarette. I hand him one
and told him to keep the bread. He gave it back and took the
money and hollered that he was independent. He was independent.
He took the cigarette and set my hair on fire. Cursed with one
no-no on me and hair ablaze, what more could happen to me? But
at least he was independent, and that's one thing about him and
Jean-Luc Godard you can't say about a lot of other guys. But I've
got Mike's marker for a small amount lost upon the gaming tables,
and we'll see what happens (May 18, 1971).

Now, I showed this piece to a student in a media course and
asked him what he thought of it as a movie review: "Far out!
Fucking Far Out!"—a level of response that the review deserves. I
am sure—simply because one doesn't have to rush too quickly
into the kingdom of shillerdom for cauterized minds to find it—
that someone would try to lay the parable-like brilliance of the
review on us (the writer as Julius Hoffman, one bum as Jerry
Rubin, another as Bobby Seale, etc.), or would screech that the
review is a piece of theater searching for a response to the film.
It's *that* kind of exercise that is most demoralizing, for it has encouraged a generation to ignore even its own, aided and abetted
the long slide into a state of nonbeing.

Thus, too, one is not surprised that McLuhan's brood has difficulty in dealing with the heavily *iconographic* psychedelic poster.
The television does not orient one toward visual detail. The
perception can only be "global"; and it's no accident that the
term is *not* McLuhan's, but Piaget's, describing the general sensory impression as opposed to the differentiated intuitive impression that motions toward the concept. The global perception is
generally dominant through the age of four. But our now *college-
age* children of television who are not oriented to visual detail,

who simultaneously must struggle to articulate and explain visual experience, yet who are attracted to the McLuhan-inspired total-configuration posters, cannot, if asked, really handle the complexity of inner, multiple, and symbolic images in that "psychedelic art" which employs iconography. I am thinking here of some of the more surrealistic pieces of Alan Aldridge (e.g., in the *Beatles Illustrated Lyrics* volumes) or Lee Conklin's dense multiple kinetic symbolism in his collection, *Veeva La Mutation Copulation*. The phenomenon of total bafflement with which both students and others interviewed confronted these works of art is only confounding if one accepts the hype that this is a generation that has been reading *Mad* magazine for a decade and, we suppose, is excited by the densely detailed underground comix by R. Crumb, Gilbert Shelton, and imitators. But when one's perceptions have not been encouraged to advance beyond the "global" stage, it is highly doubtful that the detail is perceived at all, let alone remembered.

The TV eye, too, is unaware of detail on the large motion picture screen, even when it is as blatant as Stanley Kubrick's use of brand names in *2001* (one of the key elements, fittingly enough to the moment, in *Mad*'s satire on the film). After all, in the evaluation of *2001* that so many seem so eager to figure forth, that factor certainly has to be taken into account. A classroom discussion of *2001* in the spring of 1969 bounds from the apes to HAL, missing everything in between as if it were irrelevant. What brand names? Call them back to the voyage to the moon, and the eyes recall only the cinematic tricks, the play with weightlessness, and the "groove" of the docking sequence. One had to force the perceptual memories to recognize that the brands were even in the film, let alone ask the judicial faculties to deal with their significance.

Students writing about films: The most frequent form of paper consists of a summary of principal plot features—period! A college junior, in an open piece (i.e., "Do whatever you wish. . . . Respond! . . . Try to Itch!") on *Knife in the Water*, simply catalogued five episodes of conflict between the two rival principals, the middle-aged, complacent sportswriter and a young, aimless hitchhiker, mentioning the vertex of the triangle, the sportswriter's detached voluptuary of a wife, only in passing, skipping her willing seduction by the young man and her subsequent revelation of that triumph to her husband—and this in a mere plot summary. No description of characters or setting—no evocation of mood. Nothing. Concludes: "They drive happily home."

Or a sophomore writing on *Tell Them Willie Boy Was Here*, providing a detailed account of the major movements of characters in a journalistic who-what-where-when inverse pyramid, fading appropriately into nothingness below the apex, and concluding with a lonely moment of reflection or qualification:

> We greatly pity Willie Boy because he had been forced into a situation which he never wanted part of. The conflict between ancient Indian tradition and the strong white tradition made Willie Boy's attempt at escape seem extremely futile.

The point of citing such examples is to indicate the degree to which the motion picture industry—even the anti-industry—is engaging in an equally futile enterprise if it assumes that the bulk of twenty-year-olds can perceive any more.

A group of us were once convinced that a large part of the explanation for the terminal-patient status of our cities lay in the inability of so many of their inhabitants to perceive the particulars of their own environment. Battered into insensitivity by the obscenities that are urban life, they "feel" and act in the informational vacuum of smog. We felt that if college students in New York City could be offered a humanistically centered approach to the urban environment, concentrating on concrete minute particulars of our twilight lives, perhaps, in a few years, the gamble that the recovery of perception would result in some increase in empathy would pay off. In the course of this approach to the city, students were asked to present a project, in the medium of their choosing, on a single street of their choice, anywhere in New York City. We had read: architects and historians, poets and journalists, city planners and novelists, social critics and dramatists. We had been watchers: graphic arts and films as examples of patterned perceptions, and our own collective venture on a sample neighborhood expedition, perceiving detail and significance, levels of reality.

What happens? Three out of every four projects arrive as formal papers (the exceptions included one team multiple-media project involving three students, two movies, two or three photographic essays with explanatory statements attached), and a significant proportion of these consisted simply of generalized perceptions. What is meant may be illustrated by reference: Our paradigm author referred to groups or categories of buildings and spaces on his chosen street, e.g., playgrounds, housing projects, "small and old one and two story homes," houses with storefronts, "deserted and boarded up buildings." Without once mentioning or attempting to confront a *single* structure, he concluded: "I found specific buildings to be the most important factor in determining my image." What the image turns out to be is a dehumanized set of buildings, dehumanized by categories and the failure to connect spaces with human beings. What is of particular interest to us in light of the perceptual habits of TV's children, though, is that the author *thought* he was describing particulars. What betrays the spirit of a generation is that the generalizing perceptual habits easily transform into youthcult's corollary of Agnew's "seen one slum, you've seen them all."

This transformation, in turn, is aided by the *use* of McLuhan as an expiating guru or, more frequently, as a model. I have indicated some of those uses in the gravitational fields, but those at the core not only are more pronounced but also indicate the ways in which McLuhan can lead deceiving into a counter culture which will not survive, and which will simultaneously deepen the disease it bills itself as resisting. For example, take the guy who says he's headed for Drop City: He doesn't dig this highly specialized society, so he's going to search for wholisms—which means putting his head together in some Nirvanic experience, which, in turn, means doing nothing but worshiping a new, totally configurative Absolute. McLuhan's notion of preliterate retribalization is a convenient cover for him. I'm not too convinced, though, that there are many genuine mystics around; a salient and vivifying feature of the mystical tradition is that there never have been. Yes, with Blake, "Would to God that all the Lord's people were Prophets," but Blake did not mean a society of preliterate retribalized grunters pretending to eternal wisdom and inner vision while children are still being chartered into Saint Paul's cathedral by two's and three's under the perniciously guiding hands of the elder beadles to whom the Drop City man leaves the rest of us. Despite their overblown rhetoric, those in the core of counter cult who are real or imagined children of television have kicked both the idea and the reality of act out of the cosmos. The nonexistence of the will becomes true by ontological argument, and McLuhan becomes its high priest. After all, the guy heading for Drop City thinks he's "totally involved."

McLuhan's analysis has thus become a counter-cult religion; but one must be careful to recognize what delusions one is drinking with the electronic wine. TV's children, though, predominantly nondiscriminating in their perceptions, cannot recognize the delusions; and when they accept the theory as religion, they are setting themselves up for manipulation.

The most accessible examples fall in the realm of counter politics. There is a potential rip-off, for instance, in our attempts to actualize the notion that "the medium is the message." Think of the era of leaflets, pamphlets, broadsides. The very form spells urgency, crisis, paranoia. Pushing information in the streets. The Mimeographed Apocalypse. And coming from a freak, it must be freaky, right? I see a Crazy decked out with an armload of this stuff, and I know that whatever falls to my hand will be radical, if political, and funky, if cultural. There is no doubt that, in this case, the gesture (total: including the outfit) is the message. What the ink says is meaningless. In fact, we've seen the commercial so often that the freak might as well be selling deodorants. But watch the rip-off coming, and it's an old ploy, based on a fundamental question in behavioral inference raised earlier: Pick up the broadside, expecting the crisis number, and find something quite different. From hip capitalism to reactionary rantings to blandness.

The same type of rip-off obtains in Yippie politics (self-hyped as modeled on McLuhan's theories), whose "basic informational statement," as Jerry Rubin gladly admits, "is a blank piece of paper." The politic extends from the mystical medium man's perceptual jumps, jumps which appeal only to those who cannot perceive, who hence can be manipulated into the slogan or the sloganeering act. When McLuhan informs us that the private automobile was responsible for integrating the South and rushes right on to another similar total configuration, one does not have to look hard to find the source of the radical *nonsequitur*. I mean, you really are not required even to intuit what falls between the two prongs of this probe—just DO IT! Would-be politicized counter-culturists in gravitational youthcult respond to that "explanation" of integration with the ejaculation, "Far Out!"—no doubt express-ing a disarmingly accurate judgment. Returning from orbit, Jerry Rubin realizes just where the progeny that cries "Far Out!" was nurtured:

> *We've got to destroy TV.* Carry your TV's in front of CBS and NBC and smash them to bits. TV is chewing gum for the mind. TV turns human beings into spectators and passive receivers.

But then he goes on to indicate another form of manipulation of TV's children:

> Since we were reared on hamburgers and television, we know how important TV is for the pacification of the population. We yippies try to use TV time to shock the sleeping viewers into attention. We are obnoxious on TV, obscene, violent, horrible, contemptible, im-moral [*We Are Everywhere*, 91–92].

Certainly the electronic image of one of the Yippie children manipulated by this theoretical jag into waving a VC flag does "dynamite brain cells" (the phrase is Abbie Hoffman's). But be-cause Yippie-genre politics has unquestionably accepted that basic McLuhan fallacy which collapses form and content, the dynamite works negatively (or positively, if one possesses the ready-made revolutionist's pitch for it, i.e., it is intended to alienate—we don't want any pigs as friends). As Conor Cruise O'Brien wisely re-marked some time ago, in *New American Review #4*:

> We have ourselves made use of dramatic politics, but like our op-ponents, we have not always used it wisely. Burning has always had a dramatic impact, but one should be careful about what one burns. Burning a draft card carries a clear, specific message—recognition of an unjust war—but burning an American flag works on the public mind simply as propaganda in favor of President Johnson ["Politics as Drama as Politics"].

I'm not so much interested in what has undoubtedly become a political cliché by now, but in the fact of manipulation of TV's younger children by those (Rubin, Hoffman & frères) who issued forth from another media culture possessing the language that could formulate responses to the atrocities of the mainstream and thus direct themselves in action, *and* were informed by such McLuhan-inspired notions as (from Hoffman's *Revolution for the Hell of It*):

Fantasy is the only truth [70].

We are living TV ads, movies. Yippie! There is no program. Program would make our movement sterile. We are living contradictions. I cannot really explain it. I do not even understand it myself [84].

. . . a revolutionary artist just does it. . . . The medium is the message and the message was Theater of Cruelty [95].

CHICAGO
Produced by Marshall McLuhan
Directed by Mayor Daley and Antonin Artaud [105]

Abbie doesn't particularly care for slogans, because they contain words, and words are not information:*

America is Racist.
America is Imperialistic.
Police are Brutal.
Mass media distort.
Bah-Bah-Bah-Bah-Bah-Bah-Bah-Bah-Bah
Here we go again. None of these phrases contains information. I never once accused the police of being brutal, for example. That was not my role; there were enough liberals to do that. I applauded the police performance. They were major life-actors, performed brilliantly and never let us get away without a proper cop response. They were pigs through and through [99].

But what he doesn't recognize is that the slogan emerged from the same McLuhan-inspired Yippie mentality. It can only be used in one of those preliterate attempts at total configuration in language. And the slogan manipulates by blinding perception, a notion I think we've covered thoroughly.

More significantly, those who are drifting into the counter-*culture* gravitational field, being pulled imperceptibly, and by degrees, toward the core, are being prodded along by McLuhan's

* Both Abbie and Jerry, however, frequently translate their political theater into words, indicating that raw Doing It, without the ability to discriminate born of language, is not pure information.

religionized analyses, and prodded into deception. They may be attracted, for example, to the idea that, since the computer promises universal understanding, we might as well jump ahead to the logical extension of that notion and, in McLuhan's terms, "bypass language in favor of a general cosmic consciousness." Computers, after all, embody tribal calculation methods, i.e., the binary system. The speeds of space travel "abolish time and space and return man to an integral in primitive awareness," so why not climb on that invitation to the Nirvanic Absolutes, an invitation now mythologized by Stanley Kubrick?

What the potential counter-culturalist misses in his infatuation with these notions is that perhaps unintentional out-take from *2001*: The more the electronic media, the less the language, and, more significantly, the shorter and more superficial the range of the emotions. HAL, after all, possesses a greater emotional range and intensity than any of the plastic humanoid children of McLuhan on that trip. As Kubrick himself said, "I think clearly that there's a basic problem with people who are not paying attention with their eyes. . . . Those who won't believe their eyes won't be able to appreciate this film." Admirers of *2001* cite Blake's aphorism, "If the doors of perception were cleansed, everything would appear to man as it is, infinite," but they conveniently overlook Blake's equal insistence that one creates and thus communicates vision with the *hand* as well as the eye, and that he himself did both simultaneously. Obviously, Blake did not possess the medium available to Kubrick, and yet Kubrick never could have fashioned *2001* without language, without a mastery of conceptions. The mindless, passive responses of "WOW!" issuing from TV's children indicate the degree to which an elite in control of the tools (like Kubrick's own apes) will be able to manipulate masses.

Thus the potential counter-culturist is not very careful about who will be running that computer in the background hum, about who is encoding the knowledge for the new electronic globe, plugging us all into the value system of the month. He may even be as casual as McLuhan himself about wars, explaining them away as media extensions to be solved by other media extensions. The global village operatives will be those in possession of the knowledge of *how* to encode and, like Bucky Fuller's analogous advanced design science team, are going to keep that knowledge, hence power, rather secluded. Meanwhile, those who are embracing McLuhan's determinism are sloping off to Drop City to be reborn in the tribe, so no one will be left to challenge the information-possessors. And may we not expect the encoders to groom their inheritors very carefully? Marvelous Marsh has occasionally been called a fascist, and, as much as I hate to rely on the authenticity of an overworked entry in the politicized counter-cult dictionary, that is precisely the politic of the vision he presents us with.

Those who have been prepared for counter cult by both television and our schools (when the TV child walks through that classroom door, the worst aspects of the passivity-inducing electronic world are only reinforced by the rigidity of the linear world) are today drifting slowly to actualize that vision. If my own expiation of youthcult sins, present and projected, lies anywhere, it is in that combination of electronic media and the schools. Before the worms applaud, though, those who have been prepared to march out ought to consider just where our current counter-cult offerings will lead them, and how, if possible, one might salvage that which is of value in the Alternatives. In the process, reflect on the very act of reading, that language and print, in their accessibility and comparative freedom from the restraints of authority, remain the bulwark against the totalitarianism both McLuhan and counter cult, intentionally or not, promise us.

The Contradictions of
Counter Culture

8

Starting All Over in America:
Some Clippings from the Ideology of
Counter Cult and Its Contradictions

Having hectored—pardons—the reader into granting a measure of
acceptance to a somewhat Byzantine analysis of the roster of who's
what in youthcult and why, and having offered the rudiments of
an expiation of my own, I enter the arena in which prophecy and
behavior, phenomenology and synergies do intractable battle.

At issue is counter culture itself, its possibilities, its contradictions. It exists—in a variety of manifestations—and is growing, and
I wish to indicate, more by a collagic juxtaposition than by
weighty exegesis, the nature and effects of its expansion in light
of the spiritual constellation of those who are most likely to become its active inherents. More definitively, I wish to indicate the
divergence between the direction those who are either consciously
attracted to or unconsciously slipping toward counter cult think
they are taking, and the directions they are, in fact, taking. The
indication divides again, and circles back on itself as the theoretical and historical propositions merge: Given any counter-cult
Way, the nature and effect come to rest on the identity of the
practitioners.

Well, not *any* counter-cult Way, for the nature of those Ways that cater to the new Nirvanic drives toward old Absolutes are less likely to be subject to the possibilitarian thesis. The transcendental cults are not likely to undergo transformation by virtue of the mere identity of those who endorse their souls for deposit only in the drug and/or mystic banks. Generally, too, those who are strung out in these solipsistic worlds of oblivion are subject to cultural analysis only in the sense that they are removing themselves from all culture. This removal, one must qualify, is not applicable to Transcendental Meditation, for example, which has moved decidedly beyond the bounds of youthcult. In attendance at the Maharishi Mahesh Yogi's teacher-training course held at U-Mass-Amherst in July, 1971, were the commandant of the Army War College, college deans and presidents, superintendents of schools, brokerage house partners, and Bucky Fuller. The Maharishi does reinforce very straight middle American values and borders on the tractarian in proselytizing for the active and against the lethargic life-style. As the Maharishi's notion of activity includes business and creation, the more politicized elements of counter-cult welfare denigrate him as a counterrevolutionist. Little do these same galley slaves to slogans sense that so many other counter-cult Ways look to the same reassertion of the values of our great grandparents.

Lest we devolve an encyclopedic and ultimately boring survey, however, we are charged to concentrate on those groups of catalogue offerings which (1) potentially offer the largest draw, (2) seem to be drawing at an ever increasing rate, (3) offer counter cult the most embracing possibilities for realizing its inchoate ideology, and (4) *may* not, in realizing themselves, simultaneously wreak indirect suffocation on those irrevocably jammed in another order.

The primary order of business is to break through the multifold contradictions between the ideology and practice of counter cult. That task involves subjecting the practice to ideological judgment, a subjection warranted both in terms of its deep structures and by the implications of the increasing dispersal into counter cult. As we said early on, counter culture divides: Con I and the Otherworldly. The former tends to libertarian anarchism, the latter to an authority-centered politic. Both, however, drive toward Absolutes and simplicities, and, in practice, provide havens for either the will-less or the nillers. Since gravitational youthcult is brimful with those who, through no extensive fault of their own, can handle no more than simplistic forms of perception and cognition and who seem singularly devoid of will-energy, the counter-culture Ways, as practiced, have potential appeal as the only reinforcing set of refuges. Nothing to do in here—nothing to do out there; but at least out there I am not responsible to those I don't like. Each of the Ways, then, invites the complacency (call it inner peace or contentment if you wish) that comes with renouncing either the will or the necessity of perceiving the Other in the complexities of his Being, or both.

It doesn't have to be this way, really, and that's the object. It is possible to be committed to Alternatives in such a way that they, the individual, and those in the larger society who cannot afford the luxury of so many of the Alternatives will all survive. Of course, one would prefer a gravitational pull into legal, medical, consumer-advocate collectives, operating where they are needed and not in narcissistic paradises. But that draw doesn't seem too likely unless our notion of school and university undergoes a radical transformation (a proposition to be advanced in the last section of this collage) and unless we turn off the TV until a kid is six and the rock-drug scene until he is twenty or so (neither of which options is either possible or wholly sensible).

In order to convince that the Alternatives can make it, one must utilize a pedagogic method too many find repugnant, but which is essential in these years of apocalyptic prophecies, escalating apologetics, non-negotiable either/ors, and other explorations on the boundaries of paroxysmic urgency. Overkill is necessary to conceive candor, is necessary in the face of a pervasive naïve faith in a demoralizing myth. One does not practice the pedagogy of insult on a ten-year-old; but when the kid is twenty and the behavioral patterns are those of a self-indulgent, narcoleptic asshole, one does—*particularly* when both the profession and the spirit configure as they did in response to the formal survey, as well as in a hundred daily encounters. Soft, bland liberalese never made an impression on counterproductive counter-*politics* people, and it makes less sense to those at the core of counter culture. The very diction of abstract liberalese is both vulnerable and re-

assuring. The rhetoric of apologism has performed its tragic surgery likewise.

In culture as in politics, it is possible to strike a position that is
simultaneously more than sympathetic with youthcult spirit *and*
repudiative of the self-righteous, self-delusive bullshit that so often
accompanies it. Since it's the delusions that are strangling (and
no other word but one drawn from the diction of homicide will
do) the spirit, the rejection must be phrased in the strongest language the audience will understand, and from the point of view of
that audience's own professed values. Young people innately sense
what crap lies behind the myth-hype. You've just got to wear that
knowledge as a campaign button, 'cause every year will be an
issue year for a while.

Why have we been so concerned and forbearant with counter
cult? In part, one suspects, because American democracy passes
through periods of boredom, the corporate state presenting all the
mediocrity it grinds out in the guise of diversity in the same manner as the totalitarian state presents mediocrity almost by definition. So we look for what seems to be eccentric to save our tired
souls, express our longing for excitement, and employ both economic and intellectual resources in less dulling directions than
those to which they have been accustomed. The form doesn't
really change—only the content. Besides, it keeps the media filled
and the academic pundits, this writer not excepted, busy.

And pay more attention to it, still, for, like Blake's Tree of
Mystery, the media hype and the academic concern feed on their
own sap. What was once a small movement now casts a large
shade. A set of concentric circles of sympathy has developed, and
one can now overlap the circles as he wishes. We created reality
by presenting a vision of it that did not exist, enticing others to
bring it into existence, to live high off it for a while as we moved
on to another vision, another soon-to-be-reality. It's all very creative, and very much in the spirit of Con I culture capitalism:
planned obsolescence of Alternatives. Made easier, too, by mainstream television conditioning, so that realities may be created
and dropped at the whim of the executive board room or a weekly
Nielsen. The audience has grown into a life-rhythm with that
electronic logic, fragmented (not, as McLuhan poses, wholistic),

and without even the subliminal consistency of dream-image patterns. Thus the inevitable ephemerality of the Alternatives.

Keep in mind, then, as we ride the counter-cult circuit, that today's catalogue listing may become tomorrow's crumpled page. The electronic media do communicate more information at higher speeds than that creaky Gutenberg press. But though the electronic media themselves may date the surfaces, the deep structures are not about to change that swiftly.

The deep structures have to be distinguished by ideology and practice, theoretical behavior versus synergies. Ideologically, for example—and shades of Paul Goodman here—there appears to be a gestalt drive toward a wholism that obliterates the self, almost as a form of psychotherapy. No objections from the behavior of the Otherworldly Division: From hallucinogenics to Krishna Consciousness, the self is naught. And yet, how curious for a theoretically libertarian culture. Thus the theory often collapses, indeed, in the face of behavior in the Con I division. Communards quickly discover the hassles of dealing with the Other in compressed space and move, as we shall see, into more self-isolating nomadic ways, as if the logic of decentralization had a built in *reductio* that only ends with the anarchy of the self. The primitive capitalism born of this simultaneous and opposing move into decentralization often blisters in a social Darwinism that would cheer the dry bones of the most conspicuous Neanderthals.

Indeed, some of the new Neanderthals are bound to be superseded by others, and the losers will be TV's children, who have indeed obliterated sense of self if only because the perception of all else has been expunged. The consequences are revealed in expression: "Doing my thing" is as vague and inhibiting a notion of self as perceiving the Other in terms of "vibrations." The consequences lead to the musings of an attendant at the ALLOY counter-cult convention held in New Mexico in the spring of 1968 as quoted in *Domebook 2*: "The presence of the world is in us all the time. You don't need television or newspapers to know about the war. You can feel it." So a double-inversion: from annihilation of self, driving into counter cult, where self is reborn in its isolationist intensity, only to be obliterated again.

But grant the new sense of wholism. The thrust is away from

the mass and back toward the manageable; away from the impersonal and back toward the individual, acting alone or in small groups; away from the corporation and back toward small business; away from government by remote control and back to the town meeting, the ultimate participatory democracy trip; away from the city and toward the village. It *is* a *radical* critique of the highly organized society. It moves toward a sense of the whole self in a decentralized culture. In theory, and in the process, the self maintains its previous left-liberal politic, at least in terms of its attitude toward racism, imperialism, poverty, etc.

This fusion of the liberal and the libertarian conservative is more inevitable than revolutionary in our time. That the elder juniors are less deluded about what's happening here can be easily perceived in the fact that nearly 20 per cent of them (the second largest block) classified their own politics in terms of some combination of liberal and libertarian-conservative (see Appendix, A.24). Among the other two sub-generations, the percentage was smaller, but nearly all of those who claimed a combination, for example, of anarchist and libertarian-conservative or liberal-libertarian and conservative-radical were (1) counter-culture-oriented, (2) highly involved in all media, and (3) comparatively well informed in both mainstream and counter-culture spheres.

Grant, too (a significant aside in light of the youthcult bookshelf), the quarter from which this combination has been so heavily verbalized, in a wise fetish, for more than a decade now:

> Mailer was a Left Conservative. So he had his own point of view. To himself he would suggest that he tried to think in the style of Marx in order to attain certain values suggested by Edmund Burke. Since he was a conservative, he would begin at the root. . . .
>
> Since he was also a *Left* Conservative, he believed that radical measures were sometimes necessary to save the root. [*Armies of the Night*, 208–9.]

Or, less metaphysically, in a 1969 mayoral campaign speech to a class at the John Jay College of Criminal Justice (read: New York City Police Academy):

> I, as a man on the left, I'm talking across the board to conservatives and saying that after all these years of thinking about political problems I've come to one conclusion, which is that you conservatives

are right about one terribly important matter: that a man has to have control over his own life. He has to be able to shape his own life. He has to be able to work with his own future, and he has to know the immediate result of his work.

While doing away with remote control and centralization, and moving toward individual agency under which a man comes to know himself only when *he* acts, the mixed ideology that has come to underlie counter cult (Mailer being its first, most articulate, and most present spokesman) also holds that the problems of poverty and injustice must be solved first but, again, with primary reliance on the agency of the poor themselves, not on the distant dictatorship of the superagency liberals.

Two observations on counter-cult structure arise: If Mailer himself has become the last conservative left in America (the pun is wholly intentional), counter cult, too, in practice leans more heavily on the conservative than on the left. But there's a significant distinction: Mailer's conservatism drives toward Absolutes at the root, is entitative, and drives for them through and for the sake of the conscious existential act; whereas counter cult floats mindlessly to "transcendent" Absolutes, half so by abdication of both consciousness and will. And while the entitative never loses concrete contact with the individual, the pseudo-transcendent so often does at those very moments when it is exalting his sanctity. Following, too, is the distinction between the man whose combination of left sentiments and conservative philosophy fifes the moral necessity of memory and the culture that not only wishes for past structures without recognizing what those structures signified in history but hopes, too, to live wholly in an amorphous present that creates no structures for future memory. So it is not surprising to find counter-cult conservatism, in practice, so often tending to formless individualistic nihilism rather than Paul Goodman's vision of creative anarchism. As we'll be noting as we ponderate through the rarified centers of counter-cult offerings, the new nomads harrow and plant yet are reprobate, so their ideals defy them and grow down: The roots, the scraggly, grasping forms, stick up out of the earth.

Still, on the ideological table the fusion of right and new left, a long overdue development, has remained a comparatively unexamined cliché. We've left the thought standing, with hollow noddings, that if one scuds far enough to the left, dissolves the state, and lives in a thousand scattered self-subsisting communes, he will be hard pressing on the right. Occasionally, and in the sphere of counter *politics*, the analysis reverses the ideological roles, e.g., Lowell Ponte on the platform for a fourth party in the *Los Angeles Free Press* (August 6, 1971):

> Since my goal is to win sympathy and action from many sectors of this strange society, I categorically reject the use of the label "Leftist" for this party. Its emotional charge will add little support for any radical party, but it could alienate many potential adherents. Moreover, the term is misleading since Jefferson and other American Revolutionaries were "Leftists"; here, knowing it or not, Rightists articulate outdated Leftist traditions, but they respond emotionally to the same decentralist individualist critique that today's Left-anarchists claim as their own. The common root must be used to unify radicals, Right and Left. Our goal is to drag the obsolete Right and Left both, kicking and screaming, into the 21st century. To do that we need to drop our old semantic hangups.

Regardless of the direction of interchangeability of labels (that is, it's probably more accurate to say that Jefferson was a radical libertarian, a "Rightist"), it happens that there's nothing very "leftist" at all issuing from the platform that Ponte presents, e.g., we allow people not merely to vote *for* a candidate, but *against* the whole government; we permit the individual to specify where he wishes his taxes to go; we assign citizens (a touch of the left there) at random to perform tasks currently performed by name-less government personnel (such as turning the key on a jail in-mate just sentenced to twenty years, seizing a home for unpaid taxes, etc.). The object of all of these being to return the individual to fleshly contact with the operations of social structures which he takes for granted. In fact, there's more of an existential edge to such acts and their object (Mailer comes to mind too easily, here) than there is of what Ponte acknowledges to be the obtrusive labels of ideology.

One suspects that it is precisely because counter politics has paid only lip-service to the right-left analysis, has brushed it aside as a plausible philosophical whimsy, that counter-culturalists pos-ing as ideologues (as they do in the reflex of ignorance) fail to perceive the deep political implications of the actual forms the

Alternatives have taken. Even Mitchell Goodman is tragically guilty of this oversight in his introduction to *The Movement Toward a New America* (an indispensable and encyclopedic collage of clippings down the many metal Ages through which the conglomerate Movement has passed in its young but jaded years):

> The Movement is the act of *getting ourselves together.* Clarity. Coherence. Community. It is also a vision.
>
> I see the Movement, then, as primitive culture. . . . The Movement is anarchist in its deepest impulses: it is decentralization that leads back to community and wholeness and away from the atomized non-community of men helpless in the machinery of the centralized state. It is primitive at least in the sense that it involves a return to sensation, to the living body and its senses, its capacity for feeling and imagining the life in others—that state in which a man knows again "at first hand, through his own energies, the possibilities of life"* [vi].

No doubt, as Goodman rhapsodizes, "something is happening," and no doubt "it will take a long time." For that "decentralization that leads back to community and wholeness" only works when its agents are those who understand fully what "community" means, and whose primary allegiances are toward the community (the "left" side of the analysis), and only secondarily to "putting my head together" or "doing my thing" (the "right" quarter). But it is trenchantly the reverse order of allegiances that is most dominant in counter cult.

It is veritably because the masses of those now prepared for counter cult or actually sweeping in are incapable of "feeling and imagining the life in others" (Goodman) beyond the dull trap phrasings of the hip dictionary that the reality of new *community*

---

* Toward the ideal of returning man to sensation, Goodman sees the poet William Carlos Williams as "a prophetic precursor of the Movement." Most students I have worked with couldn't read Williams, and when, in a discussion, Goodman's proposition was tossed out for consideration, it met with very blank and incredulous stares. In fact, a couple of self-avowed radicals started harping on the very idea that "a guy who is into the language bag" can be Movement. We looked at "Yachts" for a statement of revolutionary anger— "Yachts," that horrific vision of the cruelties of raw Con I survival struggles, with the robber barons knifing through waves of proletarian bodies. I didn't suggest the Movement reading, and they didn't find it: sophomores and juniors in college blandly assenting that this was a poem about man's struggle against nature, with man triumphant. Some revolutionary statement! Mitch, friend, you are of a different generation.

is trampled. As John Sinclair of the White Panthers (footnoted earlier as a victim of mainstream paranoia) wrote in *Leviathan* (February, 1970):

> This ponk [*sic*] in EVO talked about Woodstock being like a hip concentration camp, or said something about he could dig it if there was a groovy camp like that where they would all do their own things and not have to bother with the awful nasty stuff in the world. No wonder the blacks have no respect for those creeps. But it is our job to educate the people, and it has to be done or we might as well forget the whole thing as far as I'm concerned. Because I don't want any part of a Nation of imbeciles who sit around and shoot speed and listen to bogus records, and all. I've had enough of that forever. And the other ones, the "politicals," are just as bad, too, and their culture is bogus as well. The records they listen to are even worse.

So John is doubly rewarded and told where it's at when the MC 5, the politirock group long associated with the White Panthers, splits from all politics into the growing world of "creeps," announcing in the resurrected rock journal *Crawdaddy* (June 6, 1971) that "we don't want to be identified with any political philosophy or dogma; anyone who says he has all the answers is either a liar or a fool."

Reinforcing Sinclair's analysis is Kenneth Keniston who, in one of his appendixes to *Young Radicals* (p. 341), notes that "most activists seem . . . to possess an optimism, faith in human nature, belief in the efficacy of human action, and a capacity of co-operative endeavors that few alienated students manifest." So the alienated counter-culturalists have now adopted the Reichian optimism that displaces "getting ourselves together" with "doing my thing," "straightening out my head." In fact, counter cult has found ways to establish community that only encourage transcience and superficial relationships, precluding "co-operative endeavours"—this despite all the rhetoric of community and commitment. The "coherence" of Mitch Goodman's formula is likewise undercut by the anarchism of the self that reigns in so many counter-cult Ways. The decentralization has thus led away from one atomism toward another. And in an information-stocked electronic global village, atomism is but reinforced by a primitivism that exalts only the sheerness of sensation. The ever-flung analogy between the new "tribes" and primitive societies is decidedly an unconscious pandering to fantasts. If primitive man could know his own energies and the possibilities of his life, that was partly because he was informationally isolated. The attempt at self-imposed information isolation by the children of technocracy is nearly impossible, for they bring with them to the social retreat the subterranean assumptions of the mainstream, which, however they may struggle, are too embedded to exorcise wholly.

Thus as we leaf through counter-cult offerings and behavioral patterns, do not be surprised to discover cameos of consumerism, suburbanism, primitive capitalism, elitism, and the subtle repetitions in the counter of the oppressions of the mainstream. Theoretically, we are starting all over again in America, without the corporatists, without the bureaucrats. That bodes promise. But behaviorally counter cult offers a nihilism so intense that creative reconstruction will be impossible. What that means to the rest of us may have been well summarized by Mailer when he wrote, in *Armies*, that "nothing was worse than a nihilism which failed to succeed—for totalitarianism would then be accelerated." I indeed hope that the accuracy of that prophecy—for prophecy it is—will be adequately demonstrated in the following chapters. Only one whose journeyman's papers have been stamped and colored myopic will be required to listen very hard.

But before we enter the existing behavioral patterns at the core of counter culture, the notion most critical to the prophecy has to be illustrated: the characteristics of those who are now potential practitioners of counter-culture Ways, those who will be drifting in from the gravitational fields, slowly and inexorably. For this we return to our sub-generations and, from the survey, a roster of candidates for counter cult, distinguishing between those who can forge surviving Alternatives and those for whom commitment itself will be a whim.

Start with a single archetypal profile from the latter group, a nineteen-year-old sophomore at Douglas College. Media as one might expect: high audio, minimal visual, moderate print (concentrated on the underground press, emphasis on *Rolling Stone, East Village Other, Los Angeles Free Press*). Currently into a small commune and multiple drug use. Information is a complete blank. Could not even identify the rock musicians. Counter-cult vocabulary only average. No political activity whatsoever, not even ecological boycotts. Calls herself a liberal and identifies with the Democratic Party and the Yippies, those eternal antagonists of Grant Park. High attitude ratings to Earth Day, the Hare Krishna People, Billy Graham, a volunteer army, *Easy Rider*, *Siddhartha*, and (gasp!) Al Lowenstein. With the exception of the Lowenstein rating, the signs are almost too strong for the case. A timid gesture toward a counter-cult Way accompanied by a totally configured blank mind, and an energy rating of one on the Richter scale.

Better: a seventeen-year-old Vanderbilt freshman, presenting a similar caricature but without the underground press or a dot of counter-cult activity, adds, on the issue of most appealing records, "James Taylor expresses what a lot of us feel." For some, no doubt, the attraction of the quiet, homespun Menemsha Pond fog Taylors after years of rock anger is a measure of political exhaustion. But "political exhaustion" is tragically evasive jargon when applied to the vast numbers of suspended future applicants to the Ways. Indeed, in the profile before us, what fire and rain there was must have been wholly imagined. For here the will-energy rating is zero, and the prospects for being drawn in the direction of one's sympathies, passively giving up the ghost of whatever substance of one's life remains, are closer to the model.

The 17–20 age group produced dozens of similar profiles. I admit that flesh does not pulse on the bones of data, but consider: When the flesh that has actually incarnated in counter cult reveals the same bones underneath, the assumption that other manikins will follow is not wholly unreasonable. This plastic entourage pours libations to neither counter politics nor mainstream culture, rather it drinks the genteel wines of the culture of Drop City. For them the counter-cult Ways are conveniently fluid, for unless the individual asserts control over his chosen refuge, it will simply and quietly reinforce his proclivities for wordless passivity. With that option lying around and being hyped heavily, the flow from gravitational field to core will increase: Dig! We've got a trip where you won't have to say much or do much, and yet you'll be taken care of.

It is of these that Peter Marin has written ("Children of the Apocalypse," *Saturday Review*, September 19, 1970):

Theirs is a condition of the soul that marks the dead end of the
beginnings of America—a dreadful anomy in which one loses all
access to others and the self: a liberation that is simultaneously the
most voluptuous kind of freedom and an awful form of terror.

Terror lies in freedom only when one does not wish to accept his
freedom. Freedom places a categorical imperative on perceiving
the self and the Other, and acting to construct a social world in
which the self survives, identifying one's self to oneself through
the act. If the act is essentially that of nilling—i.e., willing not to
do, or willing not to will—then the self is never identified, and the
social spaces through which it passes lose whatever force they
might have possessed through the solemn apparatus of nothingness. As one of the elder juniors interviewed for the survey remarked:

> It wouldn't be so terrible if people knew how to engage themselves,
> really engage themselves, in what they were into. People say they're
> into this or that, but they're dabblers—even in the matter of self-
> knowledge—and are into emptiness. . . . If you said you were into
> some alternative culture project and were, in fact, into it, then you
> would be taking your freedom for a reason, and for that, too, you
> have to take it from something and from some standard, and the
> problem is that we've kicked relativism around so much that nobody
> has any basis to judge himself any more. To be into *anything*—
> films, communal farming—whatever it is, requires certain standards.
> Doing something—just decently, just decently!

Otherwise, whatever value the Alternative possesses will never be
realized. The kid who is doing nothing today but sitting in strung-
out college cafeterias, sliding some hollow motions, and talking in
hip dictionary of paradisaical farmettes will tomorrow hie to the
greenfields themselves and simply continue the same pattern of
nonbehavior. In the former existence, he might say he's into
macrobiotics—which is doing nothing; in the latter, he might lie
at a commune wandering the woods for six months, painting part
of the side of a barn once. No matter how much he says he's into
communal living, he is, in fact, into nothing. If the new nihilism
commences with the proposition that nothing is communicable,
it surges into a Götterdämmerung in which nothing exists but a
phlegm of catatonia.

In *Do It!*, Jerry Rubin fantasizes:

> Kids who grew up in the post-1950's live in a world of supermarkets,
> color TV commercials, guerrilla war, international media, psyche-
> delics, rock 'n' roll and moon walks. For us *nothing is impossible*.
> *We* can do *anything* [90–91].

Back on the planet, note that what Rubin cites has been done *to*
(whether done for or against) them. What is being done *by*
them is easy, demands little expenditure of will, cognition or
emotion. In other words, what's being done by them is not really
doing anything. Rubin is correct only in the sense that a sub-
generation has been set up for noncommitment. The logical
migration into counter cult follows.

By contrast, if intellectualism had dried the elder juniors in the
late 1950's and early 1960's, and if a movement toward new forms
of perception, feeling, and activism developed, only those who
came to that movement and propelled it with their own conceptual equipment knew what it was about, could handle it and
survive. These wished for a life of perception, feeling, and activism because they knew—existentially, if you will—what a lack of
them meant. Those who arrived later, out of Rubin's acknowl-
edged conditioning forces, are really uncommitted and remain
passive players. They might express a willingness to act, or at least
the assumption on which that willingness rests—the conviction
that the order can be changed by action—but what is ultimately
expressed in behavior is the nihilism of purposeful destructive
ignorance or self-enforced lethargy.

So, in contrast, consider the survey response of a twenty-four-
year-old woman in junior standing at the Columbia School of
General Studies. Look carefully at this woman, for she is capable
of fulfilling the visions, and without the hysterical overinflation of
reality that normally accompanies the necromancers of counter
cult. She touches all the major underpinnings of counter-cult
ideology and, in fact, has already imbibed a number of its manifestations:

> Macrobiotics: was one for 10 months and gained 15 lbs.
> Communal Living: I love my privacy (& need it)

Yoga: Yes—Hatha (the physical, not meditation)

Astrology etc.: Bullshit—an easy way to categorize and negate the individual

Eastern Mysticisms: a Bahai drop-out—too unrealistic & foreign to my background & experience

Western Religious Revivals . . . . : just old time religion, i.e. the Bible & Episcopalian Book of Common Prayer

Counter cult cannot have dreamers in the woods if it wants to survive. This is no dreamer. This is also a paragon of a thorough libertarian, nonetheless oriented toward the social order.

The media involvement is universally heavy, with the expected exception of television. The responses to the audio media questions, in particular, demonstrated the discriminating perception that must accompany anyone embarking on an Alternative course with any realistic intentions of reaching port. Influential albums listed: the Beatles' *Revolver*, Jimi Hendrix's *Are You Experienced?*, the Airplane's *Surrealistic Pillow*, Dylan's *Nashville Skyline*, the Who's *Tommy*. You and I might add two or three more, but believe me, this was one of the few answers indicating that the respondent truly understood the question. Lists, too, all those "plus Jon McLaughlin and all vintage Dylan" as personally appealing. Sixteen films for the past year, including *Z, The Damned, Butch Cassidy, Camille, Anna Karenina, Ivan the Terrible, The Virgin Spring, Viridiana, Repulsion, Le Chien Andalou,* and *Woodstock.* Most appealing films: *Ivan the Terrible,* "Anything by Bergman or by Cocteau," *Butch Cassidy and the Sundance Kid, Z.* The list is from a film generation.

The politics. Protest takes the form of boycotts: grapes, phosphates, a local eating chain, and "Revlon makeup (did you ever hear Revlon talk about women?)." Lists Libertarian Conservative politics, voted for Charlie Goodell on the last occasion, and sympathizes only with Nader's Raiders. Had gone through Pentagon in 1967, Woodstock, and the 1969 Moratoriums, but no demonstrations since. Attitude section presents a moderately "radical" perspective, with 5's for GI coffeehouses, Jane Fonda, Sierra Club, small business, Allard Lowenstein, black capitalism ("why not?"), Grad ed, Mick Jaggar, sensitivity training ("it shouldn't be necessary, but I'm afraid it is"). On the last parenthetical remark, the respondent had previously noted: "I don't believe in the power of the group, only of the individual," a not wholly unexpected statement from someone who knows what counter cult is really about. To continue the strain, zero attitude ratings are granted to the 1970 Elections, Billy Graham, NOW, John Mitchell, Agnew's criticism of media ("Nonsense—true example of political paranoia"), Bob Hope, Bernardine Dohrn, urban public housing (perhaps an aesthetic sense operating there), integration by busing, open enrollment, Cuba ("Havana used to be a great town"), methadone maintainence ("just another drug"), *Love Story* ("How can he go from *Yellow Submarine* to that?"), and Tim Leary (although last year, she adds, he warrented a 4).

Other attitude notations of interest: Bill Buckley receives a 4 as "the last living example of rhetorician—forget his head!"; the Stock Exchange a 3 as "it's necessary—I like capitalism, too"; Andy Warhol a 4 ("he has some problems but I'm afraid he's right on top of it"); the NLF a 1 as "nobody has been able to give me unbiased information"; Billy Graham a 2 ("like him better if he stayed away from Nixon"); *Easy Rider* a 3 ("very romantic"); *Siddhartha* a 3 ("also very romantic"); and Earth Day a 0 ("it won't work until someone gets Con Edison under control"). The volunteer army issue was left "undecided—haven't thought about the implications seriously enough."

The politics falls into place when the question on participation in experimental education enters. The respondent had attended both the original Free University of New York in 1967, and the New School ("if you want to consider that"). She continues: "Both experiences were highly profitable & stimulating but no credit was earned so I guess they're only important to me"—a line to remember in contrast to our new unwilling stepchildren of the Academy who demand credit for stargazing.

The recitation continues. Totally into the booze-pot trip. A Janis image. Drinks a sixpack, a quart of wine, and a pint or more of bourbon a week. Occasional grass and meth. Tried coke and opium but found both boring. One mescaline trip "with intention to do more" and about a dozen earlier acid trips, "but now it's just too intense—it's been a year & a half since the last."

Information was moderate on mainstream and high on counter culture; and the counter-culture vocabulary list, along with other items, proves that it's still possible to perceive and verbalize if there's a will lying around to do so:

rip-off: robbery or a very high-priced item that isn't worth it
fascist: advocate of totalitarian rightist politics
cool: something that everyone is trying to be—go to 125th St or 2nd Ave for the visual experience
hang-up: a psychological problem of maladjustment
linear: dull, parochial, conventional outlook
heavy: intense psychological or spiritual overtones

Quibbles here, quibbles there. But read over the whole, and let it gestate, thinking deeply on it. To be sure, the respondent commented more than many others, but the sophistication and life-knowledge (she had taken two or three years off from college in order to pick up the cash to go back) convinces one that there's hope for the Alternatives and that, if the visions, stripped of politibullshit, are to be realized, we'll need a corps of similar people. One is very much tempted to employ Albrecht Dürer's self-diagnostic technique to indicate the appropriateness of this model.

When considering both the New Agrarians and the New Capitalists we will encounter similar models at the *core* of counter cult, those who are operating under no sadly overwrought delusions, who possess will-energy, information, and a discriminating perception. But these are few. There were fewer still in the gravitational field that the questionnaires and interviews touched upon. I chose the model with the strongest outlines. More typical of a potentially successful counter-culturalist might be a twenty-two-year-old City College senior, a heavy multiple-media man who has tried sensitivity training and rejected it as "fascistic," now into an urban communal living arrangement and looking to develop "some group business which would help us pay the rent." Has passed through a period of intense involvement in counter politics, now describing himself as an anarchist-libertarian conservative, who simultaneously sympathizes only with the ACLU, Nader's Raiders, and Common Cause. High information in all categories yields consistency in life-style and attitudes in light of his stated politic: Grants high ratings to both Al Lowenstein and Buckley, to Small Business and National Health Insurance, to Ayn Rand and the NLF, while obliterating Tim Leary and John Mitchell, the

Hare Krishna People and *Love Story,* Billy Graham and Mick Jagger. If this young man is politically exhausted, he has not lost by it, and the informed commitment remains. The innards have not triumphed at the expense of the Other.

But more likely than these we are liable to find the shipwrecks of political exhaustion like previously cited Paul and Meredith, in the tasteless situation comedy they call *Chamisa Road.* Paul and Meredith stomped their separate and together ways out of the Bronx High School of Science, where Paul had founded one of the early high school underground papers, then moved on to *Rat* after being tossed from the school. The two dropped quickly through the East Village and out to New Mexico, quickly through counter politics into counter culture. Their defense:

> i realized tonite that there's a reason for the way i feel—so strongly —about weatherman and the mad bombers. we lived the way they did, once. we worked with them and snuck into columbia to talk to them and layed out page after page with them . . . and james rector dies and we all made our decisions. the only way i can judge those decisions—and they seem to me to be almost opposite ones— is that we are living lives as positive as seems possible in this coun- try, and they are in jail or dead. maybe they'll be heroes in the revolutionary history books but i've got a better chance of being around to read them.

The Yossarians of the counter culture. Counter politics—indeed, anything to do with community—is too loaded with Catches, and the new elitists, in their half-visionary, instinctively defensive and cautious gestures, simply wish for that primitive isolationist world in which one doesn't even invite the possibility of a hassle. Doing revolution has been replaced with saying it:

> i really want to write something revolutionary, but i can't think of anything to say. d'you think it's a trend? maybe it should start with "neon." that's always a good beginning for revolutionary raps. "neon sagebrush." striking terror and dischord and giggles deep to the very fart of angelfood amerika. haha. that'll do it. watch out ev'body, the walls are crumbling. i don't know, somehow it just doesn't seem to catch. there's too many sides. but like we got to say something revolutionary. i dig charles manson. i hate jonny weis- muller.

So there they are out in Taos waiting for Paul's mother to open up the trust fund or Meredith's parents to send the check, so they can buy some land. Prices in the seven- to ten-grand range are bandied about, and they want to do it cash, 'cause don't want no debts, 'cause wouldn't have any way to pay them off. Mitch Goodman's "getting ourselves together" comes down to building the one-room house, and, in Paul's words,

> spend my time sitting on a fence
> whistling at the sun,
> and playing with the ants
> humming my song that don't make sense
> saving the world in my brand new pants

The perfect image of the new nihilism.

9

Elitism and Escalation Again: The Varieties of Politibullshit

Elitism in counter cult, operating blatantly, subtly, usually unconsciously, is an inevitable hangover from counter politics—at least as counter politics has been practiced among those who are most likely to abandon it for either a Nirvanic Absolute or a New Agrarian Paradise. Style politics should be a sufficient clue: It was "Free Huey!" not "Free Black People," "Avenge Che!" not "Avenge Bolivian Tin-Scrapers." Sometimes "Free All Oppressed Third World Peoples" was added, but almost as an afterthought, and the ability to relate to the concretions of individual lives, as opposed to the generalities of the slogans, simply didn't exist. Think, for example, of all the stale Lavoris of "reaching people," then look to the techniques offered, the practices of "reaching," and the results achieved: a little guerrilla street theater, waving a few VC flags, that gaggle of wooden mouthings—just whom did this politics of masturbation think it was reaching? It took the Vietvets, the Businessmen's Move, the union men who would talk to their own in their own language—it took those to "reach the people."

But with the political "exhaustion" of the nillers, who never really expended any energy to begin with, the flow of onanism from politics to culture became even more inevitable. Indeed, because the nillers generally developed an extremely elitist and exclusionary understanding of "the people" during their uterization in the universities, it is no surprise to find the number of excludable groups expanded now that we're off to New Jerusalem. The insensitivity to the Other born of the inability to perceive particulars.

Thus the white middle-class gravitational man fell fluently into the mixed bag of counter cult, melded his ideologies, called himself a socialist not because he was one but because the label would define his membership in a society apart from the mainstream, and talked of communes and day-care centers and food conspiracies—all of which (1) basically relieved him of some unpleasant duty he otherwise would have had to perform and (2) amounted to "socialism" for the middle class. The "people" who really need the communal arrangements, the day-care centers, the food conspiracies, etc., for their very survival, these people were precisely those *not* sought out for such ventures. Oh, there are those marvelous exceptions among the Sons of Los, generally the same people who are running the law communes, so to speak, but it's obvious that we're not speaking of them.

Rather of the weekend revolutionaries. The heat came down on black people on Monday. Now the weekenders are abandoning black people altogether, shaking their autistic heads over Angela and Attica from the wooded foothills where they're "making revolution." Rather more so, too, of those who never even played weekend revolutionary but sat around gawking in smoke in the university cafeterias, signing a petition or two, with a "far out!" and a "right on!" now into the endless rap sessions on free school organization at which every desperate middle class would-be freak wants to get up and do his politibullshit number. The poor, the working poor—these do not have the luxury of such time.

The economic elitism is both most obvious and most underplayed. I do not wonder that the counter-cult voluptuaries are so oblivious to the economic criteria for entering the psychedelic gates, or that so many political arguments for the New Anarchism, which purportedly springs from the culture, are so economically naïve. Hard-core culturists don't mix well with economics, and rarely will. One ministers to the soul, the other to the stomach; and while the soul will be skipping around from Way to Way in its no-speed-limit evolution, the stomach is likely to remain physiologically and functionally static for at least the next century or two.

Glancing through the counter-cult catalogue, one is immediately struck with the prerequisites of venture capital or other economic security, particularly for those items in the Con I chapter. The drive toward simpler living, frugality, the primitive, in practice is a luxury. A few witnesses called to explain that paradox. First, an article in the opening issue of *Mother Earth News*, hyping the subsistence-level trip. The author, now in his sixties, recounts leaving the plastic corporate world and heading west with his family to build his own house, manage his land, and live comfortably and simply on an average annual income of $6,500. He left for California in 1954, debt-free, and with $4,000 in his pocket (referred to as "limited funds"). He picks up his ten acres in the Sonoma Valley at $150 an acre and builds his house. He has since moved, built another house, but still holds some land in Sonoma. The value of his real estate holdings alone is twenty times his cost. With that kind of back-up, debt-free security, all families of four can live on $6,500. Millions do—and on much less.

A long feature in the *Wall Street Journal* told of a couple who followed Scott and Helen Nearing's game of abandoning the works for the woods, and eking subsistence out of the land and away from "the people." The Nearings advise the New Agrarians to save up enough money (1) to be able to buy land and materials for house-building outright, and (2) to be able to live for two or three years without any income. Even by the spartan standards of the *Journal's* couple, who bought forty acres in Bucksport, Maine, in 1968 for $2,000 (land which has since increased in value at a compound rate of 75 per cent a year), who have been living on roughly the same sum ($2,000) per year, and who spent just under $1,000 for building materials, we're talking about starting all over in America with no debts and nine thousand in the till. This is strictly for the upper middle class, and when these homesteaders came on with the politihype, e.g., "I don't want to earn a lot of money because I don't want to pay taxes to a government that's been lying about Vietnam and its intentions of solving social problems" or "We're just exasperated politically," my first reaction is nausea and my second is fear. These pretenders are, in effect, making life more oppressive and less hopeful for those who do *not* have nine grand in the mattress and who, even if they did, would rather stick with brothers and sisters in local urban communities, gaining control over their lives in their place.

Item: In October, 1969, in Jemez, New Mexico, a number of heavies and subheavies of the counter cult gathered and decided to use the New Agrarian movement to find a physical place for Woodstock Nation. Wavy Gravy, a.k.a. Hugh Romney, who also gave us Tiny Tim, took his private Hog Farm Circus on a fund-raising tour. The object was to buy acres numbering in six figures in a variety of locations and open them up for the establishment of "alternative societies." The pitch heralded "a way out of the disaster of the cities, a viable alternative." If that's the pitch, what's to distinguish the planned result from Florida retirement communities? What's to distinguish the impulse, the motivation, for a less complex and threatening existence? Leave the blacks and the white working class in the cities, yeah, and let *them* deal with the complexities.

The item raises a modification on the basic premises of economic elitism, to wit: If you don't have that mattress full of cash, the counter cult is loaded with Robin Hoods who'll make the going great. The commune operator at the Wheeler Farm in Northern California, for example, inherited a Connecticut real estate fortune and, after buying the 300-odd acre ranch, still had enough left over to live off coupons while the drifters were living in psychological ease off him.

Some fragments on the Red Clover Commune in Putney, Vermont:

1. What a courageous place to commune in! An old intellectual community with two colleges, a private school, and a museum of artists in residence. The counter-cult elitists demonstrate their ethnic group colors.
2. The Robin Hood is the heir of Douglas Aircraft, that bastion of revolution.
3. Ask them what they're doing and the pat vacuousness spills out, e.g., "We're trying to break down the monogamous rela-

tionships which a racist, sexist society has imposed on us," i.e., we're open swingers.

4. Started one of those very occasional underground rags, *Free Vermont*, and called for an uprising which they, of course, would lead. I think they once went to a welfare demonstration in a neighboring town, hung around for an hour or two chanting "Free the Indianapolis 500" and other slogans which sounded distinctly Chinese to the natives who were on welfare.

5. On many days there were seven people and four cars at the farmette, and the cars weren't the wrecks one passes in the blurred yards of the shacks of the rural poor of northern New England.

The sum of these fragments is the hollowness of an avant-garde bored with the dead rustle of its own unremembered lives, off on an insensitive power jag. More accurately, the fragments indicate the ease with which the latent goals of psychological adolescence become manifest goals; and, in the process, does self-revelation become the most telling form of self-mockery.

As in the case of the escalation of the apologists, the whole leads the epiphany of Drop City, a multidomed commune in southern Colorado. The cultural imperialism of the domers will be noted in full a few pages hence, so concentrate here on that elitist combination of technology, luxury, scavenging, and politexcuse:

Soon domed cities will spread across the world/anywhere land is cheap/on the deserts/in the swamps/on mountains/tundras/icecap/ the tribes are moving/building completely free & open waystations/ each a warm & beautiful conscious environment/we are winning

Droppers make movies/black & white snow-wind poems/flickering tv beauties with all the subliminal delight of pulsing coke ads/the crystal-molecular good sense of a dome going up/time lapse/the grunting goodness of eating & sex/we want videotape records & camera/strobes—hundreds of them/tape decks & amps & echo chambers & everything/we want millions of green energy flakes/we want to use everything new junk good bad to make limitless things/we want an atomic reactor

Droppers have learned how to build beautiful houses out of cartops for less than 200 dollars/less than $100/we know how to use solar heating/we're hip to windpower/Droppers know how to best use the government doles & poverty programs/each dollar we use is one less that goes into the making of napalm/every cent that Drop City uses is one less that goes to those insane retarded creeps in Washington. . . .

The story of Drop City will never end/it's the story of man on the road to free . . . [as quoted in *Domebook 2*].

The logical extension of electronic egoism, as fascistic as promised by its models. Let oppression and harassment rage! We're off playing with technology's toys, and gimme, gimme, gimme. In fact, we'll take some money from the poverty programs and put it where it's really needed, right here in Drop City, the blighted orchards where art, life, and play coalesce. Then justify it all by vaporizing that all that poverty program money would have gone into the making of napalm, and every mindless mutant out in the gravitational field will salivate.

Communes, domers, and assorted New Agrarians are not alone in their economic, psychological, and cultural elitism. The free-schoolers, emerging from the hyperbolic either/orist dialectics of the 1960's, are equally guilty, although with less phantasmagoria. Without attacking their option (which is a viable one), one can still fire on the failure of so many of them to convince locals in their previous communities on the need for *options* in existing schools. The now free-schoolers, rigidified by Yin-Yang reasoning, didn't see any options: It was either those old bastards or the groovy people. Get up at an open school board meeting and attack all the values of the audience and they'll never listen because you just ain't trying to convince. Then, no doubt, you're justified in walking out and going into the free-school biz 'cause the unutterable "they" were all pigs and wouldn't buy your program.

In so doing, you have created an elitist institution, depriving *some* kids in that old place of the *option* to do your educational baggie, while hustling off into the Vermont woods with some other people who can reach $1,000 an acre, and producing the very elites for America that you didn't want to produce. *Your* kids may be the only ones who *might* be able to read, perceive, and perhaps think. The others are wholly dead. Kudos!

Kathy Mulherin, Mitch Goddman's "accomplice" in setting up *The Movement Toward a New America*, forwards the story of a teacher in a working-class high school in a small upstate New York city, a teacher who was able to break through the unpliable submission to the culture from which her kids came—her kids, the greasers, right?—and move them toward self-expression, toward questioning the war, the school system, their inherited values. Needless to say, she was fired in one of those countless little horror dramas played out in community after community. But here, in opposition, are the vanguard free-schoolers, who really don't give a rap about the nasties that poor teacher went through or the possibilities for the authentic creation of a New America which her activities in White-town suggest. Instead, they're off in the exclusionary tribe, saving their kids and the kids of their friends. Competitive, too, because its assumption is competitive and its environment is Con I: *Our* children, at least, will arrive first with the best.

The deep structure of counter cult in fact reveals Con I at nearly every way-station, and one must carve through the varieties of politibullshit to arrive at that proposition. The sloganeering mentality that has politicized every conceivable human activity from the classroom to the bathroom veils the ideology and deludes those who are liable to live in the twilight electronic zombie world into believing that they are, and are equipped to be, that which they are decidedly not. Occasionally the consciousness pokes through, as in this nip of politibicycling from a letter to an underground paper:

> What is behind the bicycle movement today? It is a conscious move to a responsible reaction to the problems of pollution. It is an unconscious move from our all-encompassing one-dimensional culture. It is a new form through an old media [*sic*].
>
> The escape from centralization and dependence upon the system is what interests me most about the bicycle movement today. Riding a bicycle is a new freedom, an independence from the automobile. . . . This feeling of autonomy is basic to the American myth and character. How we use the chance to use our autonomy is to prove how free we are.

Nothing really escapes politicizing. Food is never merely food:

It must pulse as a manifesto. There's a legitimate historiographical principle lurking there, but we are more likely to detect the classic divergences between the political hype and the practical reality, the former melting away into the latter among the more conscious. E.g., vegetarianism, to one commune-operator quoted by Sara Davidson in "Open Land: Getting Back to the Communal Garden" (*Harper's*, June, 1970), is

> very very central to the revolution. It's a freeing process which people go through, from living on processed foods and eating gluttonous portions of meat and potatoes, to natural foods and a simple diet that is kinder to your body. A lot has to do with economics. It's much cheaper to live on grains and vegetables you can grow in your garden.

"A lot has to do with economics," that is, after one invoices the obvious. Compare this statement of a thirty-one-year-old with that of the nineteen-year-old communard from Darien I cited back in the excursus in to the death of language. The mellifluous child of McLuhan presented only the revolutionary *schtick*. Crystalized politibullshit—adopting the revolutionary line to cover a distinctly nonrevolutionary reality.

Because the politicizing mentality reduces, collapses, and moves toward the simplicities of the Om, even the Con I counter-cult Ways become cults. The core macrobiotics people are most illustrative, expanding the basic principle "you are what you eat" into a cosmology, a histiography, a politic. According to the "Ecological Cookery" column in the *LA Free Press* of August 6, 1971, we cannot make proper moral or political decisions because "of the constant onslaught of poor quality food, drugs and chemicals." And more:

> We feel that man is not only what he eats. He is what his parents ate and what their parents ate: he is what our ancestors ate 5000 years ago. The reason why so many of us are still relatively clearheaded and in good condition is because our ancestors, who were not exposed to as much poor quality food as we have been, presented us with good minds and strong constitutions.

Evidently, anything transpiring since Gutenberg invented type is

leprous. It's the same trip that took the LSD gang out of the cosmic merry-go-round a few years ago. Why does the issue of the
quality of food have to be co-opted by madmen who then tell us
that they are "still relatively clear-headed"? My granola they are!

I am averse to playing manic and charging a particularly small
group of January's guilty children, but in reading through the cult
literature, I was impressed with the fact that there is no single active counter-cult Way in which elitism, politibullshit, the mindless
drive for Absolutes, and perceptive abilities that lead to outright
contradictions in life-style—no Way in which these illusions combine as intensely as they do among the geodesic domers. The
Domers are convenient topoids, too, as their living spaces are often related to other counter-cult social spaces, e.g., communes
and free schools, and thus afford adequate evidence for assessing
the contradictions in these cousin offerings on the circuit.

One must always listen quite carefully to the cult evangelists,
for, as innocent as the dome-builders' activities might seem, they
proselytize heavily as if to justify a life-style. If the arguments for
the domes were confined to the architectural or based on simple
engineering principles, e.g., that curves are always stronger than
planes, or that the dome form both integrates structures and dis-
tributes forces through the convex-curved triangle—if these were
the explanations, one would have reason only to exult. But no, the
mentality of the counter-cult pitchman is too pervasive, so we are
blessed with the vast total-configuration cultural claims. As soon as
those claims are staked out (at times as apocalyptic imperatives),
one must judge the single dome not in terms of what, in fact, it
does but in terms of the validity of the claims. One must judge,
too, because the *claims*, and not the objects themselves, are drawing TV's children in from the gravitational fields.

One begins in the realm of metaphysical doming—and thus
with a modicum of sanity—in one of the most comprehensive of
the counter-cult communes, "Ananda" ("bliss," for those straights
unfamiliar with Sanskrit). The community comes in two parts,
located on some 350 acres in the Sierra foothills near Nevada City,
California, no mean real estate. We have a Meditation Retreat
and a Spiritual Community, both encompassing the dome movement, yoga and related exercises from the Hindu grab-bag, and
communalism, the Swami Kriyananda presiding. In more fluid and

politicized doming environments, the dome is hyped as primitive
in style, hence tribal, hence "communistic." The Swami takes
issue, and provides an indication of the futuristic orientation of
the dome:

> The dome is expressive of our new approach to the universe. It is in
> harmony with the scientific concept that space itself is curved. In
> its roundness it represents our modern desire for continuous mental
> expansion, for reaching out to the universe instead of boxing our-
> selves in protectively against its immensity. The dome seems in
> some way to be more conducive to the mental and spiritual har-
> mony of the dome dweller, perhaps because its more natural shape
> helps to attune him with nature instead of alienating him from it.
> Boxed houses belonged to an age when men stood in opposition to
> the world around them, in competition, as it were, with nature and
> the universe. Domed houses belong better to this age of growing
> awareness of man's need to *cooperate* with nature if he is to progress
> further [as quoted in *Domebook 2*].

In both its assumptions and its particulars, the Swami's statement is perfectly reasonable. I use it as a control. Witness the first
escalation of the politidomers, which is at least grounded in the
conscious recognition of an honored historical proposition: that
architectural styles express cultural values. But in a piece such as
Michal Rossman's "Introduction to Dome-Building" (*New American Review*, No. 12), the application is distorted more for the
political claim than for the object itself:

> From our experience in the physical world we derive the metaphors
> which undergird our understanding of all else. We were raised in a
> Way which taught us that hierarchies of importance, strong and
> weak members, were implicit in building. What would be the spon-
> taneous politics and social constructions of children who played
> with struts instead of blocks, and who early internalized a way of
> building in which all components were equally essential and effort
> evenly distributed, and the power of each dependent on and multi-
> plied by cooperation? Is the social image of a geodesic dome a so-
> ciety without strongmen? [64.]

Despite the quality of expression, Rossman is thinking in slogans
here, undoubtedly appealing to those whose perceptual memories
are short and whose conceptual abilities, trained in the global, are
minimal. First, as many of us were raised on tinker toys as were

raised on blocks, and at least quasi-spherical shapes could be constructed with struts and hubs—not unlike the geodesic. The variations on design were perhaps more limited, but there was nothing
in the concept that couldn't, with the drilling of a few more holes
in the hubs, match the geodesic. Too, the principle of equality in
tinker-toy engineering is manifest.

Second, if the strongman social organization is to be imaged
anywhere in the block structures, is it not at the foundations, at
the root? By Rossman's own criteria, then, the society that emphasized the primary strength of foundations would be a society
dominated by the "proletariat." In fact, he has only to look at a
city skyline to perceive what has happened to architectural form
under the democratic ideal: The spires have disappeared. The
weakest and yet most hierarchically visible expressions have van-
ished. From spire to flat-top. From cast-iron faces to the faceless-
ness, the anonymity of blank concrete and glass, an anonymity
from which a world of domes does not promise to rescue us.

Indeed, if there is a totalitarian style in block architecture, what,
again I ask, is to prevent a totalitarianism of domes? E.g., Rossman echoing a Buck Fuller vision: "*Fact*, while our cities choke
and rot: one year of the military budget could buy materials and
land to house 40,000,000 people in geodesics—and also to train
and pay men in military servitude to build them within this period
(65)." One does not question the wisdom of employing the military budget for other purposes. But don't let that thrust mask the
spirit of the new elitist cultural imperialist. Without asking the
people living in the rotting urban neighborhoods but still holding
on to their culture, we're going to shove one-fifth of the country
into mind-bending geodesics. The mere physical housing would no
doubt be an improvement, but the mentality that leads to this approach is the same old liberal-mass-solution-riding-roughshod-over-
individuals-and-communities farrago. Forty million people may
well involve ten million geodesic structures, as much a blight of
perception upon the land as their rival red-brick housing developments. Why do we have to buy these apocalyptic either/or mani-
festos? Can't we opt for more flexibility? A few domes, a little of
Paolo Solari's cellular structures, a habitat here and there, and perhaps some structural forms as yet undreamed of. Why does this
new consciousness have to be so afflicted with the Urizenic vision:

"One God, One King, One Law"? For that is what the spirit of cultism yields.

Thus Rossman's continuing shilling strikes one as extremely hypertrophied:

> Such technology has political dimensions. It invites user design as well as construction, in each way severing dependence upon specialists and weakening involvement and support of the system built around them, the megamachine of the housing industry. Slashed capitalization requirements weaken user control by the economic system. Aesthetically, technically, financially, the living-unit thus tends to self-determination. Geodesics are a clear example of a technology which empowers people to determine the conditions of their lives [65].

Within fairly well-defined limits, one must qualify. After all, you've got to join the union first, 'cause it's gonna be the sole collective bargaining agent for your soul, baby.

In the arena of elitist cultural imperialism, the free-school hype easily slithers into the world of the domers. Pacific High School, a domed free community located on a 40-acre gift in the Big Sur, parades its experience as "so different from anything you've done in the white middle class trip with all roads open to you from birth, color and poverty not wrecking your chances to do something." One grants the ingenuity and energy of the Pacific High School gang (to whom we shall later return), but one must also recognize that to throw a hooker such as the above is to maintain the safe distance of elitist ignorance, to wit:

1. "All roads open" is classic self-delusive politibullshit. For people who just might want to become, for example, physicians to the poor, radical lawyers, consumer advocates—all thus serving "the people"—agrarian simplicity and a world sorely limited in conceptual apparatus just washes the bridges away.

2. As I've noted before, this is merely a *new* Middle Class trip, as another ten years of an expanding cult will prove. Domes and free schools cluttering northern California, Washington, Vermont. To pretend that that development does not spell New Suburbia—motivated by the same desires under which the Old suburbias were established—is hallucinatory. To pretend, too, that such an expansion is not another white man's stunt, rough-riding over the generationed residents of now-rural communities as if

they were Sioux and we were playing 1884, is another insolvent sick joke, to which conflicts between communards and both Chicanos and Indians in New Mexico will adequately attest. I'm sure the Movement will manufacture a number of question-begging excuses, the burden of their defense finally coming to rest on that nauseating accusation, "irrelevant."

3. And following the above: To pretend that the black and the poor either could or would enter this New World is an expression of monstrous ignorance, a paradoxically elitist assumption (as the white man has been the leader here, and the black man must follow), and an attempt to mask the reality of the New Homesteader's own consciousness of his abandonment of social ill in these States.

I suppose, though, that if one is playing political hangover in counter cult, one is obliged to throw a phrase-sop to the black and the poor, just so that it appears you're not running a country club. But, in fact, the New Atlantis, whether educational or otherwise, is just as exclusive—not by design (and because the sentiments are essentially old-style liberal, that, at least, is an advance), but through social and cultural reality (and there, too, irony of ironies, the oversight is essentially old-style liberal). Social realities can be altered (though certainly not by running out on them), but anyone who thinks he's going to transform cultural reality is playing the combined roles of eighteenth-century missionary and nineteenth-century colonialist. Thus:

4. The cultural ignorance of those who assume that the black and the poor want to "do something" on the order of being an ex-middleclassman-turned-rural-carpenter under the aegis of a geodesic free school reflects a spectacular dislocation of sensibility.

What interferes with and masks the positive angles of the Dome World, then, is that hyped-up rhetoric of the builders, who draw in unprepared kids from gravitational youthcult for all the wrong reasons. The builders, for example, exalt the nontechnical, the nonspecialized, and present themselves as a vanguard of the civilization of the non-tech-spec. One has to translate such hyperboles into discrimination of degree. After all, the *Domebook* instructions rest on a technical ability to perceive and construct and, in the case of any geodesic shape, on the technology made possible by the conceptually fertile and creative mind of one Bucky Fuller. As Fuller noted to the *Domebook* interviewer who so desperately wanted to hear of the primitive, the tribal, the simplistic reinforcement:

> You have a research laboratory going on with a kid right from the beginning. . . . He's usually doing something quite mature—his intuitions are making him try those hands, but then he finds the things I've said a little earlier about what mathematics can really do for him—that one week of mathematics, he's suddenly a very different kid for the rest of his life. Very deep confidence. Then you can understand what a navigator . . . how great confidence comes to a navigator. When he can get under those stars . . . he's going to prize those beautiful tables that took so long for man to accumulate. . . . You've seen the kids just hungry for the data of my geodesics. They're hungry for it. You've got kids that are catering to that because they see that hunger and they themselves follow it. But you've got to have my data.

Geodesic mathematics is not for the primitive mind, is not for sloganeers. And while the work crews may be composed of a host of nontechnicians, the designers have to possess some decent order of calculating mind. Then, too, the successful dome-builder becomes a specialist in a sense, exemplified by the dome communes, which erect a half-dozen or so of the shelters, or by the number of radical individualists off in the woods who have constructed "two, three, many more domes." The specialty may be one of many that the builder possesses, but one is strongly tempted to hypothesize that the dome ritual, with its attendant psychological preparations and politicultural justifications, is all-consuming.

Despite the comparatively low cost of mass-produced domes, one must also recognize, beneath the evangelism of present domebuilders, the necessity of either a good burst of venture capital or a benefactor. How about a shopping list? Start with the land, and for the number of Big Sur jobs cited in the *Domebook*, that's a healthy start; and generally it's either 100 per cent cash or cash and collateral on the mortgage (collateral being something that all of us are walking around with in our shirt pockets). The alternative, by the way, is inevitable: Mortgages or even purchase money mortgages are not available to the itinerantly employed. It's no wonder the dome-builders come on with the efflorescence of "refusing to deal with the established building industry and its bankers." They don't have to. The rhetoric is an afforded luxury.

A local building supply firm was gracious enough to do the calculations for a 24'-diameter product after a list of materials provided by the *Domebook*. The firm drags no reputation as a rip-off house. The bill was $2,332, which might also just about cover a well, were it to be drilled for the inhabitants of the dome. Put the whole on even a single acre of land in the Big Sur, and a bill for five or six grand plus amenities will be presented. I don't have three friends who could come up with that collectively—and they work for a living. One might reply that there are dome kits now available for $1,200, which, with floor, plumbing, etc. can be rough-completed for about $1,800, exclusive of land and well. The Pacific High School domes averaged in at $900, but then again, they built seven of them.

The point is *not* that domes are evil or that dome-builders are dangerous or subversive or whatever right-wing paranoia rhetoric one wishes to draw on. The dome is a refreshing architectural form, a versatile and innovative form, a comparatively inexpensive form of shelter, a classroom *in practicum* for a good many people who need it, etc. But as comparatively cheap a shelter as they are, domes are in fact being built today more as a luxury item than as a necessity, and, among those who ring the praises of the *porta*-domes, as a reinforcement for a nomadic, television-commercial, eternal summer life-style. Membership cards in this Way are relatively expensive items. The differential between the shill and the shadow is becoming an old theme.

The issue, as noted in the earliest pages, lies in the critical factor of the identity of the practitioners. There are those who approach dome culture so that it will survive as a viable alternative, and there are those for whom the dome is only instant karma, a self-centered refuge of inner space, and through whose lives the form will pass as swiftly as those Bufferin bubbles and with the force of the 491st repetition of "off the pigs!"

Two opposing examples, the second of which will move us out of the dome world and into the area of what Stewart Brand of *The Whole Earth Catalog* calls "the Commune Lie."

There is no doubt concerning the harassment of some dome

builders by local building officials, inspectors, and their cop aids
(as if the latter didn't have anything better to do), all of whom
have ironically bought the politicized counter-cult "take-all-of-it-
or-take-none-of-it" presentation, and therefore equate domes with
the whole freak scene, not conceiving of the possibility that some
right-wing total abstentionist might very will dig spheres. But the
dome builder-designer who wants to live in this world and have his
dome, too, and who is not interested in mouthing revolutionary
self-justifications, can do both. Testimony from a Marin County
dome-builder:

> We learned . . . that building officials are prepared to take struc-
> tures like this seriously if they are approached seriously. We had a
> set of plans (working drawings) and a computerized structural
> analysis. The other approach is to load test the built structure pro-
> vided you can convince them to let you build it. A serious and sin-
> cere attitude is a big help. Many areas have building departments
> and planning departments. The first is concerned with whether the
> structure is safely habitable; the second primarily with its appear-
> ance and how it relates to its surroundings. Both are valid concerns
> but both can be fatal to proposed domes unless they are rather care-
> fully considered [as quoted in *Domebook 2*].

The second libretto falls off the world of communes, specifically
the "Red Rockers," a commune varying in number from "12 to
20," which built a 20-ton, 60'-diameter dome

> because: we like living together "in a heap" with one kitchen and
> lots of shared space; we dig science and futuristic stuff; we wanted
> our home to have a structural bias against individualism and for
> communism; we like doing big things together. . . .
>   Our name refers to our culture, our politics and our geography.
> We live in a high mountain canyon with no electricity and a road
> nothing bigger than a pickup can travel. We borrowed a 2500 watt
> generator and kept our two pickups busy hauling wood and sup-
> plies. . . .
>   All the Red Rockers are domebuilders, not just the men. Brothers
> and sisters, get high together, trust in the Lord, makes domes and
> Revolution together. There is no point in building revolutionary
> structures to shelter reactionary life-styles [as quoted in *Domebook 2*].

There is something stagnantly preposterous about a commune living "in a high mountain canyon" in northern California, making

revolution, thinking that what they're up to differs so greatly from the mode of the frontier caravan of the nineteenth century. In fact, the life-style, a communal anarchic libertarianism, is quite re-actionary, and, in many cases, the dome only reinforces the reaction. For there's a contradiction between the ideology of the open and potentially creative environment the dome builders claim and the stifling world that the dome often becomes; and, related to that coin, the reality of psychological isolation and conflict in the comparatively compressed space that most dome-builders can afford. The dome can easily retract into the endless summer of a totalitarian world. Indeed, I recall one of the Pacific High School domers complaining that, while they were living communally before the domes were built, bad weather "kept us inside and drove us mad with lack of space and dirt. People started hating each other." Don't want no hassles, like seasons. Mama, wheel me to the corner grocery, will ya? So we create the summer of inner space, cop-out on the life cycle, and are reborn into a world in which there's nothing to do in here, and nothing to do out there.

Eventually, many dome-builders of large structures find it necessary to partition, and thus lay the grounds for (arggh!) in-dividualist activity. As the *Domebook* instructs: "There is defi-nitely a noise problem in an unpartitioned dome. You'll need partitions if more than one activity at a time is going on. Sound permeates space as efficiently as heat." And if no more than one activity can go on at a time, have we not a totalitarian society, far more rigid than the one down the canyons? But, to cite Jerry Rubin again, let's "not let details get in the way of the myth."

10

Collected Counter-Cult Ways I:
The New Agrarians

When the Alternative-hypers inform us that to be revolutionary is to "do it yourself," we must recognize the voice as distinctly American, and the revolution resulting as against—or, to be more charitable, away from—"the people." The large movements failed in the stale marshes of mass meetings and protests in which many felt as "alienated" as they were in the corporate society. When the Movement tripped across ecology, the discovery was natural: the discovery of places that were relatively unpolluted and underpopulated and distinctly underpolitical. For those attracted to the more romantic phases and personality cults of counter politics, the discovery was more natural still. For their heroes had been the Maos and the Ches, and their model societies all agrarian, societies in which the case against The Monster Pig is more easily identifiable. The task of restructuring a technological society is finally recognized as being too demanding, and when the realization comes, its extension is logical: Construct an agrarian society away from the geosocial mainstream of North America.

New Agrarians come in a number of forms, and their motivations usually cannot be classified in the terms of counter politics. Under the general proposition of rural living, one finds both individuals and communities. "Occupations" range from crafts to farming to outright nothingness. The latter breaks into a number of categories running from dedicated self-subsistence to acid-laced woodland wanderings.

The New Agrarianism is, as practiced, an elitist activity, available primarily to those with, or with access to, venture capital. The capital investment has to be high, because our New Agrarians are concentrating on geographical locations not too far removed from "the action." For many, the agrarian impulse in Vermont or northern California is a very tenuous gesture. One searches hard to locate New Agrarian ventures in Kansas, Nebraska, or particularly the Dakotas, where farmland can be found cheaply. No, if they're not in northern New England or northern California, they are within twenty miles or so of a large and hip state university campus (radii from Madison, Ann Arbor, Amherst). Another timid gesture, which simply moves the off-campus apartment of the mid-1960's to the off-campus "farmette."

The New Agrarians are an ethnic group and, like all others, stick together. Thus, if not the outright commune, the community. For the earlier countrified waves that mean colonies of older vacationing academics, generally drinking themselves through their books on decks in Wellfleet *circa* 1959, Chilmark *circa* 1964, Peacham *circa* 1967; or artists in Stockbridge *circa* 1957, Provincetown *circa* 1960, Mount Desert area *circa* 1969, Woodstock, A.D., Taos since the last phoenix arose. The latest sprouting, considerably younger, issues from the same ethnocentric environment, the Academy and its inevitable urban aftermath. The irony falls in that the same prophets who foresaw cities left wholly to warring factions of blacks and white blue-collars and who berated the middle class for moving out to their antiseptic barbecue suburbs now leap over two tiers of suburbs to a whole range of rurals (the degree selected depending mostly on cash on hand), helping to fulfill their own prophecy of doom, egging on the apocalyptic urban night.

Talk to the kids drifting in to taste the towns and styles, and the impulse is the same as that which pushed their parents out to the suburbs: the exurban "I can't hack it." They come to the communal "farmette" in great lassitude, dragging the dead willed tails. So "farmette," a term adopted from rural real estate catalogue listings, is most appropriate to the hesitant nature of the gesture. Basically, the agrarian communes are truck gardens. After all, it's too much of a hassle to try to cultivate enough acreage to support, let us say, twenty people—even if the whole crop is consumed in the house and everyone is a vegertarian. The collapse of many such ventures, as chronicled in the underground press, stems from the concept-less naïveté that farms are "groovy," will virtually run themselves (it's difficult to be up at six feeding animals if you're still strung-out at two), and will support all residents, invited and otherwise. The guy with the bankroll eventually discovers that it's giving out because he's running a welfare operation—hardly a radical break with the system.

The hard-core agrarians survive, but being in the main in their late twenties and thirties, they bring the conceptual equipment, will-energy, and rationales built on experience and not visions. To be sure, their number has grown considerably in the years of Nixonomics. If you were thinking of leaving the city in 1969, you had to in 1970. Since, despite whatever bread you left with, you were honing the cash close, the rhetoric of economic and political survival played easily. But underneath, the sense of unease reflected in the establishment of the ethnic dogpatch ghetto, that wince of anxiousness when friends who are making decisions, and in the rush of conflict, arrive from the Winter Towns. The defensiveness, and the irony of the Big Break: "Do you know that your chances of being a victim of violent crime are one in 107 in the country and one in 7 in the city?" This is not a fad. It's an old story, as old as the parents, indeed, as old as the rhythms of the earth, the alternation between Frank Lloyd Wright's cliff-dwellers and tree-swingers, except now we're all nomads anyway, all except the rural natives and inner city poor and near-poor—who have no choice.

To claim that visionary society awaits one in the kingdom of windy space is, then, an old order of business. The Romantics, too, went to rural rides to "put their heads together," as the hip phrase runs, and to gain the perspective not available, as Coleridge noted, to one long "in the great city, pent 'mid cloisters dim." The correlation between new social vision and open space is archetypal. So if, in one sense, we are witnessing one of those cyclical arcs of the serpent history, in another, we stand before the impulse to utopias. Thus the prevalence of the rural commune within the New Agrarian movement.

In one sense, the idea of communal living has to be split from agrarianism, because the exurbia impulse is common to anyone who can afford to get out. Too, because the practice of communal living is not limited to rural space. Thirdly, because communes can be formed around social, political, and economic activities common to the desires of those who join regardless of the spatial location of communal activity. Lastly, because urban communes formed around an activity do not necessarily require common living facilities. Thus, for an obvious example, legal and medical service "communes," located where they are most needed, in cities, are more likely to be "collectives." There are art "communes," too, in which one or two dozen practicing artists might buy an old building and operate it as a cooperative, with separate living and studio quarters. If one wishes to call that type of arrangement "communal," fine, as iong as one does not add a politihype announcing the formation of a cooperative as a revolutionary act— which it decidedly is not.

Nor is entering a monastery, i.e., a religio-spiritus commune, particularly if one enters for a long gestation period. Self-subsistence monasteries have been with us for a millennium, and that, in effect, is what the collections presided over by our current crop of swamis are. To search for absolutes, one removes himself from the social flux of time, the corruptions of the world of generation. The world of generation has always made place for the retreat of holy men, but in this age of the Om and the neon motto born of the death of language and perception, the retreat is potentially a mass draw, and those currently operating spaceship America are pleased at the growing migration. Only an occasional monk proved much trouble.

The commune represents as much of a drive for simplicity and an informationally limited world as does the agrarian move, and for that reason the two dovetail quite neatly. But the reasons for attendance are primarily personal and not visionary. Talked, for example, with a group of people in their mid-twenties organizing prior to commune. One guy going because he's lonely. A girl entering because she and her husband want to have a child but don't salivate over the idea of caring for it. and therefore are attracted to the idea of passing kids around. Another living a marginal existence and reasons that the arrangement is economically sound above all else. Others looking for group therapy, and still others for an environment in which the escape from consumerhood will be encouraged.

Recognize first that, with such motivations, one cannot describe the communal movement in the ecstatic terms William Hedgepeth ballyhooed in his preface to *The Alternative*, "a radical break with the present system" and "reactionary (in the strictest and most literal sense) in that its members seek a return to something they think we once had." One is more likely to assent to the second half of that proposition, but on slightly different grounds. For example, the cult of the nonconsumer seems to reach back toward nineteenth-century and earlier frontier simplicities. But in a rural commune in particular, one does not survive unless one is a consumer (in the strictest and most literal sense). It is simply a question of what one is consuming. To replace the frill with the necessity, the record album with the tool, *Rolling Stone* with *The Whole Earth Catalog* is simply to shift the emphasis, the qualitative nature, of consumption, and to live as rural families have been existing in America for decades. A good 16" chain saw, even used, is equivalent in cost to a stereo tuner-amplifier, and no commune in a temperate climate will be able to cut and stock firewood for the winter without it. Simply to maintain a tool shed and workshop involves considerable "consumption." Need one continue?

Thus a *rural* commune in particular represents "a radical break with the present system" only if one has a significant stake in that system. Thus, too, to say that one is now conscious of turning to earlier models, and to assert that that very fact qualifies the New Agrarianism as a new social order, does not disguise the fact that the principles are the same. Give it a few years, and there *may* develop an alternative economy, and its name will still be capitalism, and it may act positively as a depressant on the wage-price spiral of the corporate capitalism of the mainstream. The whole development presages a salutary effect on counter politics as well. For if Stewart Brand is right, if communes (communities is a more accurate term, as separate family living spaces are becoming more and more frequent down on the farm) develop at least a semblance of an independent economy complete with its own form of capital, then government of some form will be thrust upon those who are, in effect, abstaining from government by their mere presence in the new Edens.

Unfortunately, such reconstructive prophecies hold little promise in light of the behavior and motivations of a vast majority of those who are currently packing off to communes, or those out in the gravitational fields who are set-ups for naïve acceptance of what Stewart Brand, in the last issue of *The Whole Earth Catalog*, called "The Commune Lie":

> One reason we promote communes is that there's no better place to make all the wishful mistakes, to get your nose rubbed in your fondest fantasies. . . . Everybody has his own version of The Commune Lie, for example:
>
> We'll let other people take care of us.
> We'll let God take care of us.
> Free Lunch. (Robert Heinlein)
> The Tragedy of the Commons. (Garret Hardin)
> We'll all be honest.
> We'll all be selfless.
> No Rules.
> Possessions are bad. Privacy is bad. Money is bad.
> We've got the answer.

One must first recognize that, frequently enough, the ideal of communal *living* breaks down very easily. We have a small crafts "commune" up the road a piece: eight adults, five children. Originally one living structure, now four. The decentralization occurs quickly under the pressure of psychological space. Agrarian society reverts to its frontier models: the schooner caravans, eventually setting up what amounts to a new *town*. Unless that structure develops, the agrarian dispersal will not survive, for otherwise the commune is too fluid, involves too great a degree of what the mainstream refers to in corporate lingo as "rapid turnover in personnel," for any possibility of economic self-sufficiency or individual sanity.

In a piece I've cited quite frequently, Sara Davidson's "Open Land: Getting Back to the Communal Garden" (*Harper's*, June,

1970), the number of communes that have survived only by virtue of the decentralist principle argues most persuasively. Miss Davidson visited a commune up in Washington, known as the Freedom Farm, established in 1963, long before it became fashionable to run Alternative. When she asked the founder of the farm how a community had remained fairly cohesive for seven years, his answer provided the candor which enables one to evaluate the directions of the new agrarian cult:

> The secret is not to try. We've got a lot of rugged individualists here, and everyone is into a different thing. In reflection, it feels good that we survived. A lot of us were from wealthy backgrounds, and the idea of giving it all up and living off the land was a challenge.

In the process, they discovered:

> It's impossible to have a commune, where everyone lives and works collectively, and free land, where anyone can settle. Some day we might have a commune on the land, but not everyone who lived on the land would have to join it.

How was that realization wrought? Only the marathoneers can tell, and their accounts are multifold. During the first few months of Freedom Farm's existence, the communal experiment was attempted, on the assumption that people would work because they would want to, contribute, if to nothing else, to the building of an alternate community, on the assumption of a "Western idea. You inspire people by giving them a goal, making it seem important; then they'll do anything to get there." No coercion. The not-so-atypical results:

> Emotional crises, fights over everything. A constant battle to get things done. A typical scene would be for one guy to spend two hours fixing a meal. He had to make three separate dishes—one for vegetarians, one for nonvegetarians, and one for people who wouldn't eat government surplus food. He would put them on the table, everybody would grab, and if you stood back you got nothing. When people live that close together, they become less sensitive, and manners go right out the window. It was educational, but we knew it wasn't suitable for raising children.

Raw Con I survival behavior doesn't fit well in a packed house. And if the insensitivities wrought from closed space alone were as intense in 1963, think how much more so they would be among a new generation that has never acquired ability to perceive the Other. The impulse for space and privacy is too intense in the conditioning of the children of their parents, e.g., six years after, a reflection by one of the Pacific High School communards:

> When school starts to my horror I find we've built a mess hall, like the army carry your plate past a counter where food is dumped on it. Too many people on the land, the price of success. Mark who digs farms and the country senses it, feels the heaviness of so many people. . . . Yet the land is still beautiful, land you walk miles over. It begins to feel like time to move [as quoted in *Domebook 2*].

It's all there: the impulse for space, small group individual freedom, elitism, the honest realization of a repetition in the counter culture of the oppressions of the mainstream; *but* also the nomadic reaction that leads away from community: "It begins to feel like time to move." For those new agrarians who look on the rural commune as a form of creative anarchism, as the "only answer" to contemporary America—for them the commune will disintegrate. Commune and anarchy have proven antithetical realities in New America in the conflict between the dominant libertarian ethic and the idea of communitas conducted under the same roof.

There are exceptions. In "Your Global Alternative" (*Esquire*, September, 1970), Hugh Gardner notes that the successful forms of communal anarchy arise only through a "probationary screening process" of prospective members. If that country club resemblance isn't enough to add to the evidence for elitism, consider the Con I spirit of Libre, a commune in Colorado, at which, according to Gardner,

> to avoid unnecessary entanglements, all adult males and females are expected to build their own private dwellings. Some of the buildings are adobe, others are domes, and one lady built her house in a perfect cube. Each house expresses its owner's personal sense of his relation to the land, and all reflect the intense ecological consciousness of Libre as a whole. This consciousness has led Libre people to a clear idea of how many people their land can support. When that number is reached, no more new members will be admitted.

There are other communes, run by Robin Hoods, at which an

entrance fee and/or annual "maintenance" charges are levied for the use of open land as individuals see fit. When there is actual cash in the venture, communal progress shapes itself easily behind that hidden leader.

The only alternative to such precontrolled anarchic libertarianism as a stabilizing force in new rural societies is manifested by the Twin Oaks Community in Virginia, a socialistic experiment employing Skinner control. Any New Agrarian communard who runs from one haphazardly controlled piece of social engineering—which is American culture at large—to this tight machine and who thinks he's going FREEEE is in for considerable bewilderment. Of course, Twin Oaks is a rather exclusive plantation, complete with entrance fee and probationary screening period, so chances are the Om generation would be barred.

In fact, there isn't much to distinguish the rigidity of a community such as Twin Oaks from the encounter-group communes, which preclude anarchy through the authority figure, the encounter group leader. The totalitarianism of close psychological space is particularly noticeable in such arrangements: the put downs of those who question the assumptions of the group, the imperative to respond to the others' emotional outbursts, the impingement of the individual's right to silence, boredom, mind. A masochistic form of behavior-conditioning, reinforced by the noncognitive state of feel me/touch-me, expresses an Absolutist drive in the same structure used by monastic communes dedicated to the sublimation of the self in the presence of spiritual absolutes and rituals on the order of those prescribed by Krishna Consciousness. What is to distinguish the proscribed primal scream from the proscribed chant? The ecstasy of *unfelt* pain?

But as Brand implies, it may be worth the mistakes, the experiments, to explode the commune lies, along with the most visionary and otherworldly of the New Agrarians. Worth these temptings of the gods to establish a permanent alternative structure with the capabilities of economic self-subsistence; new communities that will not impinge on or expropriate the freedom, livelihoods, and Ways of consciousness of the "natives," but that will work quietly and seriously at their crafts, holding to their values without the pretense of anarchy or revolution or any other false assertion. Perhaps, too, worth the consciousness-raising of existential error to dispose of the sectarian madness that, for example, in its rage against pesticides, imports disease-carrying praying mantises to play the role of natural predator or tolerates weeds in the field to the extent that crop yields are deliberately lowered, thereby raising prices beyond the point at which those who might wish to support agrarian alternatives can contribute.

To indicate the possibilities of such explosions among those who still possess the ability to recognize the living lie, I cite one of the most candid confessionals in the literature of communal America, a piece anthologized by Mitch Goodman in *The Movement Toward a New America*. The politihype fades into the realities of the soil and human flesh in the case of the self-named DRV (a very clever pun, 'cause it really stands for the great revolution going on in the hills of Vermont, the "democratic/republication revolution of, or in, Vermont"). We open with a relatively balanced statement of initial purpose:

> We were all motivated by an awareness that cities had become a destructive environment overcrowded, polluted, dehumanizing, and violent. We want to see whether there was not a more healthy and meaningful way to live, free of the system, but relevant to the means of working for radical change.

The realization arose with the voracity of a primitive beast: that New Agrarians cannot continue to think in traditional Movement terms; that the land and the mere task of survival overpowered them. The single house became too crowded, particularly with the hordes of transients who simply leeched, then moved on, so many tinseled refugees from sloganland. Ultimately the transients were tossed out, and outbuildings were converted into private residences. "Old age facilities are not built to house New Age families," is the way it goes. Besides, the facilities were "overtaxed," by that ecologically conscious mob: The spring ran dry, the outhouse filled to the windows with shit after the plumbing broke down with overuse. These had to be repaired, and forty cords of wood cut, split, and stacked for the New England winter. Necessity comes to overwhelm the politic:

> Before we moved to Vermont we all had ideas about publishing a newspaper and continuing our involvement in the Movement, as we knew it. But we had been thinking in city terms and didn't antici-

pate what we were getting into. In four months our heads have been turned completely around. [For originally,] because we were movement people living in an urban setting, we felt it necessary to describe our plans in political terms. The DRV would be a meeting place and rest area for weary activists. Or, the first wedge in the movement to liberate Vermont and bring about its secession. Or, a commune for free people to roam in the woods and do their things. . . . We fast became victims of our own hyperbole.

The land forces realization of those contradictory bits of nonsense for what they are. The location, as we should recognize by now, did not demonstrate an abundance of political courage. The farm was in southern Vermont, and purchased in 1968. Prices were high that year, and the tab for the DRV was no exception. The drop down or drop up from Boston or New York was too easy to lend an existential sense of place about the DRV. But when the open communards lost their argument to the advocates of the extended but close-knit family, and the group decentralized living space through a multiplication of shelters, and individuals began to supplement agrarian activities with small crafts capitalism, country school teaching, and other long-repressed "careers," what was conceived in slogan as a political commune on the edge of a "revolutionary" situation became a social community that reassessed values, as opposed to assassinating them out of hand, e.g., money:

> We treat money in much the same way [as work], trying to apply the concept that money is a commodity with certain desirable uses but is of far less value than building nice things, making love, creating a poem, baking bread, or watching the sunset.

Gone, with that attitude, is the naïve belief that a radical change in style alone will produce a corresponding change in power structure and distribution, and gone, too, are those typical communard communiqués to the urban poor (e.g., from a Minnesota commune writing in *Mother Earth News* No. 1: "Write to the urban poor telling them you'd like to help families get out of the city if they want," then "go out and plant a row of carrots. . . . Roll in the grass and begin again"), to which an old Marxist aphorism applies: "They wish for a bourgeoisie without a proletariat." Dissipated are the pretensions, and the long process of building a new community is in the seeds.

But our new agrarians are not building in a vacuum. Most of the new frontier caravans stake out among others. New towns must slowly agglutinate with the old. Herein lurks the disheartening recognition that the permanent residents of the DRV are the exception, not the rule. Their very language and the quality of the perception it reflects, distances them even from those communards who also have been detoxified from The Commune Lie in its more incantatory forms. For those more frequent hangnails of instant gratification (those whose perceptions have been flattened into sheet-iron obliviousness, who communicate only by gesture, Hedgepeth's "soft growls," and hip dictionary) come to realize the imperialistic and jarring effects of their flaunted counter-styles on small lost dirt road towns only through tragedy.

Here, for example, is a contrite confession of commune self-destruct recorded in the *LA Free Press* (April 9, 1971). The commune, Kingdom of Heaven, lay in New Mexico, visionary heartland of the New America. Some musings from former visionaries:

> Like I don't think any of us were really mature enough to face things—to get together. We all came from the city with all these bullshit ideas in us and now we can see that we're going to have to make radical changes inside ourselves if we're going to live a totally different life. Some people came there to do the work but because they were into a work thing and because some people weren't as ready for it as they were, they developed a very negative attitude about everybody else.

> Within the kingdom itself, the hassles that went on in there were the same going on in the world. It just didn't seem like you could get away from it.

They were joined by the more frequent form of communard, the sometime visitors, who, devoid of that will-energy, weren't into any "work thing," and from whom the hassles emanated:

> The problem was that it was a bunch of hippies trying to prove how much they loved each other. And the other people were people who were really bitter, who came there bitter and wanted to establish themselves, who wanted to get out of the whole trip because they'd seen so much in the city of a bunch of people who were trying to prove how much they loved each other.

Being incapable of perceiving the Other, though, the New Agrarians rarely look to their effects on the surrounding community, and the imperialist war joins, is inevitable. Particularly so in the hills of New Mexico, among Chicanos who want the trip the communards are skipping and who also desire (and therefore despise) some droppings from the commune life-style.

Under the sloganeered banner of anarchy, there was no control over the relationships of the Kingdom of Heaven communards with their social surroundings. Shooting speed and drinking wine, cutting the neighbor's trees down, jaunting into town with their cocks hanging out, burning money in the streets, and preaching out of the middle-class bag to gaping and furious locals. The result was a stark death, and the immediate disintegration of the Kingdom. The autopsy struggles bravely to explain, but is inhibited by its own language:

> The trouble was that if we were different on the land that was one thing but people brought their trips to town with the usual hippie-carrying-his-world-with-him attitude. We've gone through all kinds of heavy things in the city which they can't imagine and so the heavy reaction that's come about in us from the city is something they don't know anything about and they don't understand it.
>
> I don't think it was the trippers exclusively who were causing the problem. People who didn't realize what they were doing. Didn't realize that their way of acting, their lifestyle and their whole trip, including myself, were blowing people's minds. People who didn't realize that some of the other people around them couldn't understand or accept their trip.

The New Agrarians soon discover that small-town and rural visionary, primitive, tribal America is as likely to display its violence born of fear and ignorance as is urban America. More likely so in the face of the blank insensitivity of communards off on the freedom trip, not caring whether or not their Alternative survives, as long as they "do their thing," and, in the style of the invulnerable niller, expecting the surrounding peons "to relate to" them. But as George Dennison observed in *The Lives of Children*, "there is no such thing as 'freedom,' but only the relations between people." That is, the idea of freedom implicit in the new agrarian revival can only be expressed by perceiving the Other, accepting him in his human complexity, and acting with and toward him in a manner subject to moral judgment. When the possibility of moral judgment has been choked off by a pervasive apologism, when the "freedom" of Yippie theater carries into the country towns, when the whole is underwritten by a purposeful solipsism, the gesture of freedom is an anomaly, if not the very sick joke that moved the Chicanos to murder a Kingdom of Heaven communard. Freedom consists neither in the yearning for nor the adoption of a life-style diametrically opposed to that of one's adolescent uterus. Simplistic negations that fecklessly seek the Prelapsarian will quarantine counter cult in moral and cultural nihilism.

11

Collected Counter-Cult Ways II: The New New Capitalism

It's when we arrive at those little nasties called the coins, the cash that all the counter-cult politihypers with counter-pol hangovers want to ditch, that we realize how truly Con I the counter cult is. Beneath the politibullshit are children of their parents, in a way, who evidently believe that not the *idea* of the system but the *form* it has taken is what is objectionable; that, in fact, a change in drivers may bring the car under control.

Not a mere change in drivers but, with the shift to the new libertarians, a radical decentralization of the economy. Economics is something TV's children cannot understand because the concepts are too complex. They thus cannot recognize that what's being practiced out there among the Alternatives is primitive capitalism—absolutely primitive—a capitalism that may turn the Alternative into a nation of shopkeepers and craftsmen operating more on barter than on debt finance. Here's explosive potential. Blowing corporate America out of its skull. Dealing in hard goods and hard cash. *Mano a mano*. Notice the universally and staggeringly high attitude ratings accorded to small business in the Generations survey. In fact, the higher the claimed counter *politics*, the higher the small business rating. Only those old liberals held the over-all rating down to a 3.9 mean.

Split to the small enterprise, in which a man has control with his hands over the production of goods and services, over the marketing. And it seeps through the hype. When we're encouraged even by the umbra of a Jerry Rubin to discover "methods for producing books without publishers," what is meant is *their* publishers, the ones with the corporate shadows. So instead we spawn thousands of small and occasional business enterprises, a development that the overcorporated rationalized welfare capitalism of America desperately needs.

In one sense, the effort at reorganization is simply a playback, and the terms belie the reality. The ideology of this increasingly large draw on the counter-cult circuit announces that we do not like the managers and the stench of bureaucracy they have conceived, we do not see that corporate capitalism has been responsive to a genuine demand curve, so we'll do it ourselves in "alternative" institutions. The technology, too, is now available with which the little people can get back in after the second great rationalization of industry in the twentieth century. In this sense, even the politidomers are technology's children, but at least seeking to adapt it to themselves by choice rather than allowing it to be imposed. No politibullshit can hide that raw demand curve. Of course, there's an overlying spirit from counter-cult party line that confuses those drifting in: A simultaneous passionate desire to do away with the complexities of technology, and with those human complexities like perception and language as well, an impulse that may lead us not merely toward a simpler physical environment but also toward a primitive social environment in which the New New Capitalism may be doomed to failure.

The two strains come together, washed over with the politibullshit nostrum, in a series of columns former TV show writer Larry Menkin, who dates from the earliest years of the medium, did for the *LA Free Press*, "Space Time Continuum Memos." The thrust of our response to the following must lie in the question: "What makes the alternative institution so different in *form*, aside from the diminution of size and the identity of the managers?"

In "Memo No. 2" of August 6, 1971, Menkin advocates the formation of media collectives employing video cassettes for original programing of their choice as an alternative to network television. What the "Video Collectives! Video Communes! Video Co-ops!"

turn out to be, however, are new small business enterprises, resisting the insensitivity of the corporate world, the high-gloss on the libertarian:

> You can tell them to go fuck themselves. No kidding. They can't fire you. Because you won't be working for them. You'll be working for yourself. . . . They can't steal your ideas, talent, experience and then discard you like the obsolete man. Dig . . . ? Outta sight? Far out. . . . You'll write and produce the programs. You and your commune, co-op, collective associates will make and sell and distribute the soft ware. . . .
> All our sons have a chance to live again. A chance to communicate truth in a people's media. A chance to transmit information. True information. And information is power.
> Information is a gun. Information is the new revolution.

> Video cassette free information exchange, a new service for the alternate media in viedo. Share costs, profits, experiences in the videosphere of your local community. Be your own portable TV station, producer, distributor. Use your profits to create more programs; find new outlets, develop your own distribution outlets.

> HOW DO YOU DO IT? WHERE DO YOU BUY THE EQUIPMENT? HOW MUCH? Thoughts verbalized at me in light speed, flowing streamo, like this . . . if we cats, if we people, if we form a collective, a cooperative, if we learn how to work together, if it is so inexpensive, if it's going to sell like rock records and tape, how do we do it, who'll invest, if money is so tight, if you can't get risk capital, if the underground, alternate, off college press is clutching at straws to keep from going under, how do we do it, make with a miracle, man!
> I can't walk on water. I can't perform miracles. I can't tell you anything except this: do it. Get together. Raise the bread. Throw your bread on the water and it'll come back raison [*sic*] cake. Do it.
> Start. Go. Begin. 1971–1972. Now is the time. Organize your own company. Find the talent. Sell units or shares in your company. Borrow. Work and save for it. Start.

By the end of this out-take, Menkin reverberates like Nixon, for Chrissake! Even though, two paragraphs later, scaping examples of programing, he plays to an audience that seems to be a cartoon of the slick media counter-cult image: *How to Fuck* show, an Arthur Janov *Scream Along*, and, in a single character presentation

("Menkin's Mono Drama Technique of *One Actor,* no sets, few props, telling, acting out a story.") a choice of Marx, Mao, Ho Chi Minh, Nat Turner, etc.—from a guy who has just been shrieking at the alternate media people to go out and sell stock in their "collectives."

The Menkin column raises a number of issues which I try to emphasize throughout this little advertising folder on Alternative economies. Most important is the distinction between the ideology and the realities, a distinction centered in the identity of the people who can guarantee the survival of the Alternative. That is, if you're asking for will-energy and, in this case, for acquaintance with both technology and people-markets, and simultaneously addressing an audience that speaks in hip dictionary and raps like McLuhan on Speed, odds on that you will constipate both the energy and the sustained commitment. Secondly, and following, the awareness of technology and people-markets is frighteningly complex and therefore rejected by those who have already simplified perception and language to the point of nonexistence and are now out to reduce the world to a mirror of their souls. So those new business enterprises (call them "collectives" if it makes you feel better) concentrating on technological services and products, and thus more likely to demand *groups* of Alternative-seekers pooling resources and talent, will be limited in participation to comparative elites.

An asterisk to this second issue points to the disheartening realization that financing procedures analogous to those employed by the corporate mainstream will be necessary to some of these more technologically oriented alternative ventures, just as those ventures must currently rely on information available from mass corporate research labs (witness what amounts to a mass of corporate advertising for those resources in *The Whole Earth Catalog* or the *Domebook*). "Disheartening" is sarcastic, of course, and is directed at those who cover their reliance with some quasi-revolutionary rhetorical justification such as "we're only ripping off the capitalistic pigs." After all, when one speaks of "alternatives," one implies that competing systems still exist—in this case, decentralized versus rationalized business.

Lastly, of course, underneath that rhetoric, one cannot deny that the basic impulse is starting-from-scratch capitalism. Counter cult has known for some time that America has killed off free enterprise, but its response to the accompanying alienation of man from his work is hardly Marxist. Listen, for a moment, to moving force Stewart Brand's concluding comments in *The Last Whole Earth Catalog,* unquestionably the most successful of the alternative enterprises, and one which, as Brand notes, was designed to encourage others to follow suit:

> One of the main things that drove me into business was ignorance. A liberally educated young man, I hadn't the faintest idea how the world worked. Bargaining, distribution, mark-up, profit, bankruptcy, lease, invoice, fiscal year, inventory—it was all mystery to me, and usually depicted as sordid.

> I noticed that great lengths were gone to in order to prevent "consumers" from knowing that part of purchase price went to the retailer. It seemed exquisitely insane to me. You sell deception and buy mistrust, to no advantage. The retailer in fact earns his 25–40% by tiresome work, but the prevailing attitude makes him out a clever crook. Ignorance institutionalized. Would you mind leaving the room, we're talking about money.

> So along with shit, fuck, cunt, and the rest, I wanted to say to my friends, money, not to swear but to honor function.

> You may or may not think capitalism is nice, and I don't know that it is nice. But we should both know that the WHOLE EARTH CATALOG is made of it. . . .

> So I invested, comrade. I took the profits from old investments and put em into a new one, a brand new naive hopeful unlikely business with ditto in charge. Investing in yourself has hard truthful edges; I hope you get a crack at it, and can stay as sweet as you were as a dependent.

> Why am I saying all this? Because many who applaud the CATALOG and wholeheartedly use it, have no applause for the uses of money, of ego, of structure (read uptightness), of competition, of business as usual. All the things, plus others, which make the CATALOG, and make the selective applauders into partial liars, and me one too if I aid the lie [438].

Even in closing down *The Whole Earth Catalog* after four issues (during which cash flow jumped from $225,000 in calendar

1969 to an estimated $1 million plus in calendar 1971*), partly
for tax purposes (*WEC* could not have maintained its tax-free
status as "primarily an educational prototype" if it continued),
Brand indicates that the effects of discontinuance could and
should be considered in terms of classic capitalistic economics:

> Our stopping is primarily an economic experiment. Rather than do
> the usual succession things [and thus grow into an unwieldy and
> impersonal corporate venture] we prefer to just cease supply, let de-
> mand create its own new sources. Our hope is that those sources
> will be more diverse and better than we have been or could have
> been if we continued.

> There's money in this business. We made some in spite of our-
> selves [438].

In other words, encourage the process of decentralization, and
thus the establishment of an ever growing alternate economic system. In an interview with Sara Davidson recorded a year earlier
(*Harper's*, June 1970), Brand waxed evangelistic on the possibilities:

> "What we want are alternative economies and alternative political
> systems. Maybe alternative ecologies. You can't do this with six
> people." Brand points out that new social programs "are always
> parasitic, like newborn babies. They feed off the parent culture un-
> till they're strong enough to be self-sustaining." The communes in
> New Mexico, he says, can eventually develop their own economy
> by trading goods and services and paying in tokens, "like the casinos
> in Las Vegas. The climate is great for experiments now. There's no
> end of resources for promising ideas. But people had better hurry,
> because the avenues will start being closed off."

Given the identity and experience of so many of our current
communards, the actualization of Brand's vision is unlikely. Hard-
core, long-distance commitment to such projects, and the knowledge which could actualize the experiments, is fairly thin among
spin-offs from the audio media culture. Notice, though, the possi-

---

* The unaudited balance sheet for *WEC* as of April, 1971, *before* receipts
from the last, and unquestionably best-selling, issue, shows sales running at an
annual rate of $600,000. Ratio of current assets to current liabilities, even
taking account of corporate income taxes (to which *WEC* is not subject) was
7:1, not merely respectable, but, in the absence of long-term debt, amazing.

bility for competition which Brand leaves open both in his concluding statement to *The Whole Earth Catalog* and in his earlier interview in *Harper's* (i.e., "People had better hurry, because the avenues will start being closed off"). To the extent that Brand and others are children of their great-grandparents, the "experiment" of stopping the WEC was a measured success. Now here we have *Mother Earth News*, one of the more prominent gap-fillers for that demand curve, providing the overview for the New New Capitalism in a First Number borrowed editorial, and borrowed, not so coincidentally on hindsight, from the street sex capitalist *Cavalier:*

> So okay. So it is possible to break loose . . . but where's the bread going to come from? Can you actually do exactly what you want and still cop the loot? Damn right. In fact, you're more likely to make vast quantities of cash if you *are* joyfully in tune with yourself.
>
> Let's stop and lay down some ground rules right in front: We presently live in a society that puts a price tag on virtually everything, right? Right. And that can be a real drag, right? Right. Because you always wind up having to put in your time on a job you hate just to get the necessities of life, right? Wrong. . . . There's no reason you can't make that work *for*, rather than *against*, you.
>
> It's easy. First, decide what you really want to do; second, start doing it (as long as you're not putting a bad trip on someone or something else) and third, figure out some way to exchange what you do for what you want and need.

The roots are profoundly American. From Thomas Jefferson to Do-It-Yourself kits, we are dealing with Con I. The only factor that differentiates the manifestations of this spirit is the time environment. That is, we are looking to *earlier* models as a way to reconstruct the present and the future. Brand's ideal alternate economy, for example, would eliminate the middlemen, the overheads, the surplus baggage centuries of mercantilism and now corporatism have engrafted on individuals attempting to provide goods and services for others. The basic impulse is back to a more simplified economic state, without unnecessary external controls. Some elements of the counter culture adapt the earlier models to the contraction of space and time, and within existing economic and social orders (Brand's project and its imitators). Others disregard the contraction and the existing orders and live in a cruel self-imposed hoax. Among the former, the impulse is away from *surplus* consumerism, not from consumerism *per se*, basic possessions, or from money. According to Brand, the attitude is best expressed by Ken Kesey hisself: "you don't make money by making money: you have that in mind early on, but then you forget it and concentrate entirely on good product; the money comes to pass," echoed by the Horace Greeley editorial board of *Mother Earth News:*

"Go where you want to be and pick up the free percentage that's always there. You'll soon be considered an authority or a craftsman or—at the very least—a fixture in your chosen field. When the money comes down, you'll get your share."

An exemplar from an item in *The New York Times, circa* July, 1971. A couple in Hawaii, John and Lisa Harvey, running a health food store, and believing that

> the evolution that changed them from anti-Establishment dropouts to successful proprietors will become an increasingly common phenomenon among the young, particularly when they are married.
>
> But although the Harveys say that making money is where it's at, they are not interested in a new car, a house in the suburbs or a fat savings account. The young couple are hoping to start a noncoercive, tuition-free school teaching peace and encouraging creativity with the profits from their natural food store, "The Good Earth."
>
> "John and I have done the whole bit," said the 23-year-old Mrs. Harvey. "We were flower children, we took drugs, lived in communes and gave away all our possessions.
>
> "But when it was all said and done, we still had to decide what we wanted to do with our lives. A school, which would offer an alternative to the standard 12-year sentence children get as a birthday present, was the answer."
>
> Mrs. Harvey laughingly recalled their naivete in thinking "it was such a good idea everyone would contribute money." When the contributions failed to come, the two realized it was back into the Establishment, at least half-way, or no school.

It's not really "half-way," but a leap to values which the Establishment itself has betrayed. The more this directed phenomenon spreads, and the less it is accompanied by the hyped politic which operates as a kind of paranoid self-justification, blinding the fantasts and precluding a lengthy stay, the less, I think, will be the anger, vulnerability, and feeling of disposability of the young.

Unfortunately, in the more politicized counter-media, the models of the politidomers disparage the work of the Harveys as hip capitalistic rip-off. But one must confront the motive forces of the emergence and continuing growth of alternative capitalism as it has arisen specifically, and nearly exclusively, among the young. We recognize well by now that American society, in heinous cooperation with the Academy, extends adolescence by about ten years without propping it with any social sense of being or purpose beyond the empty gratulations of epigraphic platitudes. Trying to carve out a position, a social organization and climate that would provide something less amorphous and despairing than that inherited state, the young first turned, instinctively, to their immediate environment, the university. Thus the demand for relevancy and student power—some sense that one is controlling one's own destiny as much as possible in a society that seems paradoxically fearful of the prospect of young people's becoming adults. The effort fails because it takes place in an institution that is isolated and insulated. No matter how much one may control his academic environment, he still does not fully control the direction of his soul.

When the peculiar set of circumstances that coalesced in the late 1960's forced students into an economy with few job opportunities, the myth of the education-job indispensability equation was thoroughly exploded. The "practical" grounds on which so many had surged into the Academy for their union cards became dispensable. The exit—of the middle class, at least—from the university was on.

Confronting the options for controlling their own environment, on the one hand forced into the reality principle of the economy and on the other aided by a growing counter culture that demanded highly specialized goods and services,* they began to copy some of the early hip capitalists and discovered that in small en-

---

* E.g., the attitude toward meat intense enough to rival the strictures of an orthodox religious sect, i.e., either no meat, or meat from animals raised without benefit of the clergy of antibiotics, opens up a host of possibilities for the New Agrarians and shop-keeping "collectives."

terprise they could indeed control their lives and values in a far more encompassing and meaningful fashion than the university-encouraged retreat left open—all without abandoning the political sensibilities that define the community of youthcult spiritual interest. Indeed, in the process of advising prospective entrants, Stewart Brand indicates at least some of the values that can be reinvigorated:

> Small business is based on earned trust. Send cash-with-order in your first dealings with another firm. Pay bills scrupulously on time. Keep exact, open books on all your accounting. Small businessmen respond faster to honesty than any other kind of person: most of them couldn't care less what you wear, smoke, or think if you're straight with them and don't care what they wear, smoke, or think [*The Last Whole Earth Catalog*, 438].

If, in the process, one sends back profits into "the community"—in the form of donations to a day-care center or through a project such as the Harveys' planned free school—one will find, without any politibullshit, that he is following an old practice of small businessmen, who are more likely to be in intimate contact with and play supportive roles in their communities. Flesh on flesh. Proving it on the pulses. Not the abstract and distant donative hand of the corporate foundation. The message is "Do It"—but not draped in Rubinian paranoia and violence. As George von Hilsheimer, writing in *The Last Whole Earth Catalog*, said of free schools (and the principle is the same), the way to keep your ideals realized as going propositions "is to be compulsively sure" you want them, "hardnosed about business, and WORK. America's most lamented four letter word."*

As likely a form as the small retail operation in counter-cult capitalism are services and crafts, which generally involve individuals operating alone. The services are directed toward the counter community and born of the barter marts in the small underground papers, e.g., "Thirty acres of standing hay . . . for instruction in

---

* Von Hilsheimer reminds the dreamers: "Opening and keeping open a free school has much more to do with being tough, anal, compulsive, cantankerous and agile than with love. The *real* genius at Summerhill is Mrs. Neill who sees to the kitchen, housekeeping, bills *and billing*. I cannot too strongly tell you how all those nice folks you take in for nothing will be the first to run screaming to the fuzz about how vile you are—meantime owing you for the medicine, food and clothes you bought their brat."

sewing, VW repair, housebuilding, plumbing, carpentry," "Mechanical work for a zinc sink," etc. The crafts are necessarily directed toward the mainstream economy (as they often offer nonessential consumer goods), a mark of the necessary parasitic relationship between the two "economies." In crafts as well as services, individuals may market together but work alone, and the arrangement reinforces the nomadic libertarianism of the counter-cult life-style with a vengeance, to wit, and not so much between the lines, the following insertion.

AN INTERVIEW WITH HARRY, THE BLACKSMITH

Harry, the blacksmith, is a double drop-out: (1) from a small college in New York City and (2) from a smaller college in North Dakota, where he went "because I wanted some place in the Midwest where there was an opening. When the Placement Service said North Dakota, I had to unroll my plastic puzzle map to find out where it was."

Why did you go into blacksmithing?

Because I didn't want to be a doctor.

That's why we're all doing what we're doing—nobody wanted to be a doctor. A prophetic metaphor. But what was it that moved you to choose smithing?

I was working summers in Colorado for a great old guy who ran an inn and had made all the ironwork—gorgeous gates, lattice work, stuff like that. He said there was a course in smithing down in New Mexico, so I paid my $300 for a six-week course, but left after four weeks when I figured I knew about as much as the instructor did.

Where did you go?

I went to a little town in New Hampshire which the AAA didn't even have on their maps.

Why there?

I wanted to get in with the New Hampshire Crafts Association, which was nearby; and also, that was the only place where I could find a barn for a forge and workshop in the middle of February.

Why did you leave?

It was a bad scene for business. See, I have to charge more for my stuff—like carbon-coated stainless steel knives or gatework—

because I don't go in for arc-welding. Arc-welding isn't being a blacksmith. So you go to these fairs, too, and the Crafts Association takes a third cut, so you've got to price even higher—unless you want to sell under the table without writing it up. You know, "You really like this knife? What's it worth to you?" So you sell a fifteen-dollar knife for seven or eight, but if you didn't do that, people would just be standing around grooving on watching you and not buying. I always attract these crowds, but it's always everybody else who's selling.

Business should be better here in Vermont. Even with the Crafts Center's cut, you've got a lot more nifty-gifty traffic.

I'm really not counting on that. I'd really like to sell in major quantities to interior decorators and architects in New York.

Harry is Buck Mulligan without the bravura style. With middle spread, flying beard, and crinkled intensity, whether in jest or for survival's sake, he would be cast as a blacksmith in any remake of the first Revolutionary War. In one sense, he's fighting the second; but with that last sentence from the excerpt, he indicates where Con I will go, what it needs to survive. Raw bartering at flea market tables may produce a borderline survival kit for the craftsman, and even there he is relying on the corporate economy that produces all those consumers whom counter cult dislikes so much. But simplified existence does not mean borderline survival, as those without the trust funds or other monthly disbursements soon discover. So the individual craftsman starts looking toward larger markets and marketeers. He can remain close to the production of his work, can maintain an intimacy with his hands, but must recognize that his survival cannot be predicated on other New Agrarians and Hip Craftsmen who are returning to the tribal garden and are not in need of his labors. Harry, twenty-three, knows that:

"The ones who come and gawk at you most are all these hip travelers, these kids who think it's all a groove and want to get into it or something like it. Then you ask them whether they want to buy, and there's the whole bag. They don't. So how the hell would they survive?" Another local craftsman, Paul the Woodworker, points to the way in which this same brood, wanting the whole world and wanting it *now*, rips-off its own:

"I once made one of those barter deals with a couple of these commune kids down in X. I figured, what the hell, they seemed cool enough, and I was in for the good vibrations—you know, that innocent line, we'll trade you some vegetables and help you chop your wood for some wood bowls. So I tell them I'm splitting wood on Saturday. On Wednesday they drop by some mouldy squash and about enough carrots to feed a rabbit, and of course they don't show up on Saturday—nor ever again. That whole line is such bullshit."

Paul is thirty-one and has been woodworking for five years in the same general area. He keeps a centralized market in the tourist trade. Harry may develop the ability to work nomadically (though, considering the physical requirements for a blacksmith's shop, that's hardly likely) if he is able to reach a centralized buying market among the "interior decorators and architects" in New York. If these men are cameos of the Alternatives, they know that they can survive only through that kind of stability and long-term commitment. And alternative decentralized economies can only grow around the long-distance runners.

As roguishly charming as Harry may be, and as fine as his work, he still exhibits those impatient, nomadic strains which will undermine alternative breaks from the corporate. Indeed, a notable number of hip craftsmen project that unfortunate possibility. The most distinct aversion is to marketing, particularly to direct selling, as they somehow believe everyone will come to them, a belief partly acquired, perhaps, from observing the slick media jumping all over anyone who comes on in *de rigueur* form. Place, too, spells commitment, so the new drive is away from operating one's own outlet and toward descending on towns—occasionally, when one needs the bread—and laying something on the local nifty-gifty outfits. The operators of those, many of whom are now older New Alternatives members, dropping from the corporate-commuter synapses, would gladly underpin the craftsmen if they could be assured of a steady source of supply. But because the younger seekers simultaneously admire the independence of the traditional craftsmen and bore easily, migrating to other "scenes," they rarely hit the same town twice. They may be working out of a barn in New Hampshire one year, in Idaho the next. Primitive capitalism becomes anarchic capitalism and courts oblivion.

The older operatives both admire and grate at the independence and radical individualism of these occasional seekers. One tale of an April order for July 1 delivery of a mass of finely wrought jewelry: The craftsmen turned up on May 1 with the goods, and since, as itinerants, they operate on cash and carry, demanded that the store man take the stuff then and pay, incapable of realizing that no nifty-gifty joint that dances to the summer tourist trade has any cash on hand on May 1, particularly a sum like the one at issue, $150. Presented with a veritable "non-negotiable demand" that he either accept the goods c.o.d. "or you'll never get anything from us again," the older Alternatives man spoke the malediction, "Fuck off," and remarked later that "I would never expect to receive anything from them again anyway. Look, you go to a crafts show loaded with those people, and the sample work is spectacular, I mean, some of them, if they can stick with it, are really talented. But you go to the shows, and if you get 30 per cent of what you order, you're doing well. Most of us can't operate like that, so I know I'm not going to those shows any more; and I've got to feel sorry for those of them that come through."

In so many words, what hope there is for some permanent Alternative tends to atrophy from within even in the deep structure of Con I capitalism in counter cult. It's a function of both the practitioners and the itinerant anarchism which the rugged individualist ethic encourages among those in that paradoxically odd state of grace, wanting the world and wanting it *now*. With this observation we are led back to counter-cult ideology.

12

More Clippings from the Ideology of Counter Cult: The Consequences of Anarchic Libertarianism

Proposition: The *practice* of counter cult often reveals more strictly right-wing ideology than even the combination of left-libertarian. The New Nihilism in the broader reaches of youthcult proliferates not by willed destruction but through the paradox of nilling. When one wills not, freedom comes to consist, as the Country & Western song muses, of "just another word for nothing left to lose." Nil, and one not only denies all authority but denies the Other as well. Nothing is left to lose beyond the self, and because the self no longer relates actively to others, it has been singed into an indifference under which it can no longer bear witness to its own unmoored motions. How uneasily does the New Nihilism sit with the left-libertarian ideology! How willingly can it bed down with that craggy nineteenth-century frontier politic and its more recent extension, the Paradise *now* of Nazi decadence! How willingly *does* it bed in the subterranean structure of counter cult!

Such is inevitable among those with limited conceptual equipment. We've been unconscious of the potential projection: Anarchic libertarianism, coupled with a search for new Absolutes, can yield a fierce fascist authoritarianism. One doesn't even need Con I competition for that development, particularly when the mass turns purposefully mindless. If the Hell's Angels have now taken up residence on the fringe of counter cult, we have a living metaphor for one of its principal structures.

After all, we began with a return to the self and reinforced that return through a group politic—rallies for hair, Gay lib, etc.—all asserting the individual's right to control his own body. Then we forked, with one portion logically seeking the isolationist self, moving into homogenized rootlessness, the other simply content with a supererogatory laissez-faire.

On the isolationist self: Complacent with the community of spiritual interest formed in the collective libertarian movements, some chose to remain wholly within them, at first talking only to "brothers and sisters," then only to the self. As the Other became more and more of a hassle, unperceived beyond "vibrations," the retreat intensified. It became an unwilled odyssey without mythic dimensions.

I recall one who journeyed, first shrinking into a print collective, a convenient form of isolation (as opposed to a legal or medical service collective, in which one might have to confront in the sensory portions of the society other than one's own). From there (and on inheritance) because group work involved progressive chaos and entanglement and because the collective announced its intention to live communally, it was into a VW bus with the old lady and off on a nomadic expedition. On a winter evening in their first landing place, they sat proselytizing for women's lib, and he sent her into the kitchen to do the dishes while he, raggedy in pomposity, slumped over a chair holding forth in sundry movement clichés. Gradually he removed himself from every activity in which he would be directly confronted with the Other, the tenuousness increasing in wandering a nation of ephemeral "scenes" in that bus which came to define the limits of his existence. Looking for space, not people—a hidden canyon, an empty ski trail, a deserted fogged beach—and even in falling into an occasional radical project, the same, e.g., a media venture on the Coast, making tapes for the unseen masses while parked in the bus outside of a removed shack near Mendocino.

One is reminded of that 1970 *Esquire* college issue, in which, following the commune trip, fleeted the hype for the new nomad who can jump through spaces and environments like the early *Counter Cult* nineteenth-century huntsman, with technology providing both the materials (the house-car) and the psychological setting (mass anomie). Such counter-cult nomads, revelling in a kind of formless rejection, are practicing a brand of individualism that the shills for the "new consciousness" have falsely tortured into a motion toward regroupment in community. Such a sly transformation is also confusing to those in the wings who are drawn to the "new life-styles," but haven't yet taken the plunge. As Keniston wrote:

> The quests of most alienated Americans are private quests—for personal sentience, for intensified subjectivity, for kicks and stimulation, for individual artistic expression—the alienated express themselves more to achieve self-definition than to persuade others.

But even self-*definition* has become a subordinate clause, as the increasing number of counter-cult wanderers float like a Sargasso Sea, semiconscious of only the vaguest *parameters* of the self, oblivious to the inner substance—if, indeed, there is much.

To fortify evidence, one adds the statement *Esquire* issues on behalf of one of the new nomads:

> I choose this way to freedom because it offers me the best of two worlds. I can live most of the time away from the regimented, congested, indefensible cities, yet still profit by "exporting" my labor into those cities [shades of Harry the Blacksmith]. I have the freedom and security offered by mobility; yet I possess what is in most respects a permanent residence. I can fully enjoy life right now, yet live economically and accumulate capital for further ventures. Finally, I can "opt out" alone, while I look forward to trade with others who may choose similar or complementary ways of life, my liberty does not depend on their decisions.

The freedom of the self, then, no longer depends on the existence of the Other. In fact, the statement contains an implicit moral assertion that the existence of the "Other" may well inhibit my freedom. Moral anarchism follows. The ideologic posture pamphleteers that the libertarian nomad is cutting ties of state control over himself (a classic conservative cliché) and runs the program out to the end of the maxim: "What one can't control, one doesn't really own." But what obtains in anarchic capitalism, which has also produced an Ivan Illich in education, is the total abdication of judgment beyond the self. It's different in this existential tinge from the morality of the Yippie cop-out, and it is radically Socratic. Casting off the ropes altogether, instead of merely attaching ratlines, seems morally perspicuous and psychologically convenient.

No wonder the response to Ayn Rand (remember how one defined himself as a "radical" by heckling her on the college lecture circuit in 1961?) was hardly negative on the Generations survey. Among those calling themselves "anarchists" or some combination involving anarchist (even "anarchist-radical-general leftist," in one case) *and* among those with actual counter-cult involvement, the attitude rating accorded to Rand was consistently higher than that accorded her by everyone else. As Hugh Gardner speculated in that *Esquire* spread on the garden of alternatives, if you asked one of the new furry libertarians to explain himself, "he just might tell you that most modern longhairs are really right-wing anarchists like himself, but just don't know it yet. Give them some experience in communes, he just might say, and they'll figure it out."

Commune, as we've observed, so often works against community among those who cannot wholly kiss us. As a symptom of reinforced rootless isolationism, start with a small counter-cultural artifact, tent domes, and the drive toward portability. The designers are, in effect, acknowledging the fleeting nature of the counter-cult relationship, the fragility of what is now aphorized as the "one-year community" (better make it, "one year or less") by allegorizing portable hip. "Getting ourselves together" has rarely lasted more than a week, except among the hard core. Ephemeral hitchhiking relationships increase. As a twenty-year-old college student picked up by a *New York Times* correspondent researching the new open-road easy riders commented:

> On the road you get a feeling of not being anywhere. If I don't have a destination, sometimes I feel lost. That's also good—to have no structured thought in your mind and to experience new things without having a basis to relate to them. But it's also scary sometimes.

Or a silent Om-ing threesome who rode with me somewhere in Connecticut, sitting stonily (no doubt relating to each other through vibrations), figuring they might head for Boston and split up there—or maybe before. In fact, one stayed, heading north, because, as he said later, the other two "were a drag." Combining, recombining, dispersing—almost unwilling stepchildren of a nihilism born of the feeling of inadequacy in the face of the mere complexity of another human being.

Laissez-faire, in matters both social and economic, follows. Angus Black concludes his *New Radical's Guide to Economic Reality* with a pitch for a platform that would be heartily endorsed by Barry Goldwater, Milton Friedman, and the Young Americans for Freedom, capping itself with the aphorism, "Less government today; even less tomorrow." In fact, the whole book, despite its title, despite the rhetoric of the Pig and occasional Marx name-dropping, configures as a right-wing tract, advocating monetarism, flat tax rates, voucher education, abolition of the minimum wage, abolition of rent control, competitive medical services, and accompanying rejection of National Health Insurance.

Likewise, even in some of the more advanced polemics for women's liberation, we find what William Shannon, writing on the *Times* Op-Ed page, once referred to as a "laissez-faire approach to parenthood." Often, indeed, the underlying motivation for commune-joining among young adult families is that the intellectual, moral, and emotive responsibilities for child-rearing are lessened. "The kid makes too many demands on me," said one friend heading for passed responsibility, "like it really gets in the way of your self-development." The cover rhetoric asserts that by placing the child in a communal child-caring arrangment, one is teaching him anarchism and its attendant values. If one means *right*-wing anarchism, yes, but by example (although one is tempted to hypothesize that "teaching" anarchism is a contradiction in terms). For the arrangements frequently place the kid in an ephemerality of relationships that will, in time, force him back into himself as the sole arbitrator of good and evil. Transcience reinforced. A mirror of the larger society—but with a vengeance.

Free schools, too, echo this line. If there's no written philosophy, the assumptions are still thick. Do something or do nothing: the individual as sole resource, however much the theory holds community to dominate. Independence, autonomy—you either pick it up or you don't, and what you pick up is of your own choosing. Nobody, presumably, cares. Laissez-faire, and the robber barons will out. After all, those who pick it up join the counter elite of the New Jerusalems, while those who don't abandon even that possibility. A friend remarked that her ten-year-old in an open classroom experiment "spent the whole year playing chess in the fifth grade. At first he loved it, but now he feels that he wished he had done something more concrete. At least playing chess is a thinking proposition, but that isn't the issue. There are too many kids for whom that sort of freedom pays poor dividends." The Movement here contributes not to the democratization of society but to its precise converse.

If the full Con I ethic, social Darwinism, runs strong in counter cult, one is not surprised. It's the logical extension of the anarchic-libertarian route. Even, and particularly, among those who announce their abhorrence for that ethic, the life-style runs counter to the intended spirit. E.g., Lou Gottlieb, formerly of The Lime-lighters, operating a religiomysto commune in northern California, told Sara Davidson: "From the first, the land selected the people. Those who couldn't work hard didn't survive. When the land got crowded, people split. The vibrations of the land will always protect the community." If one doesn't work, the Robin Hoods hedge on intolerance. Hard by the Gottlieb Farm lies the Wheeler Ranch, at which our Connecticut real estate heir presides, openly "contemptuous of people who can't pull their own weight" (Davidson).

Bucky Fuller reinforces through his theory of the "outlaw area," a place or resource that is virgin, so anything goes. The species diversifies, decentralizes, by discovering the alternatives it is forced to discover in these "places." All technological creativity, Fuller adds, has been developed in what previously were "outlaw areas." The new outlaws think they are likewise creating, but reflect: Those to whom Fuller refers had some equipment to begin with, and therefore were not chaotically tasting everything in a desperate attempt to stay ahead of the baddies on the other side of the frontier.

And not necessarily by design does the social Darwinism flourish. One looks to the raw jungles of the former hippie neighborhoods. The new street people, all under twenty, are far more into hard drugs, illiteracy, and impatient violence than their predecessors. They're falling off the campuses and high schools into the street, and however much many may battle with the bikers, they are all part of the nomad faction. The community is fragmented by mutual trashings, rip-offs, hasslings, and swarms of parasites who arrived after the flower neighborhoods have been institutionalized by Yippie flyers and the media—slick, establishment, and underground alike. The peasants came looking for the easy indulgence and found that the appelation "brother" did not stop a mugging at knifepoint on East 10th Street. They were forced to adopt such ways themselves. The Speed culture cooperated: the speed freak loses all sensitivity to what other people are saying, feeling, thinking, and becomes compulsively aggressive. Couple that behavior with an ethic that begins and ends in self, and one has chiseled out a militant right-wing tableau.

No wonder the Yippies have mimeographed panegyrics to the development: The social and educational divisions in Amerikkka must be expanded, even exaggerated, as a prelude to Revolution. The Hoffmans have gotten savvy: You can't have a revolution with an intelligent middle class, not even assuming that intelligence to be wrapped in Marx. The object is to create a class of mindless subsistense-level ekers fighting for a raw survival over scraps, eliminating the middle class, magnifying the poor and illiterate, and thus artificially creating a social chasm into which revolution can easily plunge. But the gist of that vision, I suspect, is not quite as likely as the following options.

13

Some Brief Visions, Fantasies, Prophecies

One particularly piquant vision of the effects of the growing and projected dispersal into counter cult was offered to the readers of the *New Republic* (April 3, 1971) by two professors of sociology, Peter and Brigitte Berger, from Rutgers and LIU respectively, under the title, "The Blueing of America." Their prognosis, somewhat simplified, runs thus: The uppermiddle classes drop out to the new agrarianisms and capitalisms, leaving room in the power system for someone to fill in and keep the computers running. Who fills in? The children of the working class, predominantly white, some black. The effect is to fortify the class system by providing upward mobility while others move down and out. Thus the unconscious irony of the cultural revolution: It will indeed give power to the people—well, if not the people the revolutionists were thinking about, at least people other than themselves. The system doesn't change; only the drivers of the car are switched. To this one would only add the qualifying note that the new drivers may have been affected by their move through the gravitational fields of youthcult, and may not have been.

The timbre of the Bergers' prophecy is suffused with the reasonable, but several double-takes are warranted. One immediately agrees that whatever vacuum is created by the abdication of the counter-culturists will attempt to close itself in the mainstream.

Questions: (1) Which counter-culturalists is one talking about? The Stewart Brands? If so, that will indeed leave a vacuum. But the average TV child drifting into counter culture has little equipment for mainstream power structure roles anyway. (2) Will abdication actually create that much of a vacuum, or has the technocracy evolved to the stage at which all it requires is an axised elite, with everyone else dying off by attrition? (3) Assuming there is a vacuum, will there be enough bodies to fill it? And (4) if so, what kind of bodies? For if the supply is limited, then power will indeed be concentrated in the hands of a very few. Rigidity will set in at the top, and the class structure will retract to the bounds of a medieval estate.

On the availability of bodies of the children of the working class. Perhaps my experience teaching in two universities dominated by the lower middle class, living in a few lower-middle-class/working-class neighborhoods in Chicago and New York and in a small working-class mill town in New England, has been fundamentally different from that of the Bergers. One persistent perception of the late 1960's remains unshaken: Most of the kids in those neighborhoods were not particularly interested in either education or power, the Bergers' prerequisites for the Blueing of America. Typical of their concerns, quoted in *Phoenix* (August 3, 1971): "All we want is some peace and quiet so we can drink our beer, smoke our smoke and screw our chicks." And on a Brooklyn stoop corner, pupils the size of pin heads, staccato acne of monstrous proportions, they tap dance on meth and on the "heavy vibes at the Fillmore last night, man. This street? Who gives a shit about this dumpy neighborhood? This rat-fuck city . . . only them young asses who head for Recycle on Saturday morning, and I'd like to lay into a piece of them. Oh, sweeeeet snatch!—Yeah!"

The street-corner-hanging life-style, now tragically augmented by speed, has not merely persisted but intensified. Long hair and bell bottoms on such corners bode no new sensibilities.

Granted, an increasing number now go on to college. But the highest attrition rates among my former students were precisely among those whose backgrounds suggest potential mobility to the Bergers. Even before attrition, that group evidenced perhaps the most brutalized minds, the least literacy, sensibility, or perceptive ability. Black kids from ghetto areas can at least overcome their polluted school environments because their social structure forces them to acquire perceptual survival kits at an early age, and so often their lives literally depend on the swiftness and depth of their wits—the con, the laugh, the cultivated style of cool. Working-class kids, on the other hand, are burdened doubly with a rigid family structure, with fathers who lock them in rooms for weeks at the age of seventeen for minor infractions of that iron blue-collar morality.

Thus the college attrition among children of the working class involved as much induction into counter politics as into counter culture, for they have fathers to revolt against, and are not interested in the search for new authority figures. If the Weathermen were loaded with aristocrats, the Crazies around our way were stocked with junior blue collars. And among them, the YIP program has its greatest appeal: It's pure street corner and reinforces a life-style they already possess.

Still, assuming there will be enough around who actually march through college and follow all those certification programs the counter-people reject, then move on into custodial positions, what genus of custodians will we be blessed with? Racist flag-wavers, the Wallace kids—those who spat at us during a neighborhood peace march in Brooklyn? I doubt it. These generally don't go to school. Instead, I suspect—and very much invited by the Generations survey—a group more insensitive because less perceptive, less informed old-line liberals than we've had cycling around the halls of power in the past. The survey correlations: Those under twenty-five who indicated lower-middle or working-class backgrounds and who simultaneously did *not* indicate counter-culture or -politics involvement *or* highly positive counter-culture attitudes strongly tended to be

1. exclusively audio-media-oriented
2. but more likely to register moderate to significant TV viewing indexes
3. less likely to have participated in social or community action programs
4. but equally likely to have participated in a peace protest or rally

5. less likely to have boycotted anything
6. more likely to identify their politics in single, traditional categories of Liberal and Conservative
7. and less likely to evidence political consistency
8. more likely to rank low in information in all categories
9. and more likely to respond positively to counter-culture clichés *and* corporate clichés *and* liberal issues clichés.

If the counter-culturalists are doing little, these people are doing less. The quality of the Blueing, then, might have the effect of filling the vacuum, yes, but will still leave power in the hands of a fiendish elite. The new body habitus anemia is universal. It's not a class problem, and therefore its prospects, even assuming the Bergers' prophecy, transform an inkling of fear into a pulse of dread.

But from the Bergers' premise one facilely springs into an alternative fantasy, and a desperate poker game ensues. Compose the young and hip heading for the woods to play homesteader, anti-consumer, or self-sufficient commune. Or enter the monasteries of Krishna Consciousness, Jesus Freakism, *et al.* Or nomad, doing the nineteenth-century Hungarian gypsy number. Or to the loner or crafts collective business. Perhaps a few million effloresce in an unwitting vendetta. It doesn't take much to open up an abridged version of a sci-fi tale to unwind through the alienated circuits over the miseracordia of a few years.

Envision that billiard table of consequences. We begin by knocking upwards of $20 billion out of the mainstream economy, initially yielding widespread unemployment in all media, advertising, consumer electronics, and garment industries, an unemployment which later spreads through the education industry as at least a third of the colleges in the country close. The multiplier effect sets in. Increased homesteading by displaced education people. Demand for goods and services drops to Depression level.

Basic economics unctions into political vibrations. As the media close, information becomes more centralized, restricted and controlled by the John Mitchell barbie dolls. Blacks and the white working class, traditional sufferers of unemployment, are now desperate enough to shoot at mere sounds of each other. Their conflict exacerbated by the loss of government revenues for education, housing, transportation—those items to be cut first in yielding to demands for a massive domestic police force to patrol the desolate urban plains. All while men in power gain sinecures, and options on replacing them nearly vanish. They now control what's left of the Academy, so fully condition their successors. The decentralization of a population that has yielded up information in favor of the restorative atmosphere of a past world renders effortless the task of dividing and conquering, the agents being all those rednecks in the volunteer army that was once so naïvely promoted by the now departed.

At some point in here, the vision opens itself up to at least four options: (1) the possibility of mass government depression deficit spending creates at least statist employment for the blue-collars and blacks, while the New Jerusalem people become the official rural poor; (2) the same, but with some of the original counter-culturists flowing back into the power structure, rising even faster than possible before as so many of the oldies were flushed out—a true Con I counter-cult ethic case of survival of the fittest; (3) the unemployed also head for the land, and we regress to a full feudal society, replete with local warlords and chiefs, some of whom will arise from the ashes of our current libertarian nomads, others through the new absolutes of counter-cult religion; (4) the long-envisioned fascist state is actually born, and the possibilities for resistance are nil among the shrines of isolationism and ignorance.

I suppose the first option presents the least of evils, but whichever one of these possibilities, born into vision by an increasingly justifiable analysis of the coming generations of youthcult, whichever vision concretizes will spell bad headlines—except there won't be any more headlines.

"It's not all that unreasonable," said one in a group rap exploration of apocalyptic possibilities on a long-shadowed spring morning with enough tension between the buds to launch charged voyages, adding, "you know, unless somebody reminds you of such a simple-assed thing such as what happens to a lot of people who depend on kids for a living, you just don't think about it." Another, more defensive, was not wholly prepared to accept the disconcerting tone of the possibilities, and the interplay danced around an urban space of broken glass:

"Tribal wars! Groovy! You see, we *will* get back to the tribes, new communities."

"No, no, it really won't be tribal wars—more like family wars, hill-folk feuds."

"It actually won't be tribe in the sense he's thinking of it—sort of like tribes out of necessity, not because people will be digging each other."

"Whaddya want? Look, we all come out of American society where we're all divided, out of schools where we're split apart, and you take those habits with you no matter how much of a cultural revolutionary—even political revolutionary—you think you are."

A setting filled with appropriate metaphors to impel the dance toward the Educational order. The search for new communities and alternate cultures is partially foredoomed by the awful isolationist activity of the schools from whence the searchers issued. The will is short-circuited by an artificial conditioning process, the soul is fragmented by imposed roles, and the whole carries over into the colleges to such an extent that all the renovation in those slums won't deal with the rotting land on which the buildings sit. We must think of some other order of perceiving our education. We no longer have the luxury of a debating society.

The Complicities
of the Academy

14

The University as Wheelchair

What feeds the hidden ideology of counter cult? What nourishes
the motivations? What accounts, too, for the chain-reaction
deaths of the soul's functions recorded earlier? The culture is too
vast to reduce, to offer simplicities, or to sloganeer in rebuttal. But
at the end of our excursion into the congeries of McLuhan, I
offered the tentative combination of media and schools as worthy
of serious attention. In this final corner of the collage, what has
been telegraphed as the university "crisis" and its alternative must
be sculpted—if not with talmudic care, then at least in a series of
overlapping, and hopefully encompassing, accretions.

University, and not school, and this focus for a number of reasons, although the two are really inseparable. I am simply not
equipped to speak of primary and secondary education and am
tired punch of the casuistries of gurus in that field. University,
too, because the age group under consideration is what it is, and
because the place presents us with the opportunity for dealing
with vast numbers of the generations at issue. University, still
again, because our effulgent enshrining of the institution has rendered it an unwitting accomplice in the drama of alternatives
bound for failure that is slowly unfolding.

We have inherited, and with satisfaction, a conditioning process
under which millions have been wedded to the university mentality, who perceive all problems through the looking glass of abso-

lute mental freedom which the university environment provides. Lulled into bogus security, they dread breaking from it when they confront a world beyond the campus gates. Consequently that world is perceived as if it were a university.

The epiphanic moment, the indication of the absurd intensity of the tie to the Academy spoon: When Yale rumbled up to prepare for the Black Panther rally on May Day of 1970, the crystalizing event was the handing of contempt citations to Panther heavies Dave Hilliard and Emory Douglas at the New Haven Federal Courthouse. At the mass hysteria meeting that ensued, the following were among the suggested reprisals: Burn down *Yale*, occupy some halls at *Yale*, boycott classes at *Yale* (that one passed), demand that *Yale* contribute a half-million to the Panther defense fund, kidnap the *Yale* president, Kingman Brewster. X hits Y, so Z, in reprisal, hits Q—not X. Brilliant! But before the easy dismissal, think: The responses were the perfectly logical consequences of a pervasive cultural opiate that prevents young people from scourging the authentic Manichean hydras. They embodied the extensions of that uniquely American assumption: The school does everything.

As Peter Schrag has wisely written ("End of the Impossible Dream"), the school in America

> is our answer to Karl Marx—and to everything else. . . . Thus, if the school system fails, so does the promise of equality, so does the dream of the classless society, so does our security against the inequalities of society. The school system has failed. [*Saturday Review*, September 19, 1970.]

The mere fact that 30 per cent of the country is in school, and nearly 5 per cent is tied to the universities in one way or another, fits neatly into our unwritten expectations that education will resolve everything from family disputes to technological cul-de-sacs to a particular local crime to the very itchy enigma of what to do with young people between the ages of eighteen and twenty-four (and perhaps beyond) in a post-technological society with a dwindling demand for labor.

So, to come bouncing illiterate out of high school and immediately to blame the university for the failure of the public schools and the society they represent, i.e., for what one is, is a logical but tragic consequence of the shipwrecked incubation chambers. That is, if one is, to begin with, quasi-literate and conceptually disfranchised (by both coercion and choice) and then arrives in a place where a previous, more literate generation found its dissatisfaction, one is tempted not only to follow suit but also to vilify that place for all suffering, cosmic and personal.

The source of the illiteracy, by the way, is well-identifiable. James Herndon in *How to Survive in Your Native Land:*

> *In all public schools in the United States* the percentage of kids who cannot really read the social studies textbook or the science textbook or the directions in the New Math book or the explanations in the transformational grammar book is extraordinarily high. Half the kids. The school tells everyone that reading is the key to success in school, and no doubt it is, a certain kind of reading anyway. Does the school then spend time and effort teaching those kids who can't read the texts how to read the texts? Shit no, man. Why mess up a situation made to order for failure? [95.]

Yet a multitude of those kids who can't read are figured forth into college, where they're now someone else's problem. In the meantime, we've stuck them in front of a tube and then slammed earphones on them for a few years, and to celebrate the death of language we bury it in the same crypt with perception and will.

In one sense, the university presents us with the last opportunity to recover these lost functions of the soul and perhaps to strengthen the possibilities for the survival of cultural alternatives and for the resurgence of social commitments born of an acclimated sensitivity to the Other. Thus the importance of the university in this concluding portion of my ruminations.

We must assume—with solid *a posteriori* reason—that our high schools will continue to do nothing but produce a comparatively high number of hard-core shipwrecks. The social imperatives are too powerful to allow simply passing the buck down, even if the high schools withdraw into an ever-increasing complacency, figuring that the colleges will function in crescendo as extended high schools (with a little curricular pizzazz), filling in the inevitable gaps.

After all, we're now wedged in a situation in which the colleges are impelled to start all over again with many kids, start back by using each class as a perception lab: "What color is that chair?

What else can you say about its physical properties?" Attempt every stunt conceivable to force the gears of mental operations into motion. The old apoplectics with the yellowing note pads stumbling up to read their lectures aren't about to try it, let alone perceive the radical problem, and younger college instructors are under a command to discover the methods since nobody ever talked about the *vocation* of teacher in graduate schools dominated by the yellow pads and footnotes.

I suppose it's possible to harangue students, but one has to take account of their resistance to old-value formulations. Thus it's not a question of reading's being "the key to success in school" or even "the key to success" in the patterned activity of one's "career." One cannot speak from the point of view and with all the banalities of a minor corporate functionary. Rather, tell 'em that Spiro Agnew wants functional illiterates—a whole society of them, 'cause morons don't make no trouble. Only people in law collectives or Nader's Raiders make real trouble, and those people are required by their Ways to read, perceive, and act. Even here I remain unconvinced of the potential productivity of the rhetoric since so many are incapable of responding because they don't want to do law collective or consumer advocacy. Under the new hedonistic rubrics, after all, those who opt to be Sons of Los are "failures."

What the university increasingly offers the young is an environment that leads straight to Yippie morality, in which relative passivity has no consequences, in which the law of the conservation of energy is implicitly denied. In allowing this environment to become as pervasive as we have in America (and uniquely so), we have encouraged the extension of the psychological dependencies of adolescence for at least a decade, and that of social adolescence perhaps for life. There are few institutions in society to which such all-encompassing attachment is possible. We build in a rhythm of the school which, though oppressive for twelve years, soothes thereafter. Soothes because the place is *in utero*, offers both comparative freedom and safety. It's too easy to postpone the moment of birth and to act out social fantasies as if the Academy were a microcosm of the society. Since it isn't, as long as we pretend otherwise we're setting up kids for rural communes with guaranteed self-destruction clauses or total removal into the Otherworldly Divisions of counter cult.

Look what we're starting with, after all: a mass moving mind-lessly onto campuses both because they're not prepared, psycholog-ically or socially, to do anything else and because mainstream cul-tural values mitigate and dilute any possible encouragement to do anything else. The kids know. Here are some City College stu-dents passing the pipe of such realizations around:

"I'm there for lack of anything better to do."

"We go through the whole thing not realizing what we're doing, but intent on getting that degree because that's what we're there for."

"And even then that piece of paper doesn't mean too much, but you go through the ritual half-heartedly anyway."

"But it's really impossible to go through without having some contact with other people or other ideas."

"Yeah. Nobody really expects to learn that much in college. All they think is that they'll come in contact with a few ideas and a few books and a few people that they will remember and that may influence them, and that that's sufficient reason for being there."

"But compared to other things, I'm not sure that it's worth four years for that, four years of your life, if that's all you expect; and if that's all you expect, that's all you'll get."

Or a twenty-year-old Pembroke junior:

"I'm here in school because I really haven't got the courage to leave. I would like to go out and get a job but that takes a lot of guts, which I haven't got. I'm not really qualified to do anything. I'm completely dependent and what I need to do is go out and be totally on my own and find out if I can hack it. Right now I don't think I can and I'm not learning how to do that here. It's a real struggle."

In that last we have a paradigm for the complicities of the Academy. Ponder well exactly what the young lady expects the *school* to do for her: to qualify, to certify, to teach her how to "hack it," in fact, to motivate the will to move the body—let alone the psyche—through the gates. Even some Antioch students spoken to en route to these notes, students who are forced through those gates by their required strophe and antistrophe of "work/ study," remarked that they're just "wandering around, looking for something to get into, and marking time with formal education," an activity which, they added, was "a sham." But thirty years later, some of these same people, having consigned themselves to the wheelchair of the Academy, will be equally unprepared and unwilling to leave, equally dependent.

Communities of interest abound, to be sure, but given the democratization of higher education which has decreed that half our young people between the ages of eighteen and twenty-four will be in college, the academic uterus is culturally minatory— particularly if there's nothing going on among those who are its half-willing registrants. Indeed, precious little goes on these days, as anecdotes scattered through the following attest. If the spirit of those stories reverberates with that of the counter-cult instances recorded earlier, we should not be wholly disconcerted. For the present Academy—unconsciously to be sure—is artlessly institutionalizing and certifying nihilism, and neither the radical critique of the Academy nor the Alternatives that critique offers illuminate the forces behind the nihilism.

As usual, we're caught in a web of stale either/ors in which the old-line liberals (read "new reactionaries") and the various radical factions (except those that wish to destroy the university utterly) are not only making the same assumptions but also perversely nourishing the pervasive dependency on the Academy. The illustrative issue is the contention that students are an "exploited group." No doubt they are, in the odd sense that both the old-liners and the radicals in the Academy couldn't pay the rent without them, and it is therefore in the self-interest of academicians of multifoliate ideologies and pedagogies to perpetuate the myth of the *broad* necessity of the Academy, a myth wholly reinforced by mainstream parents, corporatists, and bureaucrats, and unquestioningly accepted by students. Listen, first, to an old-line liberal thrashing around in the rhetoric, however. Charles Frankel, in *Education and the Barricades:*

> Most of the odd, novel, or shocking things that are being said about the condition of students in the United States today, and many of the discussions taking place about the re-allocation of powers within universities, depend on the application of loose and unexamined analogies, drawn from other types of social organization, to the structure of institutions of learning.
>
> Thus, to take a doctrine that has achieved growing currency, students are not an "exploited" group. . . . As those who have

experienced exploitation know, it usually involves a condition more painful to endure than boring or "irrelevant" classes. . . .

Nor is the larger version of the doctrine of the exploited student any more persuasive. The word "exploitation" has been stretched so that it is used to describe the process by which young men and women, in the best years of their lives, are educated not for purposes of their own, but for the external purposes of an alien social order. The university exists, it is said, simply to provide highly trained labor to the corporations, the government, or the knowledge factories. It is, therefore, an instrument of exploitation, a tool of the military-industrial complex or the one-dimensional consumer society. [But] to be socially useful is not to be exploited, and there is not society, existing or conceivable, which does not demand that its members make some contribution to the collective good [46–47].

Frankel has the nub of the answer to exploitation staring at him through his own words, and I strongly suspect he is fearful of recognizing it. For the promoters of the exploitation theory are asserting that the individual has no power whatsoever to control his own life, once he leaves the unique university environment. The theory is a soporific for those who like to believe that they're being machine-tooled—as indeed they are if the combination of TV–audio media–high school mentality passivity leads them to lie around for four years acting out a hollow mime for the sake of a piece of paper. It's a vicious circle in which those who turn their university lives into street corner society can always escape to the argument: I don't want to do anything around here because that would mean being co-opted into pig nation. In either case they are nilling, not willing, and have less respect for themselves as individuals than does the social order they believe is "exploiting" them.

Yet Frankel and his myriad faculty sympathizers and the sloganeers of the exploitation theory all ought to project a good deal more respect precisely because some have perceived the venal ways of subliminal control by the mainstream. This very perception, reached primarily in that university insulation which allows extended periods of reflection and spectatorship, should be testimony itself to the fact that the mainstream is not rigidly and all-encompassingly exploitative. If the perception is there, those who formulate it can resist—if they *will*.

Those who have resisted, however, and resisted for maximum

effect, have not done so within the Academy. The universities as institutions are false, convenient, and peripheral targets, and only those who have broken the psychological and physical comforts of the fibrillating umbilical in the very concretions of their lives have fully recognized the fact. Of course, if there's a local chapter of the IDA (Institute for Defense Analysis) on campus, we're dealing with another issue. But far more typical is, for example, the attempt to eradicate sexism in the Academy in the elitist naïveté that supposes by so doing one is dealing death blows to the monster of sexism in the larger society. The eradication of sexism in the university is a worthy object, but the Academy mentality wrestles with such an object so intensely and exclusively as a cover for abdicating confrontation with the far more entrenched and intricate manifestations of sexism in the social order beyond the gates. The case is archetypal in that it expresses the extent to which the school in America has become the fifty-first state.

After all, it's in the larger social organization that young people have to wrest power from Nixon's answer to the yellow pads. If we make it too convenient to sit around in a university for years on end deciding how we're going to sit around deciding how to run the joint, that mentality, aided by our toleration, will penetrate thoroughly, and few will be out on crusades to pluck the heart from the beast. Instead, we're simply juvenilizing, and the results are beginning to trace their retrograde outlines in the behavioral patterns of counter cult.

But if such a convenience is not to be imposed by the existing ethnic-group chauvinism of the university community, it will be demanded by the generations coming on; and I hope that by this swath of paint we realize that their behavioral patterns and cultural conditioning render all such debates within the Academy side shows. The following set of probes expand that contention and is designed to move toward some potentially reconstructive notions.

15

*Three Overlapping Causeries in
Search of the Proposition that
Restructuring the University,
Curricularly and Politically, Although
an Immediately Profitable Move,
Is More Fit for Another Age*

I

The apostasy of the radical critique of education lies not so much
in its analysis as in its response. The response is nonetheless a consequence of an analysis that, for all its presumptions, concentrates
more on the institution than the individual, and thus lends exces-
sive weight to the very idea of the institution. The critique pro-
poses the educational *system* as part of a subtle process of social
programing by the master planners. My objection to that axiom of
the educational barricades is that it turns a cadre of invulnerable,
bumbling fools who know no more than the rest of us about learn-

ing processes and the ideal machineries of an educational community into a sinister gang of conniving geniuses. In its zeal to create a regiment of phantoms with which to do battle on the fields of repression, the radical critique thus extends too much credit to its opposition. An informed dissenting tradition should have its opposition pegged snugly, and I'm not wholly sure the radical critique does.

But the radical response falters in running that either/or gambit: It either stays within the idea of Academy, trying to force the Academy to function according to the desires of those it immediately serves rather than the desires of its hidden masters, or it urges the complete destruction of the Academy. In the first instance, the response reveals timidity by accepting the very presumption it is resisting—the *necessity* of the Academy. But one understands. The critics, in the concretions of their individual lives, would be lost without the ever present teat, and one does not bite too fiercely the nipple that nourishes. Thus they emerge with an attitude identical in *form* to that of the technocrats: Democratize the university, but suck everyone into its premises.

That proposition, however, is turned on its head in practice through the collusion of a subsidiary, to wit: If present subjects, objects, and methods have been subliminally directed toward the devouring needs of technocratic bureaucracies and power foci, then we had better do away with—the subjects, objects, and methods, dragging up another order which, in turn, will be replaced. It's like trading in the car every three years. In this halfway step toward the other alternative offered by the radical critique—total annihilation—the results are becoming painfully clear, epiphanied in a formulaic phrase of a group of students on the rap: " 'To be alienated' is a passive verb."

All this does not mean that aged, rigid curricula are productive or that innovations and relevancies are not. What it comes to mean is that tinkering around with subjects, objects, and methods of study, while perhaps having limited value, is very much beside the point, is not really a radical critique of the Academy at all. Listen, for a moment, to James Herndon on the public schools, and think analogously of the university:

> The School is not going to change. Criticism feeds its existence by giving it something to do, namely adapt. The school can eagerly join in criticism of its textbooks, for example, knowing that text-

book publishers are preparing a billion Standard Anti-Textbooks which will show up in every class or Anti-Class some fall morning along with a neat mountain of justifying Anti-Pedagogy. The Anti-Texts will prevent learning just as well as the texts did, since they are to be used in the School. A large organized group of Anti-Parents will demand the texts back. Black Anti-Texts will have to appear. On the basis of the Anti-Texts, school administrators will get to spend their time making policy statements, getting hired, transferred and fired, and answering the telephone, proving that they still exist [*How to Survive in Your Native Land*, 111–12].

Somehow we maintain the impression that the university community is so much more mature, that we've eliminated the closet minds of the assistant principals and all those annual curricular revision reports and policy-making jobs. Oh, so much bullshit! The relevancy readers were our antitextbooks, and there are more of these pimples popping out every day, in multi-media now, out-doing Mellow Marsh himself—but in purpose still assuming the centrality of the school, and in substance based on the perceptual abilities of the most talented and alienated. So we wind up with a thousand antitextbooks, which no one can read, even though half the pages are set with photographs, music scores, comix. And you know, as an aside, that there is one shitload of people who depend on this corporate demand system for a living, and therefore are not about to stop, regardless of whether, out of the 300,000 university students (out of 7 million) who can actually read these antitexts, only 30,000 will actually respond.

Contemplate the relevancy reader again. Its effect is to institutionalize and thus dehumanize alternatives and, like its critical umbrella, it validates what it would denounce. An addition, in some cases, is the totalitarian presentation of an editor's own preferred educational hypotheses, a presentation less pernicious than that in many free schools, no doubt, simply because some college-age students are capable of resisting on deep planes.

The relevancy reader announces that it's bringing together "material previously deemed unsuitable—or, at least, unsuitable for college students" (Jaffe and Tytell, preface to *The American Experience: A Radical Reader*), and placing it between the covers of a "paracollege" text. When such a matinee intro is offered in 1970, one is quite curious about the nature of this "unsuitable" material, for "unsuitable" only thinly masks the "repression" cry.

Cleaver, Malcolm X, LeRoi Jones, Abbie Hoffman, Lenny Bruce
—or Norman O. Brown, McLuhan, Paul Goodman, Gary Snyder,
Allen Ginsberg, Mailer, Artaud. With the possible exception of
Hoffman, one must acknowledge that college syllabi are stuffed
with selections from the above lists these days. And by this time
in the multiplication of the second generation of our antitexts,
millions have at least speed-skipped through Sontag's "Notes on
Camp," Leo Litwak's "Joy Is the Prize: A Trip to Esalen Institute," or Martin Duberman's "On Misunderstanding Student
Rebels," to cite some heavy repeaters.

But the pretension of not a small company of this horde of
readers grows from and appeals to the sloganeering notion that
somehow we've all been victims of a grand conspiracy sliming its
way through history, under which every work previously forced on
students in a university is fascistic at base. The surfaces may seem
varied, but they're all cut from the same scurfy stone of tradition.
The response is to present the voice of protest, counter-everything.
Even though the surfaces here, too, may seem varied . . . etc.—or
so the pious emendations of counter-reader editors claim. And let
the additional parallel not escape either: The relevancy readers are
not the choices of students. At least one could shrug for those dull
old texts that they made no pretensions, struck no poses for the
stud-of-the-year awards, and didn't enter the slippery ground of the
totalitarian lumping mentality that emerges from the total configuration of King TV.

But in the second generation of antitexts so often we are re-
galed, in drum-pounding prefaces, with the news that every writer
offered in every English course, for example, during the past half-
century has, *by definition*, functioned as an establishment agent.
Whispers of outrage!! Thus do the new counter-mandarins dispose
of Dickens (???), who did a far more forceful underground job on
Establishment England in *Bleak House* and *Our Mutual Friend*
than garret Engels with that dry dung prose of *Condition of the
Working Class in England*. *Wuthering Heights* written off as a
tractarian exercise for the Anglican Church, and thus for moral
Absolutes (!!!!); Bishop Berkeley executed for his alleged conspiracy in the vast plot of capitalism. Once dunked in the mentality of those whose commercial interests are fueled by such
imaginary creatures from the Bestiary books, and the task of
constructing one's own lists is effortless. After all, one does not

have to perceive details or to emit the slightest odor of discrimination.

By this, as usual, I do not mean to disparage the writers actually selected for the new antitexts. God knows I would rather underclassmen be exposed to McLuhan, Artaud, Mailer, Sartre, Baldwin, Arendt, Milton, Blake, Thoreau—some selected heavies from the relevancy readers—than Burton (*Anatomy of Melancholy*), Brown (*Urn Burial*), Sam Johnson, and Macaulay. But to render an elementary pedagogical distinction one is not impelled to take refuge in that either/or political reductionistic paranoia, a disease which so often prevents essentially intelligent editors from performing an honest evaluation of what it is they are so stridently rejecting in their prefaces.

I think, not so offhand, of Louis Kampf's short foreword to Sheila Delany's *Counter-Tradition* (subtitled *A Reader in the Literature of Dissent and Alternatives*), which shills for Delany's preface, a preface that, in turn, amounts to so much nondiscriminatory shopworn propaganda rhetoric for a product that can stand on its own in 1971 without that trash. Kampf is a man of passionate mind who has written eloquently on the deadening effects of the Academy and its role in the acculturation process of American society, who argued quite convincingly in his much-anthologized 1968 essay, "The Humanities and Inhumanities," that the freedom of the life of the mind encouraged in a university environment bears no resemblance or logical relation to the freedom of action beyond those walls—of which, in fact, there is less than headlined. From that premise, he continued:

> In seeking alternatives, the educator's first impulse is to suggest curricular reform; jiggle the mechanism a bit, make a great-books course out of freshman composition, even have them reading Norman Mailer and Mao Tse-tung. Such reforms, we assume, will effect a fundamental change in the lives of our students. I doubt it. Changes in the curriculum—though often valuable and necessary—may have the ultimate effect of making the acculturation mechanisms more efficient. They may make the best more cultured, but will not change its objectives.

If so (and Kampf's view here—with some diminution of his emphasis on the scabrous plot of mainstream culture—is obviously very much shared by this writer), why, three years later, come on through such a dark glass of politihype for one of these "jigglings" containing selections for freshman composition from R. D. Laing, Tom Paine, Marx, Mary Wollstonecraft, John Muir, Blake, and Malcolm X, among others? Because if one is structuring on the entitative notion that "the meaning of life is in action—whether the acts be physical or mental" ("The Humanities and Inhumanities") and that therefore we must liberate ourselves by acting outside the Academy in resistance to what Kampf, in his foreword to Delany, terms "the going ideologies," why simply substitute one blanket set of ideologies for another? Why dull the mind into totalitarian perceptions? Why commit the sin that Blake himself referred to as "one-fold vision"? Do that, and you're still going to bolo-punch the will to act.

Indeed, bumping into Kampf at the 1970 Modern Language Association Convention in New York, in a littered corner of a dim mezzanine walling notices for the convening of a rump women's conference, I asked him what his undergraduates at MIT were up to, and the answer was not merely a visibly discouraged "nothing," but also a whispered, grimly pessimistic, "If you find something that works, let us know, for Godssake!" We commiserated for a while over the difficulty of enticing students to *do*, to extrapolate from themselves even within the Academy, let alone outside of it, through the most radical cartwheels. After three years of relevancy readers, Ex ed, and all that, we've got less energy than before. But we have also inherited a new sub-generation in the meantime, a move away from the commitment of positive counter politics and toward what Keniston referred to in *The Uncommitted* as the *"principle of implicit conservatism"* in counter culture, i.e., that

> one should seek to change the world as little as possible, for no matter how numerous its present evils, they will be succeeded by other evils just as devastating if not more so. . . . Since they [the alienated] unconsciously view their own personal histories as a steady movement away from imagined past bliss, they find it hard actively to support any program that seeks to accelerate or alter the course of social history [170–71].

In such light the radical readers accomplish little, as few will actually read them, let alone respond intellectually, let alone in terms of engagement. I once asked a freshman comp class if they would like to read and discuss Andy Kopkind's *New York Times Magazine* piece, "Are We in the Middle of a Revolution?" (November 10, 1968), and on receiving a positive response, typed it up, and ran it off. Did so in the middle of a semester (Spring, 1969) during which the campus was closed down by strikes more often than it was open. And yet with the swirling forces of "revolution" about them, few were even willing to read the piece, let alone respond. Ran the piece four semesters in a row in a slightly more advanced writing course, and swiftly realized that the only way we were going to be able to talk about Kopkind's propositions (the negative answers to his own title question) and their contraries was to require a reflective paper on the article prior to discussion. And most of the papers were ho-hum summaries and agreement, e.g.:

I don't think America will experience a revolution anywhere in the near future. In fact, I sometimes doubt if America will ever have a revolution. Back in 1776, there was the Revolution because people wanted the same basic rights and everything was well organized. Planning of government was not. Today we have been working inside the system of government too long. The political system is too strong to be overthrown.

Or:

Andrew Kopkind in an essay entitled "Are We in the Middle of a Revolution?" tries to induce us into believing that there is no revolution going on in the United States. One of his definitions of revolution is the deplacement [sic] of the rulers by the ruled. He stresses that "the same elites that have held power for years are still in control." His examples are the Cook County Democratic machine, the NY Times and Andrew Cordier. He also emphasizes the issue that "the crisis of the society is expressed in the resistance of its rebels, but the rebels did not cause the crisis." These issues (no change in gov't and the crisis was already there) are why Kopkind displays [sic] that there is no revolution going on.

I suppose such responses bear adequate witness to the stagnancy of primary and secondary education, and, from one point of view, cry out for the necessity of the Academy—if for no other reason than as an occasion (more than a place) to retrain the mind to perceive, the heart to feel, the will to act. I gather that such is the position of Kampf and others of similar commitment: Take what freedom the university grants and seek its logical extension primarily within the campus bounds, assuming that the kids are going to continue flocking in as a product of the inexorable logic of mainstream culture (and thus, in terms of deep social structure, against their wills); and as long as the journaled walls provide, we might as well trill a fugue for the ongoing occasion.

But picked up two of Kampf's own students hitchhiking to New York on a road-salt late January day of 1971, and they demonstrated the futility of his enterprise among the surging generations. They admire the man because he goes up against the journaled walls, but are simultaneously turned off by the use of the classroom as a consciously political structure. "It's not that my own politics are even old liberal," said one, "but there's a point at which you're sick of being radicalized," continuing, by poignant association:

"I mean I don't know why I'm in school anyway. . . . Look, I've just changed my major from electrical engineering to chemistry and I'm a junior, and I don't even know about that, and now I'm thinking of anthropology. . . . But I've been taking more and more humanities courses because I want to read books, and so many of them turn into contests as to who is more radical than who. . . . I guess I'm just in a period of equilibrium. I really can't get into much."

"We both came out of this high-pressure South Shore Long Island scene," the other added, "and every time I go home, I tell them I'm going to drop out of school because it's doing nothing for me or I'm getting nothing out of it, and I don't think any of these big historical raps Kampf and the other guys come on with have anything to do with the reason."

So I asked them why they haven't dropped, and what they would do if they did, and met with the blank stare of incomprehension, until one tentatively and timidly offered the admission: "Life is too easy in school—I don't want to risk losing that for a while."

As Arthur W. Chickering, former director of the Project on Student Development in Small Colleges (sponsored by the American Council on Education), has observed ("The Best Colleges Have the Least Effect," *Saturday Review*, January 1, 1971), "the most important index of college success and of its social contribution may be the quality of its dropouts, not the quality of its graduates."

What was most significant in the study that prompted Chickering to that comment was the discovery that the dropouts in any given college were more culturally advanced, more self-reliant, independent, and other honorifiums on entrance to college than those who remained. In other words, the elite drop. That doesn't mean that every high-powered autonomous kid in the country drops; rather, that *within* each college, and consequently, within various groups on differing cultural levels, those who abandon uterus university are those who generally don't need its protection and insulation to begin with.

Then, too, in all the colleges Chickering surveyed, from Bible belt repression institutes to elitist Higher Summerhills,

> scores after one or two years reflected increased autonomy, greater awareness of emotions and impulses and increased readiness to express them, stronger interest in the arts and humanities, and decreased concern for material possessions and practical achievement.

The conclusion: Individual students, regardless of institution, are developing "along vectors of change set by the general cultural and genetic forces at work in our society. The colleges neither accelerate nor retard that development. They simply provide a safe haven where it can occur."

The question then arises (and for this casual observer, arises from classroom, office, and conversational experience, and not even from the results of his own survey) as to the desirability of the extreme reliance on the haven, a reliance which is psychologically embedded in those who do *not* drop. Unfortunately, but sociologically predictable, a man like Chickering, a creature of such studies, is lubricated by the logic of either/or. He cites a study that compared those who spent four nonstop college years to those who spent the same years in jobs and/or marriage, and concluded (surprise!) that the college students "became more autonomous, more flexible, complex, and tolerant of ambiguity, less dogmatic, more intellectually curious." Ergo, "wombs are good things."

One wonders. Chickering, to his credit, does anticipate by distinguishing between dropouts *per se*, and "misfits" who remain in college. The "misfit" may be social, emotional, or academic. Whatever it is, the kid is getting nowhere, yet the mixed blessing of the womb is revealed in the fact that he remains not out of wholly conscious choice, but from subliminal psychological and social conditioning. In gingerly and higher academic terms, Chickering recommends that these, too, drop:

> Continued growth for these misfits may often require premature departure. Such moves toward more challenging and fruitful environments are healthy steps; such initiative in taking charge of one's own existence and future development is to be valued and fostered, not decried and curtailed.

I strongly suspect that a significant percentage of American college students are "misfits" (a sad term), but in the sense that the womb simply reinforces the narcoleptic patterns of behavior of this particular cultural age for adolescents, and thus expedites the demise of those faculties by which the individual normally survives. By playing self-interested womb, a particular college is demonstrating manifest disregard for individual students. Chances are that the kid who sticks it out will have done comparatively nothing in his four years, and to show for the noneffort will have lost what mind and will he had on entrance. The young are suffering now in their invulnerability, and the Academy is clinging to them too desperately. Its self-serving efforts are the signatures of spiritual grand larceny.

Ten years ago, very sophomoric, green, and running eclectic over college, some myths were rudely debunked for me when I happened on the fact that two of the most noted "alumni" of the college, S. J. Perelman and Nathaniel West, had respectively been expelled and dropped. The revelation set off some weighty ticking on just what formal higher education accomplishes and raised the question of whether such "punitive" measures were really "punitive." Ten years after in the Academy, I myself felt desensitized enough to want out for a while, and became convinced by degrees that so many students with whom I had contact required a retooling of basic sensibilities, which they would never receive in the university—not because the universities do not in themselves offer such possibilities, but because those students evidenced no internal imperatives to refurbishment. No matter how hard the university turned on its head for relevance, it could not induce these imperatives, just as the kids pushing into "relevant" experimental education within the school were not confronting the cultural forces outside the school.

The conclusion, slowly dawning now, is that the Academy itself must render itself more optional—a development with cultural consequences far more profound than that of merely doing away with the punitive stigma of the "drop." If counter politics within the university asks for autonomy for students, the demand is genuine only if those who voice it are aware that that autonomy will never incarnate confined to the academic womb. The self-indulgence that needs the womb so as to trash its walls in comparative safety is hardly an index of autonomy. It simply continues by a quixotic calculus what the mainstream began.

II

A couple of indications toward the notion that experimental education, as currently envisioned and practiced, is really beside the point, a diversion from the issue. One friend who has devoted his academic career to Ex Ed has optimistically prophesized the current Academy plus "a system of learning centers, non-degree-granting institutions where students and instructors gather on an equal and amiable basis to get and give ideas," existing side-by-side in America "within ten or fifteen years." He seemed to believe that his desired "curriculum based on a system of student selected seminars . . . organized around problems or topics of interest to students" could exist in either. Likewise for interdisciplinary seminars, organized in different ways in different institutions, e.g., "some more structured institutions might organize these seminars on a chronological basis, examining different problems as they emerge in different periods. Some might be totally open-ended, with the provision that other seminars, other problems and topics, would grow out of those in operation."

Such a vision speaks primarily to the personal experience of its promulgator and others (myself included), and not to that of most university students (certainly more to the mythologizers of student reality than to the reality itself). More important, it bypasses the larger question with which such visions are designed to grapple, by assuming the Academy to be comparatively isolated from the society. Once again: Frantically frolicking around with a curriculum, organizing courses topically instead of generically or historically, etc., is old vaudevillian stuff and does not speak to the vast majority of college students who would dance with anything as long as it had style.

A former colleague of mine participated in an experimental college *within* a traditional university structure, and offered a course on "Theology and the Modern Novel," a course eventually integrated with the "regular curriculum." I recall such a subject's being offered in my college years, as well as in a very staid graduate school. What was the difference? The guy was cool, but he was cool in his "regular" courses. The students and he collectively decided which novels would be at issue. Perhaps there it is: a surface whiff of style. But the assumptions of the course, the insights, the topical direction were still determined by the instructor. Open and democratic classroom—but no radical alterations in the manner in which he operated everywhere else. The whiff ports a nuance of bitters, though, when one discovers that the rudiments of style have nothing to do with the instructor or the course but seep from the simple act of placing the course under the heading "experimental college." One can offer bullshit or fascism or banality under that heading, and people will be happy. The act has the same reinforcing effect as calling a small business enterprise a "collective." The mere boldface type distends the impression that one is an outsider.

It almost follows with logical necessity that the educational reformists, however they may borrow the sloganeering of counter politics, are still elitist, still believe in the ideal of *higher* education, still believe in Culture, still incant to the university as the center of cosmic progress, still ring-around-the-totem, except now pretending that the content should consist of whatever is not cognitive. Analogous to the ideology of counter cult, the reformists succeed in molding a high culture of nihilism, and thus serve neither their own ends or those desperate needs of the floundering social-political world outside.

As a friend who had participated in a number of Ex-Ed programs observes:

"What we have failed to see is that we have most often thown smart, good natured, disaffected, elitist children into modes which perpetuate rather than change those symptoms. We have thought that free classrooms and all that went with them would be enough. But we have not allowed for leading them into wanting and needing those things which we see as needed. Consequently, they use them for elitist purposes, for group therapy and so on. This gives a great deal of evidence for conservatives. And I've come up against too much of this, rising from my own failed 'experiments' to want to give them any more."

Ex Ed, as practiced, involves even more intense preparation for the type of counter culture that will fail and will pollute beyond ecological rehabilitation the lives of those who must remain behind the new agrarians and frontiersmen.

My friend added a shared experience among so many younger college teachers: "The very attempts to liberate and free our students depressed us." Why? One answer falls in the leitmotif of means becoming ends in themselves, of the repetition of semesters spent deciding how to spend the semester, during which time the kids are delighted because they don't have to do too much. This pattern of reaction to the corruption of the traditional Academy, however, figures forth in nothingness. The second answers plies another theme from the analysis of counter cult: Our "very attempts to liberate and free our students" may depress us if we recognize that they embody the mainstream values which have so overblown the function of the educational institution.

Example of the second: Professor Fred Snell, SUNY-Buffalo, director of the experimental college-within-a-college, College A (the lettering system for Buffalo's experimental colleges alone indexes a repetition in the counter of the dehumanizing culture of toothpastes and mouthwashes), contends that virtually all experiences are learning experiences, and therefore should be granted academic credit. I think we've played this record before. For if dear Fred is making a mockery of the certification process, of college credit systems, we're prepared to accept the contention. But one suspects that the mockery is really another poison, that it masks a radically capitalistic assumption: I'm buying an abstract blank called credit, and I can then fill it with anything I want.* The question is not whether all experiences are learning experiences—that may be (I pruned an apple tree today, oh boy). Fred's assumption arises from the stuffing of kids in four-year ghettos, the clockwork of the educational system that says you punch in here and out here and there. What Fred and so many others in Ex Ed are still doing is accommodating themselves to the clock, a clock run by other and unseen hands. And directing their attention not at the kids but at the clock.

A third depressing factor of the liberation process is revealed to its agents when they discover the necessity of establishing criteria for what is a put-on and what isn't. As soon as we're immersed in that notion, dear liberators, we're knotted up with "standards," however we dislike the term. I recollect two ulterior liberators team-teaching a course in contemporary American lit, a course filled with live readings by true luminaries of the title, a course that placed all responsibilities but the reading list on the students —and even the reading list was considerably open to student-initiated variations. All that was required in the course was an open-ended paper or project of the student's own choice. The following exchange toward the end of a semester:

> *"Relevant" student:* I really don't want to do the paper; it's not my bag.
>
> *Liberator 1:* Well, you don't have to write a formal analysis, you know.
>
> *"Relevant":* I know, but you know, my head isn't really up for doing any kind of paper. It's just not my bag.
>
> *Liberator 2:* What is your bag?
>
> *"Relevant":* I'm into poetry. I really dug some of those poets who read, like Ginsberg.
>
> *Liberator 1:* Then why don't you write a poem? That's fine enough.
>
> *"Relevant":* Well, I sort of do poetry internally, y'know? I just

---

* Indeed, as Harold Taylor notes in *Students Without Teachers*, the academic credit has been marketed by the society and the university establishment as the equivalent of the dollar sign. It is curious—to be polite—that the radicals have been so conditioned as to act on the same assumption.

don't like to write it out. It's like poetry of the mind. We talked
about that—
Liberator 1: Why don't you do anything—anything is o.k. Draw
pictures. Translate your internal poetry into pictures.
"Relevant": That's sort of trashing the thing. I'm really not into
art at all.

The exchange can be repeated a thousandfold, and it should be
obvious from these pages that not all the repeaters will be the
remnants of library carrels *circa* 1950 or refugees from the dim corri-
dors of academic conventions. Sloth and cop-outs for the self-
indulgent uses of institutions abound; and when the self fails, the
institution or its "agents" are reproved. The most honest will admit
that they're just damned lazy, and whether one offers them the
chance to do poetry, movies, drama, art, whatever form of self-
expression *they* choose, they won't do it. As one former student
noted with equal measures of disgust and resignation:
"You can't force it. I mean, kids are old enough. You can't
threaten. I had one teacher who gave an assignment to do some
reading, and only about four kids did it. So he made us do a paper
on it, and he realized that was pretty childish, so he took it back.
And we talked about it, and we told him that there are always going to be kids who aren't going to do it, and it's up to them to
decide. . . . It's not his job. It's not a junior high school. It's not
a high school."
Now, I'm sure that the extreme liberators will come back at
both the young lady who voiced the above and myself: Because
we assume the teacher to do the offering, an authority figure re-
quiring—for the sake of a certification process ingrained in the
culture—some form of expression in a course, some monument,
therefore nothing could arise internally from the students, for the
authority figure is ultimately oppressive, and the students are correct in resisting. In fact, the gurus might continue, that's just what
students are doing when they do nothing—resisting—and that, in
fact, is doing something.
As tortured as that argument sounds (with the exception of the
notation on cultural certification requirements), it abounds, and
it's a dangerous and elaborate form of deception. It pretends that

nilling is willing, a perilous gamble of a pretense, because it encourages the self-apologists and con men, and leads ultimately away from any commitment to moral nihilism. Worse, it results in practice to suburban Marxists occupying space in the Academy that kids from ghetto streets desperately want and need. Indeed, I have used that argument quite frequently to the politihyping nillers, and more frequently still after a stint teaching remedial English to a group from both black ghetto and white working-class neighborhoods during which my conviction of the accuracy of the argument only intensified. But particularly when one is addressing the one out of five who has junked himself into oblivion (see Appendix, A.17), there will be no response. The terms and arguments of "liberating" Ex Ed are tragically misplaced in such quarters. They are even more misplaced—as we shall see—because they fail to grapple with the far more embracing question of the certifying function of any school.

As one reads through the literature of the experiments in higher education, particularly the strident pronunciamentos, one is repeatedly struck by the replay, the delayed-action reformulation of issues hammered out in similar language at so many institutions ten years ago. And the media pitchmen (who generally have some difficulty remembering what they were writing about two years ago, let alone ten) are too eager to pick up on the ejected urgency. Here's Joseph Califano in *The Student Revolution:*

> They [the students] see hypocrisy first at the university and in matters affecting the university. They see it in professors more interested in consulting the government and corporations than in teaching; more interested in writing books and articles than in spending time with individual students; more interested in the esteem with which their colleagues hold them than in respect from their students. The young relate this "hypocrisy" to the legitimacy of the status of their professors. They question, in effect, the right to teach, the authority to teach, in those who are more concerned with other interests [68].

Or the Preludium from a proposal for an experimental college by some young faculty:

> The present point of view which dominates the educational enterprise at most of the colleges and universities in this country is that

the teachers have a certain body of material to convey to the students. Concomitant with this procedure is the expectation that the students must deal with this material in a critical way. In the present situation, information is conveyed by means of a text or texts and the lectures of a teacher. Discussion is encouraged but its purpose is to clarify points implicitly or explicitly made in the texts or lectures. A student who does not understand or has a question is encouraged to ask that a particular point be explained. The critical method by which material is to be dealt with is developed in students by having them write papers on material included in or related to the course. The student is encouraged to research and organize material in an original and creative way. He is expected to be critical of the material for which he is responsible, to reduce it to a particular order which constitutes his position on the matter at hand. However, the fundamental assumption which pervades this whole task is that the teacher determines the subject matter and how it is to be dealt with.

One salient issue is that those who established these critiques were educated through the waning days of the educational gerontocracy in the American university and in the first days of the restructuring of the college classroom. That does not pretend that dull lectures from stale yellow pads no longer hold forth to intimate audiences of 300 plus. Nor does it pretend that all of those stuffy geeks who thought that college was high school and who registered class attendance and ticked recitations off a roll, have all retired. But to attack those anachronisms as the most critical current moments in the university situation is to beat the expiring brontausaur. The Sorbonne students threw the pavements at that syndrome in 1968, sure, because it was all they had. They didn't even possess those disdained opportunities for critical discussion which we now malign by rote slogan. And if the scholarship/ teaching battle is being waged for the 491st either/or engagement, it seems highly ironic that the conflict has been settled, in the philosophy of so much Ex Ed, by the effective statement: "You [faculty] do your scholarship, while we [students] teach." Or if the required curriculum argument is still being cantata'd with seriousness, only the petrified keep it from lying bracken in the backwaters where it belongs.

To place all these plaints in perspective, one has only to turn to the increasingly large numbers of younger, concerned faculty, pouring out of the graduate schools in the mid-1960's determined to be teachers foremost, to relate to their students, to preclude any repetition of their own rigid baccalaureate experiences. Many of them are now so totally disillusioned, cynical, and, in some cases, openly contemptuous of both their students and their elder colleagues, that they remain in the Academy primarily for the sake of providing for their families during these phases of the Nixon economic moon.

Why the disillusion? They aren't exactly dull or insensitive teachers. I'll use a few that I know: one nominated by students for the teacher-of-the-year award at a major state university, two others who were ranked excellent to superlative by students on teacher evaluation questionnaires at a major public university, one at an experimental college who was always considered by students at his former university to be among the "grooviest" but who left precisely because the feeling wasn't exactly mutual, whatever the appearances. Two of the four above are out of the Academy completely now and intend to return, if ever, only when the situation improves. Hear them:

1: You can stand on your head with relevancy, and they won't do a damned thing. Relevancy is irrelevant when you've got people who cannot and do not respond to anything—

2: You can come in stoned, drop your pants, rap the hip, play one of the dudes, and no response. I always felt the distance should be narrowed, but there's a point at which it becomes ineffective.

2: I used to be at school seven hours a day, four days a week, with more than half of those hours devoted to open-door-come-in-and-rap office time. Everybody knew about it from the word go. They knew it wasn't formal, they could come in with a drink, a joint—I didn't care. They could come in and rap on anything from parental hassles to ethereal realms of thought. You think anybody came? I used to go over to the cafeteria to recruit raps. We used to scream about all those inaccessible bastards with the one and a half office hours a week "or by appointment"—you know, because they were too busy jerkin' off over a footnote up in the library stacks to pay attention to the kids. So we said we would never pull that stunt; that we would shoot for maximum accessibility. But when the kids don't give a shit, after a while, you don't either, and it's off to the library stacks.

1: It's really a shame, you know, because a lot of them aren't going to get by with the help of their friends. I couldn't rely on people strung out in the cafeteria staring at quotations they can't even read which are all over the walls. After two years, too, I really had to adopt a thing about attendance. None of us ever take it, but you get kids coming in two months out in the course who you never saw before.

2: Yeah, like this kid comes in last week—middle of November, right?—and in a class of twenty, you know faces. He says, "Hey man, like I'm in your course, y'know?, and like I'm really sorry I haven't been around, but I've been doing other things, y'know?" Honest, I didn't recognize him at all, so I told him that, to my knowledge, he wasn't in the course, that if he was, he would have known to have come in sooner. The first day of class I literally beg with them all that if they're thinking of dropping the course or dropping out of school, or if they're taking off for a time, or anything, to please please come in and rap about it. But no, not this guy, so we go through that whole bit and I end up telling him to fuck-off.

I really don't think they even understand or appreciate the argument that while they're screwing around stoned, they're taking the place of some street kid who really wants to be here. They whine; they don't think; they just want to get credit for walking around spaced-out. I mean, if they were doing something, I wouldn't give a shit if they didn't come in—and we don't exactly have the most uptight classes in the world. But if they were out making movies, or into community work—

1: *Making* movies? Just *going* to movies—

2: Look, you can sit around blaming yourself, saying, gee, it must be something I'm doing or that I did, or something I'm not doing, and go through that whole frigging liberal guilt trip number, and after a while it's just insanity.

1: I think I must have whipped myself for a long time before it felt good when I stopped. I was much too loose.

2: I really don't think we were catering as much as it was a case of our resolving not to change our life-styles when we walked through the classroom door. So if we dressed like freaks and said "fuck you" at home, we weren't about to change for school. . . . It's that whole psychology of the classroom, what Dennison pointed out about elementary school kids, the two cultures; and if the two cultures and the psychological readjustments shouldn't exist when a kid is six, they certainly shouldn't exist when he's eighteen, so you don't encourage that split between styles on either side of the campus gates. He [No. 1] did just about everything, certainly a lot more than I did, to break down the kids' inherited notions of the geography and psychology of the classroom. It wasn't merely discussions outside or round-tables or small field classes, which a lot of us do. He went beyond that—

1: I would have the class break themselves up into small groups of four or five, and instead of regularly scheduled classes, we would meet in these small groups, in different places, scattered throughout the week.

2: It might have appeared like he wanted to get out of teaching an 8:30 class, but what he did meant working with the students in that one class five or six hours a week instead of three.

1: And the tragedy is that a lot of them didn't show up for those. They made all the decisions. But I don't think they were ready for that type of experiment.

James Herndon, to be quoted again in a moment, would recognize with soft smile that the two gentlemen above had arrived at "the end of the road," and on grounds that simply render paltry both the whole Ex Ed/relevancy enterprise *and* the rococo efforts of the resisting Mensheviks. For, as he who was nominated by students for a "teacher of the year" award pined, "something has changed in the past few years; the assumptions we were operating on in terms of what induces college kids even to do their thing— or what they see as their thing—don't seem to apply any more, and I don't know what does." Even setting aside his more staid complaints that nobody brings books to class any more, or takes notes on what even their peers are saying, that no one wants to "get into" anything, even in a class with a teacher they admire, we all must recognize that we now have a sub-generation so numbed that it is not only baffled by freedom but deeply fearful of extensive and intensive dunkings in the realizations of its own relevancy fantasies. It is impossible for many to sustain any amount of will-energy, even when the directions are of their own choosing.

Oh, there are those students, to be sure, who can pick up the slack of academic provincialism and both create and sustain courses in penology or ecology or the Mystical Tradition or the politics of the U.N. (all valid and productive fields of inquiry) where no such courses previously existed. Again, though, these students are comparatively few in number, and (harking back to Chickering's distinctions) are concentrated either in elite institutions or among elites in other universities. One suspects, too, that such courses are formulated without strident and bogus justifications.

*　　　　*　　　　*　　　　*

"I don't want to do this paper on Proust. I can't relate to it."

"What do you relate to?"

"John Coltrane, man; like he's really the ultimate."

"Well, Coltrane and Proust were both neurotics. Why don't you do a paper on neurosis in Proust and Coltrane?"

"Man, I don't want to write about Proust at all."

"What do you want to write about?"

"John Coltrane."

"Okay, try this: why not put together on tape a jazz collage from Coltrane, and come in and read me appropriate passages from Proust while Coltrane is playing in the background?"

"Oh, yeah—well—far out!—I'll have to think about— Man, yeah—um" (slowly backs out).

Another nonapocryphal gem from a colleague of highest credibility, who later provided the logical conclusion: "Still haven't seen anything from the kid; in fact, I haven't seen him since." This is no fogey aphorizing on relevancy after Charles Frankel, who piously announces in a paradigm: "Students are not the best judges; if they were, they would not have to be students." This is an educational activist who would nonetheless echo the spirit of James Herndon's reflections on his "alternative" experiment within a junior high school:

> The year proved to be the end of a road. The end of a road where people imagine . . . that if you abdicate your total authority as an adult, then the kids will be free to choose what they want. The end of the road which says that if the adults do not make decisions about what to do, then the kids will be able to make them. The end of the road where we hoped that the students would tell us what to teach, how to teach. . . .
>
> But the students were living in the same world as we were and lacked the same answers we lacked. They couldn't show us how to teach. . . . Our classes went the same route as regular classes [*How to Survive in Your Native Land*, 125].

One former student tried to expiate when he quietly noted that "people are passive because they're afraid to try anything out of fear of failure. It's so easy not to do anything because you're afraid that you won't succeed." I had known him for some years in the college, but we were both out now, and the remnants of roles —which were never observed anyway—had been thoroughly excised. There were no imperatives for a defensive posture. Still, I responded, what do you do with the instances in which there are no *external* criteria of failure—even hidden criteria? What do you make of those cases in which the individual outlines his own learning situation, ungraded, and yet is satisfied merely with the prospectus? Recognize the double paradox: First, by the mere fact that one is in college, he is removed from the necessity of social responsibility and yet receives the chits for entry into social adulthood. Traditionally, the color and number of these chits have been defined by forces beyond the self. We now recognize the general form of that relationship to be "alienating," so we have institutionalized a process in which the social adolescent is informed that he will receive "credit" (much of what he wants, anyway) for anything he does that "relates to" him. Under such a "consciousness-raising" reformulation, how does one then judge the collegian who *still* doesn't do anything? The critique that schools cannot justify themselves unless there is measurement and failure no longer rings with such telling truth in the Academy, since so many colleges—

and certainly experimental schools and Ex-Ed programs within colleges—have gradually eliminated its grounds.

But this depressing phenomenon becomes intelligible when we realize that criteria for "success" have become so internalized on the way through twelve years of primary and secondary education structures that decompression is difficult within a continuing school environment. Fusing dynamite between the ears of the average gravitational field college freshman or sophomore will not explode the children of their parents, nor will it propel the children of television and the turntable. The combination cannot be hidden for long, as college instructors and administrators discover whenever they present all students with the opportunities for an effectual open corridor, a curricular form which, in fact, only an elite can handle within the school. The old structures have induced too much dependency, and the culture at large too much passivity.

Thus the relevancy rot is, in many cases, sorely mistaken because it assumes that eighteen-year-olds fresh from the deep freeze we have consigned them to possess experience to which conceptual frameworks can be related. Even our course on The Artist and the City, a course anecdoted back in the chapter on Mc-Luhan, a course designed for students who, we thought, had experienced the urban situation in its most intense form, was misconceived. Whatever materials, whatever media—audio, visual, print—we attempted to employ or encouraged the students to employ themselves were, in the main, either ignored or rejected because the kids couldn't manage the most elementary tasks of perception and conception. The deep freeze had left them with a total interest vacuum and had sent them functionally illiterate and dead-willed into an environment in which visual and verbal literacies are simply assumed.

Came onto campus one day determined to scrap all planned curricular discussion and to take up the meaning of the verb, "to relate to." The raps, however, were short-lived—and I didn't say a word until they were over—because those who participated, at first eagerly, gradually found that the verb was so amorphous in its application in contemporary dialogue as to be meaningless. Self-defined relevancy reduces to multiple solipsisms. If the soul is large and vulnerable enough, it can relate to all things—assuming we grant a relevancy of degrees and textures, positive and negative. But I was more concerned than curious that the dominant usages of the verb in the raps echoed in the passive voice, i.e., the students expected the world to relate to them. There was no active search for relation. It followed that relevancy was defined wholly in positive terms; that is, the conversationalists could not conceive of a negative response as embodying a relation. It followed, too, that the objects and events in the world that were marked as touching upon one's life were (1) those that touched upon the external life only, and even then from a generalized distance, e.g., the War, and (2) fairly limited in number and range, indicating not immature, but *invulnerable* souls.

One cannot "teach" even the criteria for relevancy in a school, certainly not when those who are in the school have known little else but school. And thus Herndon is oh so accurate when he notes that "all the talk about *motivation* or *inspiring* kids to learn or *innovative* courses which are *relevant* is horseshit"; and Ivan Illich, too, in his critique of free schools:

Attendance through seduction inculcates the need for educational treatment more persuasively than the reluctant attendance enforced by a truant officer. Permissive teachers in a padded classroom can easily render their pupils impotent to survive once they leave ["The Alternative to Schooling," *Saturday Review*, June 19, 1971].

While I might reserve judgment on both of these pronouncements as applied to elementary school, they inspire a resounding "Yea" when applied to gravitational youthcult in college. If there were any sustained and substantive response to the Ex Eds, to the opportunities for the relevancies, to the democratized counter-classrooms, then a moment would reverse the judgment. Again, I'm not as much interested in the theory as in the behavior; and the student cited in limpid dialogue a few moments ago, he who declined to do what he claimed "to relate to," to read aloud passages from Proust to a jazz background by John Coltrane (which is like doing nothing), is far more indicative of the temper of what we're likely to be up against than the behavior of either elites or the black kids (who are generally too much into their own orientation to fall into honky excursions into the realms of nothingness).

Thus, as much as I honor Paul Goodman for minischools and other alternatives for those who are unable to handle total freedom, and for his unwillingness to take Illich's despairing plunge into the cosmic anarchy of the deschooled society, he reveals the basic oversight of the Ex-Ed man when, in a 1968 article in *Saturday Review* ("Freedom and Learning: the Need for Choice," May 18, 1968), he passes on to students the advice

> given by Prince Kropotkin in "A Letter to the Young": "Ask what kind of world do you want to live in? What are you good at and want to work at to build that world? What do you need to know? Demand that your teachers teach you that."

What's oversighted about it? Think on the Kropotkin advice. For one has to know how to ask the questions, how to formulate the concepts that lead to a coherent notion of the "kind of world you want to live in"; how to perceive and determine "what you need to know"—and not only that, be willing not only to ask, formulate, perceive, and determine, but to *act* on that knowledge as well. These tasks are ancillary to the demand to be taught such knowledge. They require the scintillant interplay of those now bedimmed functions of the soul. And while perception, conception, and expression may require the aid of some form of schooling, one cannot school the will. The advice Goodman passes on seems so futile in our time and experience.

III

Recall the latent right-wing anarchism in the counter culture; consider how radically capitalistic the cult of relevancy is and, more important, the ways in which it opens back into a reactionary mentality: It's the radical individualist saying, "Hey, I'm paying for something, so you give me what I want." But he's never going to get it in any *institution*, because an institution caters to the Other as well. Still, he has tried to impose his baggie on institutions and hence on others, again, paradoxically, placing the burden on the institution and not the individual. The failures of so many "Alternate Universities" adequately testify to the distance between the multiple ideas of individual educations and the implicit structuring the very idea of an Alternative University involves. The University Without Walls, a collection of alternate colleges through which students may flow, sampling at random without degree requirements, might edge a bit closer to satisfying the raw demand curve; for here the radical educational capitalist can pay for what he wants when he wants it—assuming plenitude and breadth of supply. The University Without Walls proposition would serve those who demand a greater degree of control over their educational lives but who simultaneously would be baffled by the freedom implicit in an individualized degree program in which one creates his own courses from ground zero (a task comparatively few even feel capable of accepting).

As for the "radical capitalist" analysis: Look, these are the terms of such developments. If they offend those who are committed to alternate education and who simultaneously think of themselves as New Left, I seriously suggest that they need their consciousnesses raised. Ponder well the concept of paying for credit for participating in a social action program—a frequent construct of the Alternate Universities. Isn't that a bit absurd, particularly in terms of suburban Marxism?

If the idea is to remix education into the life-process instead of holding the two apart, then it seems to me that there are far better ways, more ideologically and psychologically consistent, to achieve that end. The universities, established *and* counter, will resist, the former simply because there are too many jobs at stake, the latter out of that inscrutable Asian (and Nixonic) injunction against "losing face."

Begin to advance a proposition I have some doubts about, but in light of some of our collective experience with Ex-Ed institutions over the past few years: Let the established and counter colleges together adopt a national flow-through extended U., wherein the radical individualist can pick and choose and pay (or not, depending on the requirements of the schools) over a course of decades. An indication of the motive forces of such a proposition might well lie in replay-associations on a couple of the more notorious of the Ex-Ed institutes, Old Westbury and Cal Arts.

Enough has been written about the Westbury experiment for me to stay away from it for fear of catching a severe case of the redundancies. A few glaring facts ought to be rerun, though. The first centers on the easy slippage of the hype. The Academy rolled out its PR presses here to establish the school, and to drag in those faculty and kids who were looking for "authenticity." The hype operated subtly, as demonstrated on the application form right from the opening question: "List and answer one or more questions you think should be asked of people applying to Old Westbury." Groovy, right on, with it, right? But the slickness doesn't hide the fact of the institution. Here was the State of New York playing hip capitalist, anticipating future student demands on the basis of current student movements. Bad biz, though, reminding one too keenly of a Boeing management that simply assumed the company could go on stuffing planes down the throats of the Afganistanian National Airlines for the rest of the century, and, when that failed, the Pentagon. Hasn't anyone learned that we're all headed for irrelevancy in the morning, and that pouring concrete and passing out press releases and performing spot-commercial antics is the last way to provide "authenticity"?

Instead, spend your money to hold your staff while the programs are stretched out in time and space. Let some alternate U. open up courses in macramé and auto repair and astrology, and if a student based on your campus wants you to set up duplicates, let him know that with the floating education extension plan he doesn't have to hang around the Yard, but can go over to Macramé U. If the kid thinks the suggestion is punitive, that's his problem, because in so thinking he is worshiping the certification of the traditional Academy in the same manner as his parents undoubtedly do. If he accuses you of being reactionary, he is playing a self-indulgent, slothful, elitist fantasy game and should be told as much.

The natural association follows, and bears repeating after Old Westbury: The Academy cannot afford to cater to elitist whims. Old Westbury accidentally happened to serve as a racial group therapy session, and thus demonstrated an unplanned value in its short, resignation-ridden existence. But Old Westbury, true to the tradition of the Free U.'s founded by the same suburban Marxists who later head for communes or politidoming and think they're doing something radical, to a great extent turned into a playground for self-indulgence with credit—Augean bullshit that no shilling will wash away. You get some pampered suburban freak like the one Tom Powers describes in his *Harper's* "Autopsy on Old Westbury" (September, 1971), who spends "one entire semester polishing a four-foot high piece of bark," then creates a course, "Poetry of Life," which she describes thusly: "Now I hear beautiful music. Then I paint a mind picture. Later I walk in the wood. Reverently I study my wood, know it. Converse with a poet meaningful to me. Make love"—and you've got a television set for the uncommitted. Repeated at the $2,600-tuition New College in Sarasota, Florida, at which, as the aforementioned *Underground Guide to the College of Your Choice* teases:

> Last semester a group of freaks sort of took over a dorm and tried to start a Free College [this within what the *Underground Guide* has already described as "a new experimental unstructured private school"] with such courses as "Freaking." They got a professor to sanction it and got credit for just living communally in the dorm.

Talk about radical capitalism! $2,600 for credit to freak out. And to try to humor or rationalize the concentric circles of nonsense that institutionalize "Freaking" or "The Poetry of Life" for academic credit, and to pretend that those participating are not eminently prepackaged children of their parents' values is a distinct disservice to both the university and the individual.

Even in such a case, the argument between the fogeys and the radical academic libertarians is a side show, because they're still carrying on the dialogue within an institution and are, at the root, relying on the same assumption: The institution is the center of any academic proposition. The libertarians may not think they're making that assumption but by analogy should observe both the Socratic and Christian moral positions: They leap in opposing directions, but the self is the center of both of them. The fogeys generalize a course such as the above "Poetry of Life" into a blanket paradigm for all student-created courses, and thus see the collapse of Western civilizations inherent in the form of the experimental college. Even when they are fully sensitive to the motivations for less frivolous and self-indulgent ventures than "The Poetry of Life" and understand the paradox of institutionalized relevancy, they seem incapable of breaking through their own genteel yet stale assumptions; e.g., from a recent commencement reflection:

> The desire for courses in the contemporary is both a tribute of sorts to the university and a rather touching, but also pathetic, testimony.

It is as though reality were not endorsed or at least not comprehensible unless there be a course to give it a familiar form, a local habitation and a syllabus. To make a revolution it is necessary to have a course in revolutions. If Vietnam is in agony we must have a course in Vietnam. Contemporary literature is puzzling and exciting so we need more courses in contemporary literature. The desire for an intelligent understanding of whatever it is in the immediate world that we find most urgent is altogether laudable, but the demand that it must be fulfilled by being institutionalized, and that the formal structure of the university is the institution of fulfillment, is not necessarily laudable. It is not when it springs less from a strong mind's need to discover what sorts of questions are possible and more from a weak hope that if only you could take a course you would know the answers.

Formalize the question in the form of a course, and we push institution in the way of open knowledge, and thus, paradoxically, murder the "relevance." Get the revolution and the A.B. along with it, and one sometimes wonders which is more important to those who demand.

But you see, too, that the author of the above is answering the relevancy cult in its own terms, falling into that fogeyism that discusses the issue in terms of past and present, the value of tradition, and a level of blah that is employed to smother even the slightest deviation from nineteenth-century curricular lines. Excluding, he excludes absolutely and, along with those he is criticizing, assumes the primacy of block-knowledge-on-the-installment-plan education.

But that obviously is not what college education is about; and if the terms are brought into meaningful focus, the question of relevancy assumes a valuable role. That is, higher education assumes basic literacy, and should seek to train in as many manifestations of modes of perception, conception, and thought as possible. The fact material is secondary. The forms without concepts are empty, sure, but I'd rather be empty than blind. The high schools do enough of the blinding—which is certainly one factor that mitigates our previous assumption of basic literacy in an eighteen-year-old. But if one grants the lambent value I've placed on the Kantian formula here, then relevancy assumes quite a different dimension, i.e., it is already institutionalized. Filling in the blanks, discovering the concepts, forming the perceptions are tasks then up to him who has grasped the *forms* of cognition. What material one uses in arriving at the forms is only peripherally subject to the judgment of "relevance."

Since both the radical critics and the fogeys are in league in the deep structure of their confrontations, neither one particularly cares for the notion of the university as a place of higher-thinking training. The critics' objection is most illustrative because it reverberates to counter cult's drive for new Absolutes. One cannot conceive of the university primarily as a ground in which thought processes are acquired, they hold, for then the very nature of the institution would feed the relativity and instability of the world. Our experimentarians want a new central myth; no matter how hard they ply the trade of individual consciousness-raising, they ultimately pierce through the individual to a cosmic structure or point of reference, thus granting absolute values a constituency more intense than do the campus reactionaries.

The Ex-Ed institutes turn out to be as highly structured as the formal Academy, and—shades of the politidomers—far more elitist (primarily in the naïveté of their conception). Consider first an open letter from the "University in Exile," a statement of purpose and invitation published in the *LA Free Press* (July 9, 1971). The "University in Exile" is located in one of the most academically protective, tranquilizing, and nepotistic of all university communities, Hyde Park in Chicago. There is a significant group of students that, once arrived in Hyde Park, usually doesn't leave for two decades.

The writers of the open letter claim that they have been fired from academic positions because of their politics or have been unable to obtain academic jobs for similar reasons. In the midst of the Great Bear Market in university employment, the secondary reverberations of such whining smack of the self-serving, or so one suspects. But, having been denied their chosen channel and, like so many others who have made the nonstop school trip, being unable to do anything else, they saw their "alternative" in a new academic community, oh boy, a community in which

we would like to attempt to combine intellectual and political, practical work and develop a learning center in which people could explore ideas, do research and at the same time acquire practical skills and serve the needs of the people.

Admittedly a broad notion, but a noble statement nonetheless.

The program? The academic portion is so dull that one wonders what these people thought mainstream American universities were up to these days, e.g., "deal with the various academic disciplines . . . in a critical and interdisciplinary context." True to the form of curricular organization at most Free U.'s,* to the academic one adds a vocational school in two divisions: One keeps the professionals occupied with training in paralegal, para-educational, and paramedical work; the other instructs in tasks more of the hand (known in counter-cult circles as "survival"), such as "printing, photography, auto repair, typing, plumbing, etc." Then an odd division for "retraining professionals . . . to use their skills to serve the people." That must involve some group therapy work, for the only applicable retraining of doctors and lawyers, for example, would be that of the heart and will.

From program one moves into the inevitable Big Three of the political grounds for the counter-academy: the mutual arrangement of course, curriculum, educational philosophy (the last being a droll privilege, since the core group has already stated the philosophy, and anyone interested in exile to begin with will be buying it); the assignment of extra-academic functions like secretarial, janitorial, and administrative to all members of the community "to avoid elitism and reduce costs"; and establishment of a day-care center.

But the place inevitably will be elitist both by the definition of program and by its very existence as a haven for those seeking the exile passport from middle-classdom. A fine piece of educational counter-cult masturbation will ensue. *Among* the middle-class academic refugees who arrive there will be no elitism. There also will be a little critical academic work—enough to keep the founders

---

* If one extracts from experimental college catalogues, experiments within colleges, or experimental colleges within colleges, one can easily rearrange a very consistent grouping of courses, e.g., topical and interdisciplinary treatments of traditional academic subjects, survival (home ec, appliance repair, etc.), games (photography, dance, candlemaking, etc.), group therapy, relevant polemics (e.g., a white racism project for whites), action polemics (e.g., "Radical Confrontation," women's lib, and action program), occult ways (Tarot, *I-Ching*, yoga), and simply very staid academic subjects.

happy slapping themselves on the back. Therapy for the overcon-
sumers. Taking the place of imposed course content will be much
discussion within that "mutual arrangement" jazz, talking about
talking about how to spend the semester (or whatever new order
of time is determined). The resonances indeed are keen with the
geodesic domers, for the training in para-everything will be taken
by the exiles and *not* by any significant number of "the people,"
who, as anyone who has taught in an experimental program knows,
want far more structured and formal situations and, among the poor
and the black in particular, want an accredited institution that will
grant that piece of paper. The kid from 47th and Cottage Grove
who our exiles believe is going to hop in to become a para-some-
thing will more probably be gravitating to community organizing
through the Stone P. Nation or to a very straight academic program at Chicago State or both. One cannot assume any significant
number of such people willing to leap from educational poverty to
the rejection of academic affluence, no matter how stultifying we
know that affluence to be. It takes the full experience of overcon-
sumption before one can discard the whole bag.

If it is not surprising that the new libertarians of counter cult
are emerging from the middle class, from the culture that can afford the initial investment from which their new "freedom"
springs, then it should not surprise either to find "Alternate"
educational institutions such as the "University in Exile" attract-
ing those who have the middle-class psychological security of
academic and worldly options. These educational suburbans issue
from a society of structure and that form of control Marcuse refers to as "repressive tolerance" (a sociopolitical variation on cultural desublimation), and, in what they subconsciously believe to
be a constructive reaction, charge into what they think is anarchic
freedom with no relics of social control, an Edenic locale where
they can sit around smelling flowers, but not eating apples.

Their expectations are often rudely debunked by the inexorable
progress into structure born of the very notion of school itself.
Thus it was at the California Institute of Arts, an ironically Dis-
ney-endowed free-form total community of elites in the performing and visual arts. As initially conceived, Cal Arts was to consist of a group of interacting "schools" (e.g., Critical Studies,
Theater, Center for the Study of Technological Experience, etc.)

within a professional institute. Students and faculty in each of the schools would formulate their own curricula; there would be no grades—bah-bah-bah—the whole Ex-Ed schtick. But hardly the radical free-form expected by student and faculty arrivals.

The radical free-form caved in under the sheer amount of organization that actually transpired. The school broke up into subdivisions, each acquiring an identity, becoming a "collective" or community with a distinct ethos and highly particularized stake in the organization of the whole, and fighting, despite itself, for special privilege. The result precluded interaction between the subdivisions and fragmented the community.

As one who went to teach at Cal Arts because he had been bored and frustrated in turns by both structures and students elsewhere related, the curriculum-planning demanded more time than the curriculum and ended up having little to do with the announced purposes of the subdivisions. Automobile Mechanics was introduced into the curriculum of the Critical Studies Community by the incipient counter-cult survival suburbanites, over resistance by faculty who were chanted down as (guess what?) fascists, then folded after a few weeks when students complained that they "couldn't relate to it." Their choice, their discovery; and the only euphemizing one can offer for that experience is that such failures may be of value for the same type of audience that believes rural communes will run themselves: It brings them down from the apocalyptic expectations trip. Indeed, as one student noted after the wreckage of the first year had cleared:

> To have thought that an environment of freedom would be already established on arrival from Chicago was ridiculous. I was too willing to accept the gift without thinking that somebody would have to work for that freedom. So now the magnificent renaissance locale is past. . . . It has cleaned up from its o.d. and is now trying to work toward a real school in a real time on a real earth [as quoted in the *LA Free Press*, May 14, 1971].

There is a point, after all, recognized by the likes of a Stewart Brand or the DRV communards cited earlier, a point at which *absolute* freedom turns into anarchy and ceases to be *authentic* freedom (a distinction we'll take up in a moment). When students create a course in Urban Studies and do field work that involves neighborhood organizing or community design, we're talking about something far removed from Automobile Mechanics, "The Poetry of Life," Astrology, "Freaking," or Candlemaking. The Urban Studies course demands a *shared* experience, even if the sharing lies in mutual reporting on individual projects, and thus becomes a center for the distribution of ideas and perceptions. The others make no such demands—certainly not in practice—and are but in resonance with that counter-cult syndrome of anarchic radical individualism heading both to the Right and to failure. They do not need the school to foster them. By allowing itself to be an accomplice before the fact, the school will aid in the destruction of the most promising visions of the community of spiritual interest that is youthcult writ large. As former faculty member Jay Neugeboren observed of Old Westbury ("Your Suburban Alternative," *Esquire*, September, 1970):

> The College . . . was, after all, merely another part of the consumer society, another stop in the suburban shopping center, one where students who did not have to work for a living or for expenses could talk endlessly about their *right* to choose and plan and have all the varieties of courses and programs and educations their minds could imagine. The school, like other so-called experimental colleges, pandered to the students' unhappiness with things as they were, to their dreams of things as they should be, and to their desire for instant gratification—to their desire that all things be immediately and easily accessible and "relevant" to their emotions, their lives.

Neugeboren's summary remarks on his own process of disillusion raises, by critical association, a distinction that lurks behind every line of these accretive causeries, a distinction that informs the whole enterprise, namely the crucial difference between authentic freedom and nothingness, the latter so easily born of absolute freedom. The Academy provides what Hannah Arendt has called the absolute *condition* of freedom in relation to the general social order. That is, phenomenologically, the Academy presents an environment free of sociological limitations on the self. Theoretically, the self, provided with this condition of freedom, can move either into absolute freedom, that of essential solipsism, or into authentic freedom, the freedom dependent on the Other.

What so often obtains in behavior, however, is a paradox which the experimental college has now etched in bold outlines: Young people both reach desperately for and slip into absolute freedom in an environment in which absolute freedom is denied by the very fact of institution. Thus the young lady who creates her "Poetry of Life" course within a school and for "credit" is not really acting in absolute freedom in relation to her self. But the *condition* remains, and she is acting in absolute freedom in relation to the larger social order. For he who builds a cubicle around himself and acts in a world of objects, processes, abstractions, and cardboard human beings acts in what is essentially a world created by his own invulnerability, and in one sense possesses absolute freedom. He is limited only by the properties of the objects and processes, and by the capacities of his mind and body. He creates no point of reference beyond the self, perceives only his own phantoms, and in fact is under no imperative to perceive, conceive, or express at all. He expects the world *to relate to him*, and is liable in that invulnerability to make no *active* gesture toward any social order, mainstream or counter. This passivity often dissipates into nothingness; *authentic* freedom, the freedom that always obtains in an active relationship, is choked off among the weeds.

Freedom, after all, is a moral and political judgment, and it is impossible to judge an act to be "free" in the moral and political vacuum of solipsism. Thus did we note that Yippie morality does not really express freedom. The Rubin-Hoffman program so often pretends that the Other does not exist—or at least succeeds in rendering the Other such a cartoon that it is quite convenient to ignore him altogether. The same pattern obtains in the dehumanization of sloganeering counter politics of all name brands, and in much counter-cult posturing. She who polishes that piece of bark is not acting in authentic freedom. He who slouches to Drop City and telepaths messages to the urban poor is not really acting in freedom. And, more critically, those of the vast gravitational fields rocking out their terms in snow oblivion in institutionalized repetitions of their suburban world rarely act in authentic freedom. Rather, theirs is an absolute freedom which melts into nothingness for them and oppression for others—subtle oppression, yes, but oppression nonetheless.

As I've noted before, such human behavior expresses not anarchy but nihilism. Nihilism all the more because language, perception, and feeling have died, and even the new absolute freedoms come to yield the slave morality of "I will but I cannot." The poisoned alternative this nihilism offers to the world of Agnix is devastating. No wonder, looking down the days of youthcult, one despairs.

16

It Doesn't Have to Be That Way

Everyone waits for a prescription, a formula. Signs demanded. I confess to being a bit hesitant, uncertain, and unfashionable—but three items are mixing in kitchen bowls. One is a variation and advancement on some modest proposals already flickering around educational circles, and concentrates on the reformulation of the function of higher education in individual lives. The second, and adjacent, proposition involves a quasi-program that already existing proposals tragically overlook. The third has very much to do with the pedagogical process of this book itself and the values of that process under the assumption that we're going to be stuck with the Academy as it is for a while, i.e., that it will be impossible to seduce anyone on the first two counts.

The first advocacy: extended higher education, downplaying its certification function. That is, we've come to recognize that a breathing spell, a hiatus in the process of formal education, is becoming a necessity before education ceases to have any impact at all, and, instead of our current crop of illiterates set up for a Drop City guaranteed to fail, we wind up with subliterate "educables" set up for instant manipulation.

In this it may appear that I am following the spirit of an old Paul Goodman montage in *Compulsory Miseducation*: to require students to defer entrance into college, and to spend two years in a "maturing activity," e.g., ordinary working, community service,

volunteer service, etc. The idea is not only to break the "lockstep
. . . so that the student may approach his college studies with
some intrinsic motivation, and therefore perhaps assimilate something that might change him," but also to give the prospective
student "enough life-experience to be educable on the college
level [124–25]." As a basic statement of both the problem and the
proposition, Goodman's simple formulation is oh so very very
right.

But the Goodman stance has two limitations in practice. First,
he advocates the approach only for the elite small liberal arts college where it is not as potentially productive as it is in the state
university. The brightest kids out of high school are those most
likely to postpone, perhaps permanently, their higher education.
And these, who are also most probably psychological adults,
stream from the elite high schools. In the back of my mind somewhere is an article in the *Boston Globe* that dealt with the incipient trend in this direction, and the kids and figures cited were
drawn exclusively from the finest public and private high schools
in the area. But it's the average semiconscious, inanimate psychological and social adolescent who needs to be jarred.

The second limitation—and by far more significant than our
customary misplaced elitism—is revealed in the notion of a *single*
break. Instead, I propose an unscheduled series of breaks, resulting
from a massive reformulation of our attitudes toward higher education so that education becomes part of a natural life rhythm and
extends over a decade or more. The educational and social environments will come to blend—not in reality, but for the individual.
The passage eases; or should we say that instead of a certified and
measured transition from one culturally defined evolutionary stage
to a social adulthood for which TV- and school-conditioned youth
are likely to be eminently unprepared, we allow for a happily
heretical trajectory along which self-definition proceeds at a psychologically manageable pace.

As Edgar Friedenberg observed in *The Vanishing Adolescent,*

> one defines oneself by clarifying the meaning of one's experience.
> As an individual, he is responsible for achieving more clarity than
> the school can give him; for the school's cultural biases will in any
> case camouflage many vitally important phenomena and relation-
> ships [78],

an observation no less applicable in the higher reaches of the Academy, even in its most experimental divisions. The nicotine school environment obfuscates by its very overwhelming and continuing *presence* in the social and psychological lives of the young, precludes the dynamic situation in which clarity can be achieved. Besides, if one's experience is fairly well limited to the school, the paramenters of the definition of self may be somewhat contracted, to say the least.

So in offering this first of three unleavened loaves, I am emphasizing the psychological hygiene of the process. Whirl someone through a monolithic environment from *Sesame Street* to doctoral robes, an environment with the consistent and monotonous rhythm of a seasonal industry, and one builds up passive expectations, limits the development of emotive and social ranges. The integration of educational and life processes should certainly break down the inhibiting psychological barrier of the school door or the soothing ciphers of the campus gates far more than will manipulating curricula.

By this I do not intend to meld the two environments, e.g., by introducing automotive mechanics into the university, particularly to satisfy the witless deprecation implied in the whim of the week. It would not be the university itself over which one would exercise control *as much as* it would be the fluidity and pace of the interplay. Thus, too, we're not talking about *scheduled* work-study programs on the Antioch model, during which, as a couple of current Antioch undergraduates on the occasional rural-crafts lam reflected with a comparative measure of disgust, "so many screw off for credit, and a *system* [italics mine] of screwing off doesn't seem to be worth it." When you're outside the school, you're outside the school, and there's no reason to march around with a credit stamp. If "alternative" education centers develop at which one can "study" macramé or smithing, terrific! And if one is compulsive enough to carry a dossier in his hip pocket, the fact of "attendance" at such places can certainly be noted. Likewise for more legitimate yet informal educational structures such as our existing *Whole Earth Catalog* replacement models, or the counter-media, or what Ivan Illich foresees as "Reference Services" and "Skill Exchanges."

Necessary to this particular systemic restructuring is the option of a *floating* extended education, that is, a higher education over lapses of time *and* in more than one institution, preferably more than two. Such passages may work against endemic academic provincialism and toward the discrimination in educational values born of differential perspective. If one wishes to be certified, then a particular university might require the equivalent of three years' residency, for example, but broken at least once, and only after evidence of attendance at one or two others.

By loosening binds to the educational punch clock, it may be objected, I run the reckless risk of circling back on my own analysis of rootlesses in counter culture leading to horrific visions of the fruits of anarchic libertarianism. Not really. First because the nomads are now fleeing from the Institutions altogether, possibly frightened by the rigidity of the social function of the Academy. In my fancy, however, the institutions of higher education remain, altered internally from time to time, but refunctionalized. The university turns away from its function as a screening and certifying instrument, and I see that turn as encouraging use, not rejection. The whole reduces not to the Illichian despair of deschooling society, but to the idea of attenuating the university's social role. By concentrating on individuals and not institutions, then, one can transform the scabrous value system that has burdened us all at the altar of the Academy.

The second tentative warranty against reinforcement of rootlessness may be illustrated by one particularly encouraging development in the more radical of the free schools (a development that hints at the period of educational regroupment and rediscovery I think is both necessary and inevitable in the next decade), namely, the discovery, after a time, of the need for structure. Somehow, watching others do nothing in an anarchical situation moves those of energy who are simultaneously committed to the idea of a school to the attempt to structure. With structure, however moderate, the cop-outs dissolve. The development is prophetic in the following sense: Current educational forms are rightly meaningless to so many young people because they have been imposed, not discovered, because they have been instruments of the society, not instruments of the self. The complaint has been raised, the issues taken, sometimes authentically, sometimes as an excuse for lack of will-energy. The Academy has been handmaiden to the extent to which it has lost its viability. But the cooperation, again, is based on a false premise: that the center of attention is the institution, not those who come to it.

So we must pass through a time in which young people are not bound to the Academy, so that when they unearth it themselves, it will be a less formulaic place for them. Seating X number of students on academic policy-making councils or introducing an interdisciplinary studies curriculum, fine individual steps as these might be, do not deal with the social myth of school. Such measures will never solve the paradox of the eighteen-year-old who is dissatisfied with school yet afraid to leave its social bounds. He slides into college with no conception of purpose, feels alienated primarily because he is being washed in a vacuum, everything done for and to him, and attempts to solve the problem (in a most sensorily telling manner) by attacking the immediate institution and its values by forcing the introduction of a course in automobile mechanics or the Tarot pack. Even if he drops the course after three weeks because he "can't relate to it," he feels as if he has aided in the creation of a counter-institution, and that the nettle of his own boredom will vanish.

It won't, and by catering, the Academy will aid neither itself nor him. If he wants to be out building domes or wrenching around in engines or playing with the soil, he should do so. But apart from the idea of function and certification. If he wishes to come in from time to time to engage in the life of the mind, then the Academy should carve a place for him, indeed, far more places than are currently available for occasional students. By this route he will happen on educational structure, and either accept, reject, or modify it in terms of his own being. But when he does so, the action will be informed.

We once passed through another hour during which our leanings were toward condensed education—advanced placement, three-year degrees, and all that. We've even had a few more recent extensions under which education transforms into a year-round proposition through the age of nineteen. Such compression would be the work of manics, yielding social and cultural insanity. In pomp and circumstance, with ruffles and flourishes, the spiritually defoliated strut out with glowing certificates, remaining both psychological and sociological adolescents, falling exhausted into the waiting arms of psychological and social negations. If the lock-step results in dementia praecox now, what intensities could the average psyche withstand under the inelasticity of compressed education?

If, on the other hand, adolescence as a process of self-definition through struggle with the larger cultural order can somehow be mixed with responsibilities to self, if we can remove the academic teat, then at least from the point of view of the Academy, those entering will be infinitely more committed to being there than they are now. After all, were not the most exciting students generally those who had been walking up and down this earth for a time? From the perspective of the student, the rhetoric of conversion looks toward fewer hang-ups about being in college, toward the idea that you, not your parents or the society, are deciding to do this.

Harking back to Jay Neugeboren's concluding reflections on Old Westbury and the associative issue of the qualities of freedom, what else would this particular fancy accomplish, if realized? Young people would be indirectly forced to relate to both the Academy and that which lies beyond it, forced into an active and hence authentic condition of freedom. No gratification would be instant; and in discovering that "all things" are *not* "immediately and easily accessible" (Neugeboren), they might happen on the root of "relevancy," discover what was enduringly "relevant" to their lives. They might realize, as did the student recalling the degeneration of absolute freedom in the first year of Cal Arts, that authentic freedom is relative and can only be constructed, that even the most radical free school is not really "free," because someone is still defining what ought to transpire, what the goals and values of the school are—and this in the same sense that relevancy readers do not in themselves introduce freedom to the college audience insofar as they are concocted by elders who have rendered some implicit decisions on educational goals and values. Such freedom as students might build in the Academy would be both integrated with and conditioned by the authentic freedom dependent on the Other that may be demanded outside the gates. To those liberators who may grant even partial agreement with the proposition that all the reticent signs suggest a coming move of youthcult spirit toward *right*-wing anarchism, the option of this more flexible educational form should be considered seriously.

Consider it, too, from the psycho-social positions—present and future—of the young. They are being presented with a progression of stupifying change in geometric multiples at precisely that point in their lives at which the inner being is most in flux. In these vertigo years, they are being presented with two alternatives, both of which too easily induce passivity and malleability: the Academy as it stands, and our existing forms of counter culture. Inherent in both are an artificial removal process and great latitude for the avoidance of depth. When the first game doesn't work, it's too easy to slouch off to the second. Protean man is diluted. From Academy to counter cult hardly exhibits a protean quality. The outer man is not frantically charging from one commitment to another, 'cause the inner man is frightened by commitments in the surrounding gyres. Yeah, after Robert Jay Lifton, there *is* "an interminable series of experiments and explorations," but after a while, these experiments take the same form, and in the younger reaches of youthcult, the sense of the self fixes as a total blank. If we're interested in encouraging the young to order their inner and outer worlds to the simple extent to which they can ascribe coherent meaning to their lives, then it seems to me that neither alternative structure available is adequate. Both are noxious utopian forms, which do not encourage catastrophe and its analysis, and therefore encourage neither learning nor self-definition.

To be sure, there are a number of pressures working against my little formula for education beyond, let us say, the age of sixteen. The Academy itself, as an interest group, will certainly be foremost. There are too many jobs at stake, too many hangers around universities who have never known any other environment. Reacclimate attitudes toward higher education so that it becomes more occasional, and jobs become just as occasional. Parenthetically, though, that development might well prove as salutary for the Academy as for the students. That is, the professoriate may be forced to develop styles and points of view conditioned by vectors other than the Academy. In fact, their own professional organization has already recommended that they adopt far more occasional residency in the university. In the October, 1970, issue of *Academe* (a publication of the American Association of University Professors) a report of the AAUP-sponsored Project to Improve College Teaching suggests, among items that distinguish themselves from institutional clichés, a parallel to my extended rhythmic education vision, "increasing opportunities for teachers who may wish or need to seek a temporary or permanent change from a teaching career."

The closet bureaucrats, too, holding outlandish purchase on some small piece of power, will scream. Their jobs have been—well—too orderly. The computers alone may be able to handle the new order, but the programers won't. And when, in the course of determining what was really "relevant" to their lives, students may well downplay demands for participation in faculty appointments in favor of demands for effective operation of admissions offices and thus for the power to determine the character of their most immediate community in the Academy, administrators will fulminate. The reactionaries, too, in their perverse anticipatory logic, will sense the preclusion of their principal burden of defense: that kids who have never been anywhere else but school are unequipped to govern their educational environments. It will be people, not systems, who will resist.

Opposed, too, and not so startlingly, will be those students who may just be placed on an existential tightrope. The harsh reveille necessary to exorcise the soothing assumptions of the school, and hence to foreshorten social adolescence, will create limit situations for the sleep-walkers. That tingling moment of self-knowledge when it is said, in effect, "Okay, baby, you want to do your thing, you want to find your head? Well, you're not doing your thing here, and you will never find your head here, so why not migrate to an authentic existential edge, a border, and feel what you're doing on the pulses for a while?" The subliminal social compulsion to remain an adolescent has been too willingly accepted; but that pendulum of "nothing to do in here—nothing to do out there" has to be smashed utterly if we're going to have half a generation willing both to resist the totalitarian swamp and to construct more than mere portable alternatives.

Restructuring the practice of higher education so that it is less of a time-bound certifying imperative is an inadequate repackaging by itself. Without another and adjacent option, at least for a time, some of the effects of the outflow from the decertified universities will be socially and psychologically negative; the kids may just take the jobs of the poor blue collars and the blacks, and/or so many of the young will be baffled and unprepared that the counter-cult nomad faction will be tragically but measurably strengthened. How do we manage to induce authentic freedom without throwing the chaff like a counter-cult Darwinist dinosaur?

Perhaps some of those instructors currently chafing in the Academy and wishing for a differential life-style for a while, who also possess both sensitivity toward the young and a modicum of operative worldly knowledge—perhaps these, along with many recent graduate students who are finding the job crunch in the Academy more than unsettling, may be of crucial assistance. They might consider forming small groups to establish hard-nosed "ventures" toward which the outflow can orient itself. Not out in the canyons and with no politihyping, separate from moderate "establishment" connections but not Drop Cities, and not impinging on the communities, life-styles, and survival kits of the black, the blue-collar, or the urban poor. By virtue of the backgrounds and (one hopes) commitments of such potential "co-ordinators," these "ventures," while not formal learning situations, would provide a "community" in which there was an ever present form of direction, counseling, training in perceptive and expressive modes—along with whatever vocational skills the "venture" may require. In other words, these venture-communities would be quasi-educational—not by design, not for certification purposes, but by virtue of the visions and operative styles of those who "manage" them.

What is meant by "venture" here? Not necessarily small business employing the young exclusively. Not necessarily "employing," either, but in those applicable instances, involving partnerships—"collectives," if you prefer. Profit, nonprofit—does it really make a difference? Business, public service, educational projects after the Portola Institute, cooperative farming (as long as there is something to be grown seriously, and as long as the venture does not settle as a mindless rural commune of self-styled laureates), whatever imagination devises, provided it is in intimate and daily contact with the non-Academy world.

The vision is not utopian. It doesn't require tremendous social leaps—at least after we determine ourselves to the integration of formal education in natural life-rhythms. And the seas are not wholly uncharted: we simply replace our current counter-cult client regime of spaced-out Robin Hoods, ego-tripping Esalen leaders, manipulative trashing organizers and slogan manufacturers, illegitimate and promiscuous self-crowned holy men, and the like with a gang whose very business is to guide without playing guru, martinet, or false comforter. A monthly catalogue of openings in hundreds, perhaps thousands of such groups, advertises and recounts their products, services, projects. With Academy refugees coordinating, the products and services will optimally be directed toward all "the people," not merely the elite new life-style experimenters. A touch of the establishment may be necessary in initial financing for some of these ventures, and here our abstract and too often perniciously acculturating Foundations could contribute as much to education through such indirect channels as they now do through the Academy funnel.

Our refugees could still operate this new workaday world as an educational situation, still in learning-process contact with those to whom (presumably) they had formerly dedicated their lives; and, in many possible instances, also serve larger communities in paralegal, medical, consumer, skill-training, ecological, etc., projects. But some crucial fragments of advice are necessary to those who would begin:

1. Keep the size small, but don't play the nomad game, or you'll ephemeralize.
2. Make sure those coming in are aware that your game is iron —away from the Establishment, but looking to survive, not to fail or to entertain.
3. Use every day as a life-classroom, seeking to develop deep and detailed perceptions, quick yet balanced responses, flexibility and range in expression.
4. The finest index of your own compassion—realizing what we are inheriting from mainstream conditioning—does not include catering to elitist whims, Paradise Now onanists, mindless trippers, and the like.
5. Stay away from commune—indeed, from involvement in any living arrangements. Let people live by themselves or run their own communes if they choose. Otherwise, you'll have fermented yet another institutionalized dependency resem-

bling the college dormitory in function too keenly. Keep the structure community and not commune, particularly as the latter often generates the noxious dependency from which the young must be severed.

6. Whatever the venture, stay sweet and as unco-optable as possible. Serving all the people is one gesture; being a slave to the mainstream is another, and a more than merely nugatory, fate. What this means, in part, is that you don't plunge into rural trinket-manufacturing and similar removal gambits. By removal you are very much being co-opted. Besides, learning situations have difficulty germinating in nondynamic or noncritical ventures.

7. Laugh away. Certainly one of the greatest survival staples in the emotive life is humor. If we're now dubiously blessed with one of the most humorless generations to bleed down the pike in plastic in some time (granted, the world of their social adolescence wasn't particularly funny, but then again, when has it been? Think, too, of successive ghetto generations who have survived brutal environments through humor), what's coming along may bleed in angry pus. The absence of humor, the inability to perceive the pastel ironies in one's own behavior inhibits self-definition, "putting one's head together." The ironies need to be underscored and laughed away. They are necessities not merely of the emotive life but of the perceptual, conceptual, and expressive lives as well.

8. Behave as an equal and ally, while honestly recognizing that you aren't equal. For those whose previous behavior in the Academy has expressed sensitivity to the needs and desires of the young, that shouldn't be a difficult proscription to follow.

9. Finally, remember that, despite what the mainstream has done to these kids, and thus both for what they are and for what they do to themselves, you love 'em, otherwise you wouldn't be thinking about spending your life with successive dealings of them to begin with. So it's not really difficult to be both angry and concerned, cantankerous and understanding, cerebral and emotional simultaneously. Only the either/orists, political reductionists, apologists, and manipulative caterers would deny that.

Again, such ventures may serve as centers for a time, both edges and regroupment enclaves in which and through which the young may pass, alternating with the Academy (if they so choose), for a decade or more. The quality of what emerges will depend absolutely on the nature of the initial coordinators, their vision, their willingness and ability to break the rigid and unnatural life-rhythms to which the certifying school-obsessed mainstream has handcuffed both itself and its children.

Of course, one cannot guarantee that this new order will result in the refurbishing of the will and the perceptive-expressive faculties. As I've implied, if the order is brought on too suddenly, it will leave both the onrushing generations and the dependents of the Academy in a state of cultural catatonia, and we might well witness an even greater move of the mindless into counter-cult Alternatives that manage nothing constructive. Recall that it took the British nearly a quarter of a century to acclimate expectations under Open Corridor in the grade schools, and that elementary school teachers who attempt to dunk American kids into it overnight find, if they are at all honest, that the resulting chaos undermines the very principles of Open Corridor. We have enough of an epidemic of spiritual vertigo in youthcult now.

Hedging on the possibilities of actualizing my own visions, I am forced back on unfashionable waxing and, while shifting focus, continue to hold responsibility to devolve upon individuals, not systems. Reform the systems or create alternate systems, yes, but revolutionize individuals. That doesn't mean some eroticized amorphous unction such as "consciousness-raising." It means hard-core reality punching, a task that can be accomplished best by two groups: a cadre of level-headed instructors in the Academy who, by dint of life-style, possess strong rhetorical credentials with the young; and secondly, those of the young themselves who possess both the faculties and the will for advocacy of nondestructive alternatives, and whose first task as burgeoning Sons of Los is to chop down the Tree of Mystery among their peers. Both groups face a monumental task of engendering a retooling process and cannot rely on existing institutions to work for them. We've just got to start calling the cards where they lie without fear of being wallpapered with day-glo slogans. Practicing a little whistle-blowing, in one sense, is very much the thrust of this book: no more bullshit, no more false apologetics, no more willful avoidance of the confrontation with insanity. That does not mean turning into an uptight ogre or a stale-lecture-pad reader. It does mean making oneself more available and vulnerable, becoming a campus activist who will talk *from* the disposition of the ideology youthcult imagines for itself and *against* youthcult's own malignancies.

Assuming that the Academy is not about to undertake the responsibility of rendering itself more optional, of attenuating its certifying function, both groups of potential reconstructors who sense keenly the urgencies about them are under the categorical imperative to adopt a policy of unstructured illusion-puncturing encounters with the mass of now railroaded, adolescentized, and desensitized lotus blossoms of youthcult. If we let pass the scattered incidents recorded above, we will, by negation, refract the parents who, more often than not, seek those putatively non-hassling strategies toward the children: Buy them off, send them somewhere, call the cops, call the shrink, or just push 'em on to college and out of the house—i.e., we would not even be thinking about them. We would agglutinate into a Silent Minority.

Whatever reconstructive strategy one chooses, though, he should avoid that internecine habit of self-flagellation. By blaming himself for what students or peers do or do not do, by assuming total responsibility for the failures of twenty-year-olds, he will be undermining any possibility that these kids, many of whom no doubt have been tortured by the secondary schools, will ever feed themselves or experience the authenticity of both feeling and freedom. And particularly if he is interested in establishing strong Alternatives in the society, he cannot afford to abet the dire effects of the electronic culture–castrating education combination.

The most immediate goal is the dissolution of all self-serving false posturing. Cleanse the doors of perception which the new verbal and nonverbal regiments blind, and we may all just get somewhere. An uninstitutionalized fusion of thought, passion, and language that reaches beyond the moldy dialectics of these past years of our mutual degeneration may just actualize the prophetic vision of the bricks of our beginnings.

Appendix

General Characteristics of Core Group in Survey*

| | Age Group | | |
	17–20	21–25	26–32
1. Age distribution			
Group total	260	150	120
Breakdown	17: 18	21: 48	26: 19
	18: 54	22: 30	27: 18
	19:108	23: 24	28: 24
	20: 80	24: 26	29: 19
		25: 22	30: 16
			31: 10
			32: 14
2. Sex (per cent)			
Female	51.6	45.4	53.3
Male	48.4	54.6	46.7
3. Class background (per cent) †			
Upper	3.1	2.7	5.8
Upper-middle	22.3	33.8	25.8
Middle	50.1	50.0	47.5
Lower-middle	21.9	11.8	17.5
Lower	2.6	1.7	3.4
4. Race (per cent) †			
White	90.1	91.3	92.5
Black	6.9	1.8	5.0

	Age Group		
	17–20	21–25	26–32
Oriental	0.7	5.3	0.0
"Spanish"	2.3	1.6	2.5
5. Percentage *not* attending college or graduate school, 1970–71	1.2	24.0	47.5
6. Percentage holding advanced degrees	0.0	5.3	24.2
7. Percentage of group interviewed	13.1	11.3	11.7

* Summary of responses to Questions A.1, A.12, and A.13.
† Tables are derived from answers to questions A.12 and A.13:
A.12. Ethnic and class background (your own description):
A.13. Education and occupation of your parents (your own description):

POLITICAL AND CULTURAL INVOLVEMENTS

	Age Group		
	17–20	21–25	26–32
A.11.* Are you into any of the following?:			
A. Group therapy	7.7%	11.6%	11.2%
B. Macrobiotics	2.3	6.7	7.5
C. Communal living	3.1	3.3	2.5
D. Yoga	4.6	6.7	6.3
E. Astrology, numerology, etc.	6.9	10.0	3.7
F. Eastern mysticisms	1.6	11.6	2.5
G. Western religious revival movements	0.7	0.0	0.0

A.14. Have you had any training or experience in the visual or plastic arts?: What, specifically?:

Considerable	2.3%	8.3%	12.5%
Moderate	5.4	13.3	6.2
Minimal	5.4	11.6	11.2
None	86.9	66.8	70.1

A.15. Have you had any training or experience in the performing arts?:
    What, specifically?:

Considerable	12.3%	15.0%	16.2%
Moderate	13.8	11.6	22.5
Minimal	9.2	16.7	3.7
None	64.7	56.7	57.6

A.16. Have you participated in any social or community action programs
    during the past year or so?:
    Please describe briefly:

Ecological	11.5%†	31.6%†	40.0%†
Charitable	19.2	16.7	10.0
Social action	1.6	13.3	22.5
Other	7.7	8.3	2.5
None	70.7	58.4	52.5

* For questions A.2 to A.10, see Chapter 2. Some Survey questions are
not reprinted here because in the author's judgment they were informationally unproductive.
† Percentages will total more than 100.

A.17. Indicate your experience with, and the frequency with which you use,
    the following:

	17–20	21–25	26–32
Soft liquors			
Frequent	17.7%	28.3%	37.5%
Occasional	35.4	35.0	40.0
Minimal	29.2	18.3	3.7
Hard liquors			
Frequent	6.2	14.3	20.0
Occasional	21.5	26.7	38.7
Minimal	30.0	28.3	22.5
Grass, hash			
Frequent	13.8	16.7	13.7
Occasional	23.8	21.7	30.0
Minimal	15.4	20.0	22.5
Tried once	3.1	4.2	2.5
Barbiturates			
Frequent	0.7	3.3	0.0
Occasional	1.9	4.7	0.0
Minimal	10.0	4.7	8.7
Amphetamines			
Frequent	2.7	0.0	0.0
Occasional	7.7	11.8	5.0
Minimal	11.5	8.3	13.7
Organic hallucenogens			
Frequent	1.9	0.0	0.0

	17–20	21–25	26–32
Occasional	4.6	6.7	3.7
Minimal	4.6	3.3	6.3
Synthetic hallucenogens			
Frequent	0.7	1.7	0.0
Occasional	4.6	6.7	2.5
Minimal	8.4	4.7	12.5
Hard narcotics			
Frequent	0.7	0.0	0.0
Occasional	1.9	0.0	0.0
Minimal	5.0	4.7	3.7
Heavy multiple drug use	5.0	6.7	2.5
Moderate multiple drug use	13.5	11.8	10.0
No drug use	30.0	28.3	25.0
Total abstinence	10.8	5.3	5.0

A.18. What products, groups of products, manufacturers, stores, brand-names, etc., have you boycotted during the past few years, if any (and if the reason would not be obvious, why?):

	17–20	21–25	26–32
Grapes	13.9%*	33.3%*	47.5%*
Lettuce	4.6	13.3	26.2
Coca Cola	3.1	6.7	8.8
Other heavy political†	0.0	3.3	10.0
Other moderate political‡	10.0	16.7	13.7
General ecological	11.5	23.3	22.5
General economic consumer	3.9	5.0	15.0
None	63.1	40.0	33.2

* Percentages will total more than 100.

† Indicates boycotts of 3 or more products, etc., other than grapes, lettuce, and coke, or 2 or more national manufacturers (e.g. G.E., Schick-Eversharp, Dow, Technicolor) for strongly political reasons.

‡ Indicates boycotts of one or two products other than grapes, lettuce, and coke for mildly political reasons, or no more than two local merchants for local political reasons.

VOTING

A.20. Are you now registered to vote?:*

	17–20	21–25	26–32
% Yes	24.6*	70.0	97.5

If you are over twenty-two years of age, when was the last time you voted?:

1971	—	6.7%	5.0%
1970	—	40.0	44.0
1969	—	5.0	7.5
1968	—	3.3	12.5

Have you "sat out" any major elections since 1960, or voted for a fourth- or fifth-party candidate?:

% Yes	—	11.2	16.3

* Survey conducted between April and June of 1971; 26th Amendment not fully in force.

A.21. Have you participated in any political or quasi-political rallies, demonstrations, sit-ins, picket lines, etc., during the past three years?:

	17–20	21–25	26–32
% Yes	56.9	63.3	57.5

For what causes, in a university or school setting?:

	17–20	21–25	26–32
Peace	50.0%*	51.6%*	20.0%*
Racial	6.1	5.0	2.5
Educational	27.1	18.4	8.7
Ecological	8.5	10.0	0.0
Other political	7.7	6.6	1.3
Other nonpolitical	4.6	3.3	0.0

For what causes, elsewhere?:

	17–20	21–25	26–32
Peace	23.8%*	36.7%*	50.0%*
Racial	7.7	6.7	3.6
Educational	4.6	3.3	0.0
Ecological	8.4	16.7	18.7
Other political	2.7	10.0	16.3
Other nonpolitical	0.7	0.0	0.0

* Percentages are of gross number for group, and will total more than the percentage of those who answered "yes" to the first question.

A.23. Were you present at any of the following?:

	17–20	21–25	26–32
Newport, 1960	—	1.7%	15.0%
Washington, 1963	—	1.7	8.7
Golden Gate Park, 1967	—	0.0	0.0
Monterey Pop, 1968	—	1.7	2.5
Pentagon, 11/67	—	1.7	8.7
Chicago, 8/68	0.0	4.8	2.5
Woodstock	7.7%	6.7	5.0
Moratoriums, 10/69	35.4	41.7	48.7
Altamont	0.0	0.0	0.0
D.C., 5/70	6.1	10.0	6.3
D.C., 4/71	6.9	6.7	1.3

A.24. How would you describe your politics—in general?:

	17–20	21–25	26–32
A. Reactionary	0.7%	—	—
B. Anarchist	1.5	—	—
C. Liberal	36.9	42.0%	45.0%
D. Centrist	3.1	3.3	2.5
E. None	16.9	5.3	5.0
F. General leftist	6.8	8.6	12.5
G. Libertarian conservative	6.1	5.3	3.7
H. Socialist	1.5	6.7	—
I. Republican	—	1.7	—
J. Conservative	5.4	3.3	5.0
K. Bolshevik	0.7	—	—
L. Maoist	0.7	—	—
M. General rightist	—	—	—
N. Radical	0.7	3.3	5.0
O. Combinations of the above:			
C-G	3.1	4.6	11.7
C-G-N	3.8	—	5.0
C-F-H	2.3	4.6	2.5
B-F-H	0.7	4.6	—
B-G	1.9	3.3	0.8
Others	7.0	3.4	1.3

A.26. With which of the following political or quasi-political groups do you identify and/or sympathize (circle all that apply)?:

	17–20	21–25	26–32
A. Democratic party	30.8%	43.2%	52.5%
B. Minutemen	—	—	—
C. Weatherman	8.5	5.8	5.0
D. AFL-CIO	4.6	8.3	5.0
E. Youth Int'l Party	10.8	—	0.8
F. Young Amers. Freedom	10.8	2.6	1.7
G. Mattachine Society	1.6	6.7	6.7
H. Black Muslims	5.4	4.2	15.0
I. Common Cause	9.2	18.3	45.0
J. New Democratic Coalition	10.8	16.7	5.0
K. Black Panthers	10.4	15.8	20.0
L. Urban League	11.5	20.0	28.6
M. Hard Hats	3.1	1.7	0.8
N. ACLU	26.9	48.3	55.0
O. Republican Party	10.8	11.7	7.5

	17–20	21–25	26–32
P. None	19.9	10.0	3.8
Q. Youth Against War and Fascism	16.9	8.3	8.8
R. UAW-Teamsters	1.6	3.3	3.8
S. American Legion	2.3	—	0.8
T. Nat. Org. of Women	23.1	17.5	18.8
U. SDS	6.2	5.3	7.5
V. John Birch Society	2.4	—	—
W. Nader's Raiders	43.8	48.3	67.5
X. American Independent Party	3.1	—	—
Others	3.8	8.3	8.8

INFORMATION: MAINSTREAM AND COUNTER, CULTURE AND POLITICS

B.2. Who is your Congressman?

	17–20	21–25	26–32
% Correct	44.7	65.0	72.5

B.3. Who is—

(percentage of reasonably correct responses)

	17–20	21–25	26–32
NHL scoring champ, 1970–'71	24.6	26.7	17.5
Leader of Al Fatah	3.1	11.2	15.0
Director of "Gimme Shelter"	4.6	6.7	16.3
Secretary of Defense	68.4	83.3	85.0
House Minority Leader	22.3	35.0	42.5
Prime Minister of India	68.4	81.6	75.0
Commentator-director, *First Tuesday*	6.9	11.2	13.7
Premier of the U.S.S.R.	46.9	61.3	57.5
President of the U.A.W.	10.0	16.7	12.5
Author of *Cat's Cradle*	28.4	46.7	60.0
Director of SCLC	16.1	61.3	43.7
Chief Justice, U.S. Supreme Court	33.1	51.7	62.5
President of Chile	17.6	46.7	53.7
Secretary of State	40.0	63.3	65.0
Author of *Sexual Politics*	28.4	56.7	70.0
Nat'l League Rookie of the Year, 1970	4.6	3.3	1.3
Senate Majority Whip	8.4	11.2	15.0

	(percentage of reasonably correct responses)		
	17–20	21–25	26–32
Male Leads in "M*A*S*H" (both)	36.9	38.3	50.0
Lead Vocalist of The Who	20.8	11.2	13.7
Speaker of the House	13.8	28.3	32.5
Originator of the geodesic dome	12.3	40.0	41.8
Coordinator of Common Cause	3.8	23.3	46.3
Astronauts of Apollo 11 (2 of 3)	14.7	3.8	10.0
Author of *Magister Ludi*	15.4	33.3	36.1
Mayor of Newark, N.J.	45.8	40.0	45.0

B.4. What does each one of the following people "do for a living"?:

	(percentage of reasonably correct responses)		
	17–20	21–25	26–32
Robbie Robertson	10.0	15.0	19.4
J. William Fulbright	66.1	80.0	96.2
Art Buchwald	66.1	83.3	100.0
Pierre Trudeau	63.8	78.3	86.3
Arthur Janov	3.8	11.2	13.8
Pete Maravich	63.8	58.3	52.5
James Earl Jones	62.3	73.3	73.8
Robert McNamara	24.6	48.3	60.0
Eric Clapton	72.3	58.3	42.5
Carl Stokes	42.3	63.3	92.5
Moshe Safdi	1.5	10.0	27.8
Robert Finch	12.3	30.0	55.5
Wilbur Mills	24.6	36.7	65.0
Gladys Knight	70.0	60.0	46.2
Gunnar Jarring	30.7	55.0	63.7
Jimmy Carter	7.7	11.2	16.7
H. Ross Perot	20.7	28.3	58.3
Joe Dallessandro	19.2	33.3	38.9
Lon Nol	18.4	38.3	46.2
Katherine Graham	0.7	3.3	13.9

B.5. All of the following people have "made the headlines" in a political or quasi-political context during the past year. In brief, who are they? That is, why did they make the headlines? What did they do that was significant in any way? Or what position did they or do they hold that is significant in any way?:

(percentage of reasonably correct responses)

	17–20	21–25	26–32
1. John Sherman Cooper	13.8	30.0	42.5
2. Bernadette Devlin	65.3	83.3	85.0
3. Alex Rackley	13.8	28.3	35.0
4. Ernest Medina	56.9	78.7	81.2
5. Sam Ervin Jr.	7.7	18.3	37.5
6. Ti-Grace Atkinson	23.8	35.0	53.8
7. Curt Flood	47.6	56.7	52.5
8. Nicholas Johnson	6.2	18.3	28.8
9. George Jackson	8.4	23.3	30.0
10. Jean Louis Trintignant	8.4	25.0	41.2
11. Bella Abzug	46.9	51.6	66.8
12. Tony Boyle	6.9	21.7	42.5
13. Cesar Chavez	45.4	71.6	77.5
14. Yukio Mishima	18.4	43.3	55.0
15. Peter Boyle	19.2	18.3	18.8

B.6. Indicate the (political/social) significance of the following places:

(percentage of reasonably correct responses)

	17–20	21–25	26–32
1. Lop Nor	0.0	3.3	13.8
2. Presidio	5.3	26.7	42.5
3. El Arish	4.6	16.7	11.2
4. Bogside	2.3	8.3	20.0
5. 17th Parallel	36.1	53.3	55.0
6. Isla Vista	6.2	18.3	22.5
7. Pinkville	5.5	15.0	28.8
8. 38th Parallel	26.2	50.0	56.3
9. Plain of Jars	3.1	21.7	23.8
10. Soledad	20.7	43.3	52.5
11. Altamont	32.3	36.7	45.0
12. Prudhoe Bay	3.9	10.0	23.8
13. Angkor Wat	10.0	21.7	33.8
14. Block Island	0.8	3.3	7.5
15. Ussuri River	6.2	15.0	16.2

I have presented Section B as it appeared on the questionnaire minus the data on one question that hindsight proved to be rather silly, i.e., "Name as many *current* U.S. Senators as you can," a question which was nonetheless used for determining borderline cases in the classification tables that follow.

The following tables unscramble the items of Section B, and present a different type of breakdown of responses. There were seventy-five items in questions 3, 4, 5, and 6. The first set of tables involves the distinction between "popular culture" information and "general" information. The second division distinguishes between "mainstream culture information" and "counter-culture information." The difference between the two divisions might be illustrated as follows: the "NHL scoring champion, 1970–71" (Phil Esposito) would be classified as both a "popular culture" information item and a "mainstream culture" information item. Likewise, the significance of Nicholas Johnson (renegade quasi-radical member of the FCC) is both a "general" information item, and a "counter-culture" information item.

I don't think there would be too much quibbling on the general categories of the first division: The popular culture items derive from the worlds of sport, entertainment, and the arts. But the classification becomes somewhat subjective in the distinction between mainstream and counter cultures. Some pigeon-holing will undoubtedly wrinkle noses, e.g., I have placed Curt Flood in the counter culture (only after he ran off to Spain and started appearing in articles in the underground press), and Ralph Abernathy (Director of SCLC) in the mainstream. Still, the general idea behind the classifications should be clear by example: Gladys Knight is mainstream, Eric Clapton is counter; Angkor Wat is mainstream, but Pinkville is counter. I am sure dozens of such distinctions could be argued among the *cognoscenti,* and I am sure the underground press will yowl "rape." I do not wish to beg such questions, but none of us can afford to swim in a mucky pond of *reductios.*

Following the blocks of median scores under each of the divisions, I have also indicated the percentage of each group that possessed significant, moderate, and minimal information in each category. I did so for the purpose of providing some broad but definite indicators for the correlations discussed in the text. The cut-off percentages for the "significant" and "moderate" categories are quite low, I admit, but they are so because of the relative number of obscure items I included for purposes of cross-checking various responses in Sections A and C. Katherine Graham (publisher of *Newsweek, The Washington Post,* and other objects of the recent media paranoia of the Right), the National League Rookie of the Year, 1970 (Carl Morton—or is it Craig Morton?—but then again, from my own answers in parts A and C, one would not expect me to know, and, indeed, I did not know when the questionnaire was formulated), or Lop Nor (the Chinese nuclear development and testing site, which the rancid Right has been asking us to bomb for the past few years)—these are, one must admit, items known mostly to those with great skill at Botticelli and other long-run car games.

SECTION B, SUMMARY: INFORMATION SCORES, POPULAR AND GENERAL CULTURE

	Age Group		
	17–20	21–25	26–32
Popular culture median (20 items)	5.24	7.47	8.48
General information median (55 items)	11.87	20.24	27.99
Percentage of group holding:			
Significant pop. info. (50% score and up)	13.4	23.3	17.5
Moderate pop. info. (30%–49% score)	23.8	26.7	25.0
Minimal pop. info. (less than 30%)	62.8	50.0	57.5
Significant gen. info. (60% score and up)	7.7	20.0	30.8
Moderate gen. info. (40%–59%)	23.1	26.7	38.3
Minimal gen. info. (less than 40%)	69.2	53.3	30.9

	Age Group 17–20 *College and University Groupings**					
	A	B	C	D	E	F
Pop. culture median	7.9	4.9	4.4	11.0	4.4	6.9
General info. median	11.5	7.3	10.1	22.6	9.9	12.0

* See p. 30 above for key.

SECTION B, SUMMARY: INFORMATION SCORES, MAINSTREAM
AND COUNTER CULTURE

	Age Group		
	17–20	21–25	26–32
Counter culture median (30 items)	5.81	9.12	12.37
Mainstream culture median (45 items)	11.40	18.89	23.10
Percentage of group holding: Signif. counter-cult info. (50% score and up)	11.5	21.3	34.3
Moderate counter-cult info. (30%–49% score)	18.5	36.7	37.5
Minimal counter-cult info. (less than 30%)	70.0	42.0	28.2
Signif. mainstrm. cult info. (60% score and up)	10.8	26.7	38.7
Moderate mainstrm. cult info. (40%–59% score)	13.8	28.3	40.0
Minimal mainstrm. cult info. (less than 40%)	75.4	45.0	21.3

	Age Group 17–20 College and University Groupings					
	A	B	C	D	E	F
Counter cult median	7.4	4.1	4.3	11.7	3.9	6.8
Mainstrm. cult median	11.7	7.1	10.8	20.9	10.8	12.2

HIP DICTIONARY QUIZ*

A.22. Would you indicate the meaning of each of the following (if you don't know, place an X after the word)?:

	(percentage of reasonably correct responses)		
	17–20	21–25	26–32
Rip-off	42.3	60.0	50.0
Smack	50.0	63.3	71.3
Fascist	40.9	55.0	66.7
Bad	20.0	21.3	33.7
Toke	50.8	55.0	42.5
Off (verb)	14.9	36.7	34.1
Uptight	79.8	96.7	98.7
Speed (noun)	44.5	63.3	75.0
Cool (adj. or noun) †	53.1	65.0	72.2
Hang-up	76.9	90.0	88.9

	(percentage of reasonably correct responses)		
	17–20	21–25	26–32
Jay	43.5	35.7	30.0
Cop (verb)‡	33.2	50.9	50.0
Linear	13.8	16.7	36.3
Far-out	73.8	85.0	95.0
Heavy (adj.)	51.5	68.3	68.9
% Scoring 10–15	28.1	40.0	40.0
% Scoring 6–9	39.5	33.3	38.7
% Scoring 0–5	32.4	26.7	21.3
Median score	6.9	8.3	8.9

* This was one of the few items on the questionnaire in which content varied even slightly in successive printings. Thus, for example, "jay" and "cop" were *not* included on 54 of the 530 core-group questionnaires. They replaced "right on" and "popping" after the first printing. I have also eliminated from the statistics the sixteenth word, "rabbit," a rather obscure hip black dialect term for white man. Only two of the 530 respondents recognized it.

† The 1950's jazz-man's definition, "loose," was not accepted. Used as a noun, definitions on the order of "composure" were "cool," i.e., the adjectival meaning, "acceptable." "Hip," "pleasant," "tough," and even "groovy" were also acceptable.

‡ Many respondents tried to turn this one into "cop-out." That was a cop-out. An unhyphenated "cop," as a verb, generally means "obtain," "purchase," or "steal."

Section C sought attitude responses to a number of names, places, works of art, contemporary issues, etc., all of which could be related to patterns of media involvement, counter-culture involvement claims, political attitudes and activity, and information possessed as indicated by a respondent in Sections A and B.

The single question read as follows on most questionnaires:

"Would you indicate your response to the following by placing a number ranging from 0 (most negative) to 5 (most positive) in front of each item. If you do not recognize the item, please place an X in front of it."

The "X" indication thus served as an extension of the information "exam" in Section B, although in many cases (e.g., "IBM," "General Electric," "Graduate Education," "Labor Unions," etc.) the "X" was obviously taken to mean, "no answer," or "no opinion." Many respondents specifically inserted such remarks for a number of items, most noted among which were works of art. I refer to comments on the order of "Haven't seen *Easy Rider*, so don't have an opinion." The percentage figures for the "X" column, then, do not necessarily represent a fraction of the whole group, rather a fraction of those who indicated that they either had an opinion or just did not recognize the item at all.

Comments were also used to qualify a number of other judgments, these centering on a few specific items. For example, approximately 10 per cent of the respondents distinguished between style and substance in the matters of William F. Buckley, Jr., and Billy Graham. And positive responses (4 or 5) to issues such as methadone maintenance or urban public housing were often qualified with the statement, "but not the way it's being run now." Still, all responses were taken at face value. When two were offered on the same item, they were averaged.

There is no doubt in my mind that the "X" percentages should be much higher in many cases, for the same people who evidenced tremendous degrees of political or social self-contradiction (read: "ordinary ignorance, illiteracy, or both") in Sections A and B indicated a similar degree of contradictory judgments in Section C. One is strongly tempted to dismiss such judgments (some of which, no doubt, could be defended, but only with some fairly sophisticated conceptual apparatus) on the "he-doesn't-know-what-the-hell-he's-talking-about" grounds. A self-styled "conservative" (A.24), who sympathizes with the Republican Party and the New Democratic Coalition(?) and the Youth International Party (Yippie!) and the Hard Hats (A.26)(?), goes on in Section B to turn up with minimal knowledge in all categories, and in Section C to lend positive responses to W. O. Douglas and Bernardine Dohrn, and negative responses to Agnew's criticism of media, Bill Buckley, and Al Lowenstein? Such examples could be multiplied by the dozen, and all excuse-mongering is just that.

The college and university grouping breakdowns reveal some significant divergences, many of which can be accounted for with common sense, and not with the theories advanced in the text. It should not be overly surprising, for example, that the nonrecognition factor on the Hare Krishna people is moderately high among students in the South and Midwest—they simply haven't seen any of the bell-clangers, and certainly have not spent an hour in a N.Y. subway car with them. Likewise, students from highly urbanized areas, even those students who claim to be into ecology, are less likely to have heard of the Sierra Club than the others—and so it goes. Even the response to the Calley verdict can be explained in this manner. The median was positive in the South and Midwest, in part, I suspect, out of the politic that respects military judgment and, too, out of that Middle American repugnance at the suggestion that we're *all* monsters. The Ivy League kids, whose median response is the most positive of the lot (again, typically, matching that of the 26–32 age group in general) are no doubt expressing a level of reasoning that can detach one atrocity from other atrocities without denying that the whole pack of them are atrocities, i.e., they all should be hung, right through the generals to the Rostows, the Bundys, and the Kissingers, indeed, all the way to LBJ; but that doesn't mean that the verdict of guilty passed on Calley is wrong. The verbal reasoning here rests on conceptual division, and thus it is no surprise that the groups with the highest language orientation can deal in it.

For purposes of this Appendix, I have unscrambled the order of the items as they originally appeared on the questionnaire and have placed them in groupings that most easily correspond to the groupings employed in the unscrambling of Sections A and B.

To aid the reader in interpreting the median response figures, the following scale can be utilized. It obviously involves some subjective judgments at my end, but judgments which, based on a working knowledge of the questionnaires, I think are justifiable:

0.0–1.4: Extremely negative
1.5–1.9: Moderately negative
2.0–2.4: Mildly negative / tepid
2.5–2.8: Wholly neutral
2.9–3.3: Mildly positive
3.4–3.8: Moderately positive
3.9–5.0: Extremely positive

In those cases in which the nonrecognition ("X") factor is extremely high, the median response figure is really next to meaningless. The cases of Walt Rostow, the Tupemaros, Railpax (as Amtrak was known at the time the questionnaire was distributed) —in which nonrecognition ran 75 per cent or better, the evaluation of the *median* response can be tenuous, at best. That obviously is not the case for the individual response, as I hope I have indicated in the text.

	Age Group					
	17–20		21–25		26–32	
	Median Response	% X's	Median Response	% X's	Median Response	% X's
Group I: Counter Cult						
Mick Jagger	2.7	3.1	2.4	8.0	2.8	2.5
Hare Krishna people	2.2	19.2	2.1	12.0	2.1	14.5
Earth Day	4.3	—	4.3	—	4.5	—
LeRoi Jones	2.5	26.9	2.5	25.6	3.0	12.8
Billy Graham	2.5	56.9	2.2	51.0	2.6	50.0
Sensitivity training	3.3	5.4	2.9	6.0	3.0	2.8
Easy Rider	3.4	—	3.2	—	3.0	—
Siddhartha	3.6	38.4	4.2	42.0	3.4	34.8
Tiger's Milk	2.4	66.2	2.7	60.0	2.0	52.1
Andy Warhol	2.6	20.9	2.3	12.6	2.6	5.7
2001	3.3	—	3.4	—	3.3	—
R. D. Laing	2.7	63.5	2.7	65.6	4.3	27.8

	Age Group					
	17–20		21–25		26–32	
	Median Response	% X's	Median Response	% X's	Median Response	% X's
Group II: Counter Politics						
GI coffeehouses	3.3	32.3	3.6	14.0	3.9	14.2
Eldridge Cleaver	2.1	5.4	2.0	6.1	3.2	—
Jane Fonda	2.7	1.2	2.5	2.0	3.2	—
Sierra Club	3.6	58.4	4.3	25.6	4.5	3.7
The Tupemaros	2.0	85.4	2.1	76.8	2.2	57.5
Ramsey Clark	2.9	17.6	3.5	16.7	4.3	9.1
Bernardine Dohrn	2.1	57.9	1.9	26.0	1.9	16.7
Al Lowenstein	3.4	64.6	3.8	49.8	4.6	25.7
Cuba	2.4	—	2.0	—	2.6	—
W. O. Douglas	2.9	49.2	3.5	24.4	4.6	8.5
Timothy Leary	1.6	8.4	1.3	6.1	1.4	—
NLF	1.8	32.3	2.1	10.4	2.6	8.5
NOW	3.2	52.3	3.2	38.9	3.8	22.8

43790　　J. M. HODGES LEARNING CENTER
WHARTON COUNTY JUNIOR COLLEGE
WHARTON, TEXAS 77488

	Age Group					
	17–20		21–25		26–32	
	Median Response	% X's	Median Response	% X's	Median Response	% X's
Group III: *Mainstream*						
Billy Graham	1.8	3.9	1.5	—	1.4	—
W. W. Rostow	1.8	77.7	1.6	58.8	1.7	32.5
All in the Family	3.6	29.2	4.0	38.8	3.1	37.5
1970 elections	1.7	—	1.6	—	1.8	—
Love Story	2.8	—	2.3	—	1.9	—
John Mitchell	1.2	21.5	0.9	9.2	1.0	2.5
Blue-collar workers	2.8	—	3.0	—	3.1	—
W. F. Buckley, Jr.	2.0	3.1	2.1	4.0	2.4	—
Bob Hope	2.3	—	1.8	—	1.7	—
ARVN	2.1	69.2	1.8	58.8	2.0	32.5
Ayn Rand	2.6	43.0	2.5	18.3	2.2	2.5
General Electric	2.2	—	1.9	—	2.2	—
Group IV: *Economic*						
IBM	2.0	—	2.1	—	2.5	—
The Stock Exchange	2.2	—	2.0	—	2.7	—
Railpax	2.6	79.2	3.0	52.0	3.2	42.5
Small business	3.7	—	3.8	—	4.0	—
Black capitalism	2.4	—	3.0	—	3.9	—
Labor unions	2.7	—	2.3	—	2.4	—
North Slope oil	1.9	59.2	1.4	48.6	2.1	14.4
Group V: *Selected Issues*						
A volunteer army	3.8	—	3.3	—	2.9	—
Agnew's crit. of media	1.1	—	1.0	—	1.1	—
Methadone maintenance	3.9	22.3	3.8	6.0	4.5	8.3
Graduate education	3.9	—	3.9	—	3.6	—
The Calley *verdict*	2.3	—	2.9	—	3.6	—
Integration by busing	2.3	—	2.7	—	2.8	—
Nat'l health insurance	3.4	13.8	4.1	18.3	4.4	8.5
Open enrollment	3.0	—	2.9	2.0	2.9	2.5
Urban public housing	3.1	—	3.0	3.3	3.0	—

UNIVERSITY AND COLLEGE GROUPINGS

	A		B		C		D		E		F	
	Median Response	% X's	Median Response	% X's	Median Response	% X's	Median Response	% X's	Median Response	% X's	Median Response	% X's
Group I: Counter Culture												
Mick Jagger	2.8	—	2.8	4.7	2.2	—	2.8	—	2.8	5.5	2.6	7.4
Hare Krishna people	2.1	5.9	1.7	16.4	2.1	52.8	2.1	6.7	2.0	44.0	2.2	22.2
Earth Day	4.7	—	4.2	—	4.4	—	4.2	—	3.9	—	4.3	—
LeRoi Jones	2.6	17.6	1.5	38.1	2.5	60.0	2.6	—	3.2	50.0	2.3	11.1
Billy Graham	2.4	38.2	2.6	32.7	3.0	80.0	2.5	52.8	3.4	71.5	3.0	74.2
Sensitivity training	3.3	5.9	3.6	16.4	3.1	—	3.2	—	3.3	5.5	2.7	3.7
Easy Rider	3.5	—	3.6	—	3.5	—	2.4	—	3.5	—	3.1	—
Siddhartha	3.7	35.3	3.3	32.7	3.4	65.0	2.6	28.5	3.6	50.0	4.2	40.8
Tiger's Milk	2.4	52.9	2.8	76.1	2.8	65.0	2.7	52.8	2.0	67.6	1.5	75.0
Andy Warhol	2.7	8.8	2.0	29.1	2.9	27.5	3.2	—	2.8	38.5	1.9	29.1
2001	2.9	—	3.0	—	3.4	—	3.0	—	3.3	—	3.3	—
R. D. Laing	3.3	73.7	2.6	80.0	3.6	65.0	3.6	63.9	2.3	83.3	2.4	63.6
Group II: Counter Politics												
GI coffeehouses	3.0	35.2	2.8	49.2	4.1	15.0	3.3	19.4	3.9	16.7	3.0	48.2
Eldridge Cleaver	2.1	—	2.1	16.4	1.6	6.7	2.8	—	1.8	11.1	2.2	3.7
Jane Fonda	3.0	—	2.2	9.1	3.5	—	2.8	—	2.8	—	2.0	—
Sierra Club	3.6	70.5	2.3	80.0	2.8	40.0	3.3	19.4	3.4	32.3	4.3	63.6
The Tupemaros	1.8	85.3	xxx	100.0	2.4	85.0	2.0	66.7	1.7	83.3	2.2	85.4
Ramsey Clark	2.4	20.0	2.8	32.7	2.9	6.7	3.7	—	3.0	11.1	2.5	26.0
Bernardine Dohrn	2.2	55.9	2.3	63.7	1.9	55.0	1.9	33.3	2.2	50.0	2.1	63.6
Al Lowenstein	3.5	55.9	4.0	81.9	2.0	75.0	4.0	19.4	3.0	67.6	3.2	68.1
Cuba	1.5	—	1.6	—	1.9	—	2.2	—	1.4	—	1.9	—
W. O. Douglas	2.3	52.9	2.4	76.1	3.4	42.5	3.4	6.7	3.1	38.5	2.4	50.0
Timothy Leary	1.9	—	1.5	16.4	1.7	12.5	1.5	—	1.4	5.5	1.2	18.5
NLF	1.9	23.5	1.4	32.7	1.9	32.5	1.7	6.7	1.9	44.0	2.0	44.5
NOW	3.1	67.6	2.1	63.7	3.8	65.0	3.9	26.0	3.4	44.0	3.0	34.1

	A		B		C		D		E		F	
	Median Response	% X's	Median Response	% X's	Median Response	% X's	Median Response	% X's	Median Response	% X's	Median Response	% X's
Group III: Mainstream												
Billy Graham	1.3	2.9	1.6	4.5	2.4	—	1.5	—	2.4	—	1.8	3.7
W. W. Rostow	1.3	76.4	xxx	100.0	1.5	85.0	1.8	33.3	2.5	67.6	1.7	75.0
All in the Family	4.0	14.7	4.1	16.4	3.4	25.0	2.7	46.2	2.7	50.0	3.3	37.1
1970 elections	1.3	—	1.3	—	2.0	—	2.1	—	2.2	—	1.5	—
Love Story	2.2	—	2.9	4.7	4.0	3.3	3.4	—	3.1	16.7	2.6	3.7
John Mitchell	0.8	17.6	0.9	50.9	2.0	25.0	1.1	—	1.5	—	1.2	18.5
Blue-collar workers	2.6	—	2.8	—	3.4	—	3.2	—	2.7	—	3.3	—
W. F. Buckley, Jr.	1.2	—	2.2	4.7	2.0	—	2.5	—	2.5	5.5	2.3	11.1
Bob Hope	1.8	—	2.1	—	2.7	—	1.7	—	2.8	—	2.3	—
ARVN	1.4	67.6	0.5	91.0	2.3	80.0	2.2	19.4	2.0	55.5	2.4	68.1
Ayn Rand	2.8	47.0	1.6	63.7	2.3	52.5	2.3	33.3	2.5	38.5	2.9	29.1
General Electric	1.7	—	1.8	—	3.2	—	2.3	—	3.0	—	1.9	—
Group IV: Economic												
IBM	1.7	—	1.7	—	2.3	—	2.0	—	2.9	—	2.2	—
The Stock Exchange	1.8	—	1.7	—	2.7	—	2.8	—	2.9	—	2.0	—
Railpax	1.5	82.4	3.5	91.0	3.1	60.0	3.0	72.2	3.5	77.0	2.0	81.8
Small business	4.0	—	3.4	—	3.8	—	3.7	—	4.3	—	3.3	—
Black capitalism	2.7	5.9	1.8	4.7	2.4	6.7	3.5	—	3.3	—	2.0	7.5
Labor unions	3.0	—	2.6	—	2.6	—	2.8	—	2.3	—	2.7	—
North Slope oil	1.2	61.8	1.3	81.9	2.7	45.0	1.4	33.3	2.5	38.5	1.6	55.0
Group V: Issues												
A volunteer army	3.6	—	4.0	—	3.7	—	3.6	—	4.0	—	3.8	—
Agnew's crit. of media	0.7	—	0.8	—	2.0	—	1.0	—	1.4	—	0.8	—
Methadone maintenance	3.9	2.9	3.9	9.1	4.2	40.0	4.3	13.2	3.5	55.5	3.6	37.1
Graduate education	3.3	—	4.0	—	4.3	—	3.8	—	4.3	—	4.3	—
The Calley verdict	1.7	—	1.9	—	3.0	—	3.6	—	3.1	—	1.6	—
Integration by busing	2.0	—	2.1	—	2.0	—	3.1	—	2.4	—	2.3	—
Nat'l health insurance	3.3	14.7	2.9	16.4	3.0	6.7	4.2	—	3.5	16.7	3.3	18.5
Open enrollment	3.5	—	2.8	—	2.8	—	3.0	—	2.4	—	2.7	—
Urban public housing	3.1	—	3.2	—	3.1	—	3.5	—	3.2	—	2.7	—